The Memoir of Ilse Seger

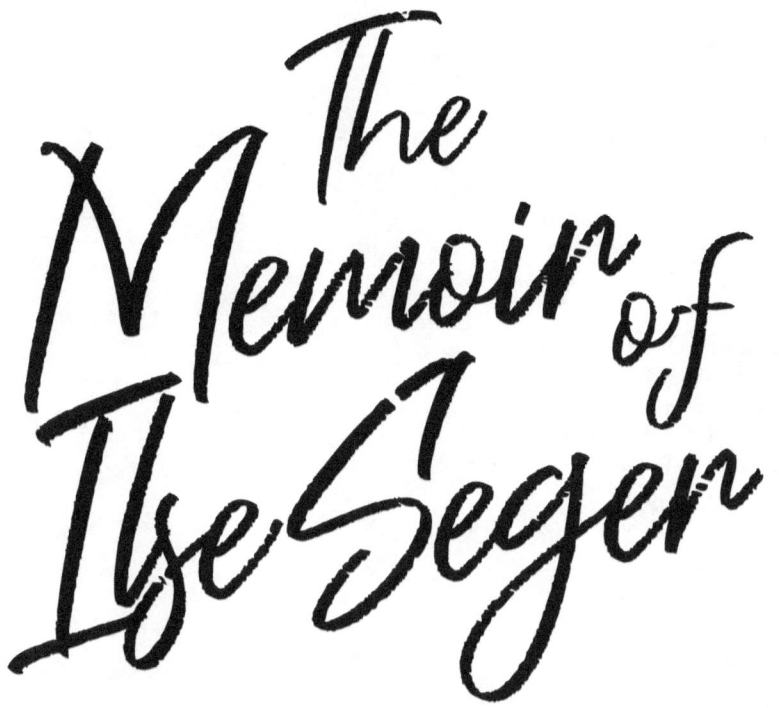

The Memoir of Ilse Seger

WIFE, MOTHER, HOSTAGE, NAZI RESISTER

BY ILSE SEGER

EDITED BY MELISSA KRAVETZ

EPILOGUE BY MARK BRANDT, ILSE'S GRANDSON

INDIANA UNIVERSITY PRESS

This book is a publication of

Indiana University Press
Office of Scholarly Publishing
Herman B Wells Library 350
1320 East 10th Street
Bloomington, Indiana 47405 USA

iupress.org

© 2024 by Indiana University Press

All rights reserved

No part of this book may be reproduced or utilized in any form or by any means, electronic or mechanical, including photocopying and recording, or by any information storage and retrieval system, without permission in writing from the publisher.

First printing 2024

Cataloging information is available from the Library of Congress.

ISBN 978-0-253-07154-5 (hardback)
ISBN 978-0-253-07155-2 (paperback)
ISBN 978-0-253-07156-9 (ebook)

CONTENTS

Acknowledgments   vii

Introduction   *1*

1 Becoming a Wife and Mother with Nazism on the Rise   *17*

2 The Reichstag Fire and Gerhart's Arrest   *36*

3 Visiting Oranienburg and Resisting Nazism   *53*

4 Under House Arrest   *83*

5 A Hostage in Rosslau   *107*

6 Meeting Marvis Tate and Leaving Germany   *142*

7 Reunited with Gerhart and Living in Exile   *156*

8 Another Separation from Gerhart and Planning for America   *194*

Epilogue   *222*

Bibliography   229

Index   235

ACKNOWLEDGMENTS

Dr. Charlie Sydnor is the reason I found my way to the Brandt family and to Ilse's memoir. He has always been a huge advocate of mine and of my research and teaching. He and I initiated a partnership between Longwood University, where he taught German history many years before me, and the Virginia Holocaust Museum, and it was through teaching with him at the museum's Alexander Lebenstein Teacher Education Institute that he put me in touch with Richard Brandt, Ilse's late son-in-law. I am forever indebted to Charlie for being a great mentor, a model teacher and researcher, and for creating this opportunity for me to work with the Brandt family. Meeting Charlie is one of the tremendous opportunities the Virginia Holocaust Museum has afforded me over the past decade; another has been the chance to use Ilse's memoir to teach K–12 teachers about political resistance to the Nazis.

It was through Richard that I also met Mark Brandt, Ilse's grandson. Mark did the important, invisible work of transcribing some of Ilse's typescript memoir on a word processor. He was also critical to making my 2018 research trip to Terre Haute, Indiana—where he and his parents were living—possible, and he facilitated the early conversations with his parents and siblings about the publication of Ilse's memoir. He has been my primary contact through this whole process and read through my initial editing of the memoir to ensure that it remained in Ilse's voice. Thanks are also due to Andrew Brandt for initiating and funding the research trip to Terre Haute. Renate and Richard Brandt graciously hosted me in their retirement community, and I feel very fortunate to have met both of them before they died. I found it endearing that Renate spoke to me in her native German as soon as Mark informed her I was working on publishing her mother's memoir. Jennifer Brandt has always responded to my many questions about her grandmother thoughtfully and eloquently. I hope at some point soon we can all be together to celebrate the publication of Ilse's story.

Swen Steinberg, whom I first met at the German Studies Association in Portland in 2019 when we presented on German refugees, assured me of the significance of publishing a memoir of the wife of a famous political refugee like Gerhart. He has continued to be a great cheerleader and resource for this project since then. Longwood University generously provided me a sabbatical in 2021, which allowed me to complete the editing of the memoir. Jennifer Miller and Hana Green were friendly and reliable Zoom writing partners during an otherwise isolated sabbatical. Stephen Shapiro, the editor for my first book, provided useful feedback on my initial book proposal. Indiana University Press, especially my acquisitions editor, Allison Blair Chaplin, and my project manager, Lesley Bolton, have been a dream to work with; Lesley was incredibly receptive to preserving Ilse's voice—something I and her family are eternally grateful for. They offered a book contract shortly after reviewing the book proposal, and everything has been incredibly seamless throughout the publication process.

My partner, Mike Nichols, has listened to my stories about Ilse for the past six years; in many ways, her story has felt like the best kept secret between us. I'm grateful for his infinite love, support, and patience and for him always being my go-to copyeditor, being the brilliant writer he is. Elijah was weeks away from coming into the world when I first traveled to Indiana and met Richard, Renate, and Mark. He's grown into an intellectually curious child alongside my work on the memoir and he will be in kindergarten by the time this memoir is published. I hope he'll get to know Ilse and find his own meaning in her story soon enough.

I'm ecstatic that Ilse's story, which I was so drawn to back in 2018 and have talked endlessly about since, will now be shared with the world. I only wish I could've met Ilse and spent some time with her because her story gives me hope about what ordinary people will do in the face of rising authoritarianism. Ilse loved her country and never expected to be in the out-group, and yet, when she and her family were persecuted and imprisoned for disagreeing with the people in power, she continued to resist. Think of her story as a lesson for all of us to hold dear in the face of societal pressure and the decay of democracy.

The Memoir of Ilse Seger

Introduction

This is the memoir of Elisabeth ("Ilse") Seger (née Hart), who was born in Strasbourg (which belonged to Germany at the time) on March 26, 1903. Ilse was the daughter of Ernst and Margaret Hart, who were both actors, which meant her family moved a number of times.[1] Ilse described her parents as "deeply involved with one another, a real love match" to her granddaughter, Jennifer Brandt, who, alongside her brothers, Mark and Andrew Brandt, lovingly referred to her as *Oma* (grandmother). Ilse was the eldest of three; her two younger brothers, whom she often cared for, were Wolfgang and Joachim. According to Jennifer, Ilse seemed "wholly unresentful" because they were a close family and her parents were "no doubt the model for her own marriage."[2]

This is the story of Ilse's life during the late 1920s and early 1930s after she met and married Gerhart Heinrich Seger, who became a member of the Social Democratic Party of Germany (Sozialdemokratische Partei Deutschlands; SPD) for Magdeburg in the Reichstag in September 1930. Gerhart was reelected for the last time on March 5, 1933, shortly after Hitler was appointed chancellor. A week later, the Nazis arrested him and held him for three months in a local prison in Dessau and then sent him to Oranienburg concentration camp for six months until he escaped the camp and clandestinely made his way to Czechoslovakia.

Because of the career, choices, and resistance of her husband, this is also the story of Ilse's early resistance to the Nazi regime as a political opponent and her life as a hostage in Rosslau concentration camp; Ilse and their daughter, Renate, were detained there after Gerhart escaped Oranienburg. She also shared how she got out of Rosslau and out of Germany with help from members of Parliament. Lastly, she discussed her first years living in exile in France and Switzerland, as her husband was on an antifascist speaking tour in the United States and as they waited to emigrate there.

Throughout her memoir, Ilse constantly defied expectations of women at the time, especially women who did not have a formal education and who were married to political opponents and exiles. While many of her experiences were due to the actions and choices of her husband, Gerhart, she managed to do everything for her family under the scrutiny of Nazi authorities, in the uncomfortable setting of a concentration camp, and in foreign countries while Gerhart was away for long periods of time. She was extremely resilient in the face of adversity and even created and sustained her own identity as a resister.

Origin Story of the Memoir

Much of what we know about this memoir comes from the recollections of Jennifer and Mark Brandt, Ilse's grandchildren. When Gerhart Seger died in 1967, Ilse became depressed. After about two years of coming to terms with the death of her husband, Ilse watched her daughter and her grandchildren move to another state.[3] Renate, Ilse's daughter, then thirty-four, "conceived the memoir as a way to help [her mother] cope with loss and dislocation—double losses, really" because in 1970, Renate's husband, Richard Brandt, got a job working at the Medical College of Virginia in Richmond.[4] Ilse, therefore, was left behind in New York without her daughter, son-in-law, or grandchildren, Mark (nine), Andrew (seven), and Jennifer (five). As Mark recalls:

> Ilse was somewhat torn; she had a large circle of friends in New York whom she did not wish to leave, but she had to let her family go far away. The 350 miles between New York and Richmond were a large barrier, especially for someone who never learned to drive an automobile. While she had friends, her husband was no longer there [in New York], and her house felt empty without her grandchildren. This was one reason that Renate suggested to Ilse that she begin writing this memoir; Renate hoped that the time and effort involved would make her mother somewhat happier.[5]

Ilse "was a voracious reader but never thought herself a writer; she insisted her imperfect English made the memoir unsuitable for publication."[6] She also did not want to compete with Gerhart, a prolific writer, but by that point he had already died.

It is unclear how long it took her to write this memoir, but Mark remembers being a young teenager by the time she finished it, meaning it took her at least a few years. She typed the memoir in English on Gerhart's typewriter on carbon sheets, sandwiched between two leaves of onionskin paper.[7] The memoir was supposed to be "an extended letter to her grandchildren."[8] This is not dissimilar to the many women who, as Marion Kaplan shows, "wrote to tell their children of the horrors they and their loved ones had experienced, to express the fears and uncertainties they had felt."⁹ Renate had encouraged Ilse to write a memoir as a way of keeping her husband's memory alive for her grandchildren so that they "would grow up understanding what an extraordinary man he was." According to Jennifer, "Oma was deeply committed to keeping history alive, anyway, front and center so it would never be repeated."¹⁰ Renate transcribed the typescript on a word processor; she started this process sometime in the late 1980s and early 1990s, working on it only occasionally, encouraged by Richard after she had retired. She eventually gave up, partially because she found the process too emotionally wearing, and partially as health issues made typing increasingly difficult. Mark transcribed the last thirty pages around the end of 2014.¹¹

Because Ilse was a grandmother writing to her grandchildren about herself, their grandfather, Gerhart, and their mother, Renate, she provides us a unique perspective—one that was intended to be private and not necessarily published. Her recounting of her experiences to her family provides an intimate portrayal of her personal feelings and fears, a stark contrast to Gerhart's two books about his experiences in Oranienburg and his early years in exile. His two books, *Oranienburg: Erster authentischer Bericht eines aus dem Konzentrationslager Geflüchteten* (*Oranienburg: First Authentic Report of a Concentration Camp Escapee*), or the English version, *A Nation Terrorized*, and *Reisetagebuch eines deutschen Emigranten* (*Travel Diary of a German Emigrant*), in addition to his many speeches about his experiences, were meant for public consumption and were motivated by his antifascist politics.¹²

The End of the Weimar Republic and the Nazi Rise to Power

Ilse's story began with meeting Gerhart during the Weimar Republic (1918–33), Germany's first democratic parliamentary republic and a tumultuous time in German politics. The end of the First World War signaled anything but stability for Germany, which had been militarily defeated and suffered almost two million casualties, and the civilian population was starving due to an Allied blockade. After numerous strikes and a mutiny within the military, the government collapsed. Kaiser Wilhelm II, who had been in power since 1888, abdicated the throne and fled the country, and Germany's constitutional monarchy was abolished. During the chaotic November Revolution, as this has become known, the Social Democrats proclaimed a German Republic on November 9, 1918.

The SPD had been founded in 1863 and was one of the first parties to be influenced by the ideas of Karl Marx. Otto von Bismarck, Germany's first chancellor and a conservative, perceived the SPD as being full of Socialists, and the party had always attracted members of Germany's industrial working class. Although Bismarck pushed the Anti-Socialist Laws through the Reichstag, thus banning any meetings, organizations, associations, newspapers, or periodicals aimed at spreading Socialist principles, the Reichstag refused to ban any members who were part of the SPD, and the party still gained support in elections. After 1890, when the Anti-Socialist Laws were lifted, the SPD was consistently the most popular party in German federal elections, and it became the largest party in the Reichstag in 1912. During the First World War, the party had split into the Independent Social Democratic Party of Germany (Unabhängige Sozialdemokratische Partei Deutschlands; USPD), an antiwar party that called for immediate peace negotiations, and the SPD, which informally became known as the Majority Social Democratic Party of Germany (Mehrheitssozialdemokratische Partei Deutschlands), which supported the war and a parliamentary system.[13] A significant portion of the USPD reunited with the SPD in 1922, and throughout the Weimar Republic, the SPD was consistently the largest party in the Reichstag. Friedrich Ebert from the SPD became the Weimar Republic's first president (1919–25). The SPD remained devoted to parliamentary, liberal democracy and in opposition to the Communist Party of Germany (Kommunistische Partei Deutschlands; KPD) and the National Socialist German Workers' Party (Nationalsozialistische Deutsche Arbeiterpartei or abbreviated Nazi; NSDAP).

The KPD formed in December 1918 from the Spartacus League, a Marxist revolutionary movement that broke from the SPD in 1914 because they disagreed with the SPD's support of the war. The KPD's founders, Rosa Luxemburg and Karl Liebknecht, led a Socialist uprising in Berlin in January 1919. During the confusing and chaotic November Revolution, General Wilhelm Groener had struck a deal with Friedrich Ebert; Groener offered the support of the military in maintaining order, including against leftist uprisings that threatened Ebert's power, in exchange for Ebert's guarantee "not to reform the officer corps or reduce the power of the armed forces."[14] As a result of this Ebert-Groener pact, the *Freikorps*, a volunteer paramilitary unit sanctioned by the SPD government, suppressed the Socialist uprising and murdered Luxemburg and Liebknecht, thus creating a lasting rift between the KPD and SPD. In 1920, the left wing of the USPD united with the KPD. The KPD remained opposed to the leading Social Democratic Party throughout the Weimar Republic and also became a threat to the growing Nazi Party.

The NSDAP was a far-right political party that emerged in the aftermath of the First World War from the German Workers' Party, which originated in

1919. The NSDAP's first followers—workers—embraced extreme nationalism and racism and fought against the growing Communist movement in the post–World War I era. The party's platform, known as the Twenty-Five Points, called for repudiation of the Versailles Treaty, unification of Austria and Germany, exclusion of Jews from German citizenship, and land reform, among other things. Adolf Hitler joined the party in 1919, became the party's most talented speaker, and then became the party's chairman in 1921 after an internal mutiny in Munich. After that, he controlled the party under the *Führerprinzip* (leader principle), in which he became the absolute ruler. The party was committed to German nationalist expansion, antisemitism, and overthrowing the Weimar Republic. The party's militia, the *Sturmabteilung* (storm troopers; SA; colloquially known as the Brown Shirts for the brown uniforms they donned), started violently intimidating political opponents in 1921. Inspired by Benito Mussolini's 1922 Fascist coup in Rome, Hitler gained national attention only after the Beer Hall Putsch, an attempted coup of the Bavarian government in Munich on November 8–9, 1923. The coup failed, sixteen Nazis were killed, and Hitler was arrested and tried for treason. After serving only eight months of a five-year sentence in a minimum-security prison and writing his autobiography, *Mein Kampf* (*My Struggle*), Hitler reorganized the party and worked toward taking power legally.[15] The Nazi Party had minimal popular support until the Great Depression.

The September 1930 election was pivotal to the Nazi Party, and it was also when Gerhart Seger was first elected to the Reichstag. This election was dominated by the Great Depression's effects on German unemployment. The election was called early in an attempt to provide parliamentary backing for the cabinet of Heinrich Brüning, who was part of the Centre Party and had been chancellor since March 30, 1930.[16] Shortly after becoming chancellor, Brüning was attempting to pass a financial reform bill through the congested Reichstag (which had fifteen parties at the time) but was unable to obtain a parliamentary majority. Because of this political stagnation, he asked President Paul von Hindenburg (elected May 12, 1925) to invoke Article 48 of the Weimar Constitution. Article 48 allowed the president to enact an emergency decree under certain conditions and rule as a dictator for short periods of time without the consent of the Reichstag.[17] The Reichstag responded by repudiating the decree on July 18, 1930, by a slight majority, which then invalidated Hindenburg's emergency decree. At that point, Brüning was unable to pass any legislation that addressed the growing economic crisis, and he also faced a breakdown of parliamentary rule. As a result, he asked Hindenburg to dissolve the Reichstag session and call for new elections, which were scheduled for September 14, 1930.

In the 1930 election, people showed their dissatisfaction with Germany's traditional political parties due to growing impoverishment and unemployment caused by the Depression. Unemployment was at 2.2 million when Brüning took office in March and continued to steadily rise until it reached three million by the time of the September election. Brüning was incapable of coping with the economic crisis, failing to pass any legislation through the stagnated Reichstag, and people were upset with the president's continued use of the emergency decree, which eroded their faith in democracy and weakened the Weimar Republic.[18] The ruling SPD party sustained the heaviest losses, losing 10 seats (from 153 to 143) and maintained only a 24.5 percent share of the Reichstag.

While the SPD remained the largest party in the Reichstag after the 1930 election, this was also a decisive election for the NSDAP and the KPD. The KPD won 77 seats (out of 577), bringing their share of the Reichstag to 13.1 percent. And the NSDAP won 107 seats (up from 12 seats in the 1928 elections), bringing their share of the vote to 18.3 percent. The NSDAP became the second-largest party in the Reichstag. After the election, the SPD suggested the KPD work with them, but the leader of the KPD, Ernst Thälmann, rejected the offer. Because Brüning still did not have a working majority in the Reichstag, he continued to ask Hindenburg to invoke Article 48 several dozen times from 1930 until 1932 in order to implement policies and work outside the parliamentary system.[19] Meanwhile, unemployment continued to rise until it reached six million in March 1932, which amounted to approximately a third of the working-age population.

When Hindenburg's presidential term ended in 1932, he narrowly won re-election in early spring 1932, dismissed Brüning in May 1932, and appointed Franz von Papen from the Centre Party as the new chancellor the same month.[20] Von Papen did not have much support in the Reichstag, and immediately after his appointment Hindenburg dissolved the Reichstag and called for a new election on July 31, 1932, in the hopes of securing von Papen a parliamentary majority. Gerhart Seger won his seat in this election, but the NSDAP also gained more seats (230 out of 608) and overtook the SPD as the largest party in the Reichstag, with 37.4 percent of the vote. The Nazis did not have a ruling majority, nor did von Papen, and the other parties refused to cooperate, meaning no coalition government could be formed to pass any legislation. Von Papen continued to rely on Hindenburg invoking Article 48 to conduct ordinary government business. He asked Hindenburg to dissolve the Reichstag in September and to call another election on November 6, 1932, again in an attempt to secure a parliamentary majority. Seger won his seat again, but the NSDAP maintained its status in the Reichstag as the largest party, with 196 (out of 594) seats and 33.1 percent of the vote. The KPD also picked up seats in both of these elections (with 14.5 percent of the vote in July and 16.9 percent of the vote in November), while the SPD lost seats (down 3.9 percent in the July election and 1.2 percent in the November election). Hindenburg replaced von Papen at the beginning of December with Kurt von Schleicher.[21]

Von Schleicher attempted to blackmail Hitler into supporting his government by creating a coalition of supporters from the left wing of the Nazi Party and the Social Democratic and Christian labor unions. His plan failed, as all factions came to distrust von Schleicher. This led von Papen to convince President Hindenburg that if he appointed Hitler as chancellor, Hitler could attain a parliamentary majority in the Reichstag. With von Papen as vice chancellor and the cabinet filled with conservatives from the German National People's Party (Deutschnationale Volkspartei; DNVP), they could rein Hitler in, von Papen reasoned.[22] Hindenburg followed von Papen's advice, appointing Hitler chancellor on January 30, 1933, but of course, they had no idea that they would not be able to keep Hitler under control.

Contributions

The stories of early émigrés from Nazi Germany and political exiles like Gerhart Seger are well documented. Seger, for one, wrote two books about his experiences in Oranienburg and about his early years in exile. In addition to his books, there are a number of autobiographies by German exiles—for example, Heinrich Mann, Leo Marcuse, Alfred Kantorowicz, Rudolf Leonhard, Arthur Koestler, Manès Sperber, Franz Dahlem, Gustav Regler, and Carl Zuckmayer. Jean-Michel Palmier has written perhaps the most recent comprehensive history of German exiles from 1933 to 1945, taking into account the "antifascist struggle" and "the conditions of life of the refugees in the different countries where they settled."[23] As Palmier notes, *Exilforschung* (exile studies) has practically become a discipline of its own dating from the 1970s.[24] Furthermore, the *Gesellschaft für Exilforschung* (Society for Exile Studies) was founded in 1984 as "a forum for the coordination, organisation, and promotion of the interdisciplinary study of exile from Germany after 1933 and its ongoing consequences."[25] The society organizes an annual conference to disseminate new research and publishes a scholarly journal, *Exilforschung—Ein internationales Jahrbuch* (*Exile Research—An International Yearbook*), as well as a semiannual newsletter. A working group within the Society for Exile Studies, *Frauen im Exil* (Women in Exile), has organized a smaller conference regularly since 2009, and they also disseminate research on female émigrés that has long been neglected in general exile studies.

The numerous books devoted to German émigrés and exiles reveal very little about women. Ilse's memoir, then, is a novelty. Ilse's account is personal, shedding light on the domestic challenges faced by a woman trying to preserve her family in the face of growing harassment and the threat of physical attack by political opponents. It is also a rare account of a non-Jewish victim of the regime, showing the risks faced by political opponents. Not only does it offer us a woman's perspective, but it presents a more comprehensive picture of what wives were doing while their husbands were under arrest, imprisoned, or living in exile. Ilse's story contributes to our knowledge of how the partners of political exiles were influenced by and involved in their husbands' political lives, but also how they created and sustained political identities of their own.

Her experience of being detained in an early Nazi concentration camp as a result of the political affiliation, activities, and escape of her husband was not necessarily unique, but her memoir is important because it gives us insight into what more than one woman experienced because of the political actions of her husband. We know, for example, that women who held leading positions in the KPD, or married women who worked alongside their husbands who were well-known KPD functionaries, were arrested and detained in Gotteszell concentration camp, a women's concentration camp near Schwäbisch Gmünd in Wüttemberg. There were between sixty and eighty women imprisoned in Gotteszell during the time of the camp's existence (March 31, 1933, to January 21, 1934). Of the thirty-nine female prisoners for whom information is available, twenty-one were proven members of the KPD, but many professed to be Communists. There were other cases of arrests and imprisonment of women in Gotteszell in order to extort information about the activities or whereabouts of their husbands.[26] The *New York Times* even reported about Gotteszell in June 1933, highlighting the detainment of the wives, daughters, and sweethearts of the political prisoners of Wüttemberg, who were being held at Heuberg concentration camp.[27] Social Democrats and Communists were also imprisoned in Moringen-Solling, a women-only camp established in 1933 near Göttingen.[28]

Through Ilse's memoir, we also get a wider glimpse of the social milieu in which the Seger's moved—Social Democracy. Her account reveals the practical and emotional support for families within this political community and demonstrates how networks could successfully work clandestinely even within the most repressive regime. The underground network of the SPD helped pass knowledge of Gerhart's whereabouts after his escape to Ilse when she was under house arrest. This network also helped him once he made it to Prague, one of the centers of antifascism on the Continent.

The Czechoslovakian Socialist, Social Democratic, and Communist parties organized and financed a number of "resistance infrastructures" in the border regions of Silesia, Saxony, and Bavaria to provide German refugees with accommodations, food, and clothing and to organize the resistance in central Germany. The contacts and networks that Social Democrats created in German border regions helped German SPD members significantly, especially after March 1933.[29] The number of German émigrés that settled in Prague was quite considerable, and it became the hub of German Social-Democracy in exile after the SPD was banned in Germany. Heinrich Mann even attested to the fact "that the antifascist émigrés were not merely tolerated but received like family."[30] After Gerhart wrote his book *Oranienburg* in Czechoslovakia, it was translated into six languages, and the underground network of the SPD illegally distributed several thousand copies in Germany.[31] In 1934, when Gerhart lectured about the book, his experience, and the conditions in Germany in several European countries, the Norwegian Social Democrats organized a lecture tour throughout Norway about a week after he was reunited with Ilse and Renate in London.[32] The antifascist movement was especially strong in Scandinavian countries, as Kasper Braskén has demonstrated.[33] Braskén and others have highlighted that interwar antifascism was a global phenomenon.[34]

By 1934, outside of Prague, Paris had become the antifascist capital of Europe and an important city of connections for Gerhart and Ilse. In Paris, the world of liberals, Socialists, and intellectuals worked together under the leadership of German Communist exile Willi Münzenberg in what became known as the Münzenberg network.[35] Gerhart and Ilse likely encountered this group and other antifascists, although they made only a few short trips to Paris for Gerhart to give lectures and to take care of bureaucratic measures before they immigrated. It was in Paris that Gerhart and Ilse encountered other German refugees at the German Club, where Gerhart had lectured and where refugees met up regularly—another indication that they likely crossed paths with the Münzenberg group. In fact, they were with these other refugees, including another former SPD member, Max Brauer, when they all learned about the Night of Long Knives, a series of murders of SA members that Hitler ordered the SS (*Schutzstaffel*; Protection Squadrons) to carry out from June 30 to July 2, 1934—something Ilse wrote about in chapter 7.[36]

Ilse's memoir is a vital source in revealing the relationship between memory and gender because, as Marion Kaplan argues, "gender mattered as people reflected upon their lives." Kaplan highlights how women's memories tended to centralize family, friends, schools, neighborhoods, and domestic experiences while men focused more on public life, including their economic and business experiences or the political environment.³⁷ Certainly this was the case if you were to compare Ilse's and Gerhart's memories of this time period, with Ilse concentrating more on her devotion to her husband, her daughter, her friends, and her domestic life, even when it was upended; Gerhart's experience in Oranienburg and his escape were the core of *Oranienburg*. This does not mean they remembered this time period differently but rather that their original gendered experiences provide us with different perspectives. Ilse's memoir is unique, however, because in addition to narrating her private thoughts and emotions, she was recounting her husband's political experience, including his work, imprisonment, escape, and exile, and thus we see more about politics and public life than we might expect from a woman. We get, in other words, her inimitable perspective on public life.³⁸

Ilse's memoir also forms part of a genre of life-writing that offers new insight into the turbulent times that accompanied the end of the Weimar Republic and the rise of Nazism. Scholars like Ingrid Sharp have given attention to women's roles in the shaping the post–World War I political landscape in Germany, including their involvement in the suffrage movement and the German revolution of 1918–19.³⁹ Sharp highlights the importance of biographies and political memoirs by and about women as a means to gain "access to the political cultures of women."⁴⁰ Hilde Kramer, for one, recounted in a fragmentary memoir her role as a young Communist in the November 1918 revolution and her time as a political exile in Moscow and then in Britain.⁴¹ While women's political memoirs from the beginning of the Weimar Republic are more common, Ilse's memoir gives a rare glimpse at the republic's demise.

Sebastian Haffner and Toni Sender expose the turmoil of the early weeks after Hitler became chancellor. In his 1939 memoir, Haffner, a law student in early 1933, commented on the disbelief and paralysis that overwhelmed people.⁴² Sender, who became a member of the Reichstag on June 6, 1920, as a member of the USPD, published a memoir in 1939 while in exile.⁴³ She eventually rejoined the Social Democratic Party and served in the Reichstag until right after the Reichstag Fire (February 28, 1933), when she went into exile in Czechoslovakia and then eventually Belgium and the United States.⁴⁴ Sender was likely well acquainted with Johann Friedrich Seger, Gerhart Seger's father and Ilse's eventual father-in-law, and then Gerhart himself because she served alongside both of them in the same party in the Reichstag. In addition to her political opposition to the Nazis, Sender was also an Orthodox Jew and went into exile almost immediately after the Nazis came to power.

Ilse's memoir differs by highlighting her unique experience as a political opponent witnessing the rise of Nazism in Germany prior to Hitler's appointment as chancellor while her husband was serving in the Reichstag and running for reelection (1930–33). She also experienced the first few years of the Third Reich, including as one of the few women in an early Nazi concentration camp in 1934.[45] Ilse's political engagement reflected the opportunities available to her because of her middle-class status and her accessibility to her husband and other important SPD members.

Ilse's resistance to the Nazis is prevalent throughout the memoir, and thus it adds to the body of literature that explores women's defiance to Hitler, the impact they had, and the moral and ethical dilemmas they faced.[46] The Nazis often took away active and experienced men, thus leaving women to fend for themselves. This was most certainly the case during the war years, when the Nazis invaded foreign lands and killed intellectuals and Jewish men or forced them to flee. But it also applied to early political opponents like Gerhart, whom the Nazis imprisoned and who then fled by escaping. Ilse, then, was forced to rely on her own resources and develop a leadership role, similar to other women who were imprisoned in concentration camps as the Holocaust unfolded.[47]

Resistance to National Socialism could be gendered, and defiant women reform what historians know and assume about models of resistance. For one, more dominant models of resistance focus on military operations or armed resistance; women challenge this narrative by performing primarily nonviolent forms of resistance. Women's motivations for resisting also differed, as they often resisted for humanitarian rather than political or economic reasons, based on their social positioning and their drive to preserve human life. And, most importantly, women integrated acts of defiance "into their everyday life activities, a day-to-day stand for what they thought was right."[48] The Nazis perpetuated the stereotype of women as passive and homebound, thus allowing women to more easily travel, stroll the streets, and not draw suspicion from authorities.[49] Ilse's resistance fulfilled all of these trends.

Ilse's story demonstrates that women had political agency even when expectations of women showed otherwise. Although she was not educated, her class status, her connections, and the reputation of her husband afforded certain opportunities for her to resist and benefited her once she was imprisoned. She was certainly aware of the political situation in Germany more than most because of her connections through Gerhart to the SPD. She found herself among a group of Social Democrats and Communists "who organized active resistance against Nazi violence and criminality as quickly as possible"; after all, they were the ones being arrested, imprisoned, and persecuted. Women took an active part in this resistance, but it was the men who became the primary targets.[50] Her defiance to the Nazis was often personally motivated because Gerhart's position, actions, and decisions threatened Nazi authorities. Her love and devotion to her husband and her daughter are the core of her story, and they also motivated her to resist. At the simplest level, a mother's responsibility to keep her child(ren) alive often drove her.[51] In other words, Ilse was motivated by both humanitarian concerns of keeping her husband and daughter alive and the political pressure of supporting the SPD and their network of friends within the party.

In Nazi Germany, there was a strong culture of coercion, surveillance, censorship, and denunciations. The press openly reported about the police state, the concentration camps, and the discriminatory campaigns aimed at specific individuals, minorities, and social groups for whom Germans had little sympathy and deemed to be bad citizens. As Robert Gellately has shown, the German people were well aware of the Nazi terror, and the majority still fell in line.[52] Gellately and Sheila Fitzpatrick have also highlighted "the important role of denunciations in the routine operation of the Gestapo and the terror system."[53] This made even the small acts of solidarity and friendship that Ilse maintained that much more remarkable. Ilse also mentioned acts of kindness, decency, and humanity from others, often from women, both before she was detained and while she was in Rosslau; these acts, too, were notable in light of Nazi terror and broaden our understanding of resistance.

Ilse defied the Nazis with acts large and small, all of them nonviolent and most of which were incorporated into her day-to-day life, at least before she was under house arrest or imprisoned in a concentration camp. Her range of actions fell under the broad definition of resistance that historians Brana Gurewitsch and Doris Bergen call attention to. Bergen defines resistance "as any actions taken with the intent of thwarting Nazi German goals in the war, actions that carried with them risk of punishment."[54] Ilse claimed to dislike the followers of Nazism while her husband, Gerhart, was campaigning for his position in the Reichstag between 1930 and 1932, as seen in chapter 1. Once President Paul von Hindenburg appointed Hitler as chancellor on January 30, 1933, Gerhart and Ilse insisted on staying in Germany rather than leaving, as many of Gerhart's colleagues did (chap. 2). Staying in Germany put them in a position to witness the rapid changes firsthand and to act accordingly. After the Nazis arrested and imprisoned Gerhart, Ilse aggressively demanded, as seen in chapter 3, to see her husband in the Dessau prison, not knowing the consequences of her actions. Also, she continued meeting with SPD friends and colleagues to discuss the Reichstag Fire when this could have resulted in punishment from the Nazis. In some of her bravest moments of individual resistance, Ilse purposefully shopped at a Jewish-owned department store during the Nazi boycott of Jewish businesses and stores on April 1, 1933, demonstrating non-Jewish solidarity with German Jews, and voted against Hitler's decision to pull Germany out of the League of Nations in a referendum that November. Perhaps her boldest demonstration of resistance against the Nazis was smuggling money to Gerhart while he was imprisoned in Oranienburg, which proved essential to his escape. In chapter 4, in defiance of Nazi authorities overseeing her house arrest, Ilse concocted a plan to talk with her mother in secret about Gerhart. She also received secret messages from some of the SPD underground about Gerhart, including an attempted plan of escape, which certainly could have resulted in further consequences for her or Gerhart or even their daughter. In chapter 5, once she was imprisoned as a hostage in Rosslau concentration camp, Ilse turned to humor as a form of resistance, especially while reflecting on the uniqueness of having her infant daughter in the camp with her.

Even the most comprehensive research on Rosslau has resulted only in succinct summaries of the camp.[55] In contrast, Ilse's imprisonment at Rosslau provides one of the most detailed descriptions of the layout of the camp, the personnel working there, the prisoners, and the various privileges that some prisoners did or did not enjoy. Her experience at Rosslau adds to our overall knowledge of early concentration camps. Some of the earliest camps were relatively benign compared to later camps, providing prisoners with a subsistence diet, the use of their own clothing and provisions, and decent medical care.[56] Ilse commented on some of these elements of the camp and, less often, on some of the darker parts of the camp. Certainly her experience, and thus her view of the camp, was colored by the fact that she was a hostage in the camp, not a prisoner, and was afforded certain privileges.

Lastly, Ilse's memoir adds further insight to *Alltagsgeschichte* (the history of everyday life) by showing what daily life was like for the wife of a political opponent of the Nazi regime. Richard Bessel, Detlev Peukert, David Crew, Lisa Pine, and others have explored aspects of everyday life in Nazi Germany but have not looked specifically at how the families of political opponents lived.[57] Throughout her memoir, Ilse constantly reflected on her identity as the loyal wife of a political opponent, her own growing political identity as a Nazi resister, and her identity as a mother and the sole support for her daughter while her husband was imprisoned and living in exile. The tension in balancing these roles is palpable, for example, when she discussed the joy, happiness, and anxiety of being a new mother, especially under the extreme circumstances she found herself in, under house arrest and then eventually as a hostage in a concentration camp.

Ilse's recounting of heightened moments of political activity are interspersed with her narration of the tedious routines of everyday "'women's work'—activities centering around food, children, clothing, shelter, social relations, warmth, and cleanliness." These so-called trivial everyday activities, however, mattered and made life among the oppressed become possible.[58] Caring for Renate gave meaning and structure to Ilse's everyday life.[59] Certain experiences otherwise stood out for Ilse *because* they were exceptional among the mundane roles of being a wife and mother. Because of her husband's politics, for example, drunken members of the Nazi Party fired gunshots into her home, barely missing her, and out of loyalty to her husband, she nervously carried a gun in her handbag to give to him at a political rally. She also gave vivid descriptions of her own resistance to the Nazis in the instances mentioned above. In addition, she remembered demanding that her daughter's crib be brought to Rosslau and giving Renate her first bath in the camp. After Gerhart had escaped and was living in exile, her memoir shows a constant tension that weighed heavily on Ilse, as she debated wanting to be a loyal wife and resister by joining her husband abroad and the fear of losing her daughter or causing harm to her family.

Ilse's "history of [her] daily life shows how mundane issues matter—and often dominate—even in extreme situations."[60] As Kaplan has argued for Jewish women, "the tension between the normal and the abnormal, the ordinary and the extraordinary, the daily and the long range" permeated their lives. The same could be said for Ilse; she too lived an "abnormal normality," but it had everything to do with her husband's position vis-à-vis the new Nazi government and not her ethnic and religious background.[61]

Notes

1. Personal correspondence with Mark Brandt, grandson of Ilse Seger, June 20, 2020.
2. Personal correspondence with Jennifer Brandt, granddaughter of Ilse Seger, February 7, 2023.
3. Personal correspondence with Mark Brandt, June 2022.
4. Personal correspondence with Jennifer Brandt, February 7, 2023.
5. Personal correspondence with Mark Brandt, June 2022.
6. Personal correspondence with Jennifer Brandt, February 7, 2023.
7. Personal conversation with Mark Brandt, February 1, 2023; personal correspondence with Jennifer Brandt, February 7, 2023.
8. Personal correspondence with Jennifer Brandt, February 7, 2023.
9. Kaplan, *Between Dignity and Despair*, 8.
10. Personal correspondence with Jennifer Brandt, February 7, 2023.
11. Personal conversation with Mark Brandt, February 1, 2023.
12. Seger, *Oranienburg*, or the English version, *A Nation Terrorized*, and *Reisetagebuch eines deutschen Emigranten*.
13. They informally used the name Majority Social Democratic Party of Germany from 1917 to 1922 to distinguish themselves from the Independent Social Democratic Party of Germany,

although those affected preferred the old name Social Democratic Party of Germany. See Luban, "Die Novemberrevolution 1918 in Berlin," 54; Hunt, *German Social Democracy*, 23–5.

14. "The Weimar Republic," *Holocaust Encyclopedia*, United States Holocaust Memorial Museum, https://encyclopedia.ushmm.org/content/en/article/the-weimar-republic.

15. "Beer Hall Putsch (Munich Putsch)," *Holocaust Encyclopedia*, United States Holocaust Memorial Museum, https://encyclopedia.ushmm.org/content/en/article/beer-hall-putsch-munich-putsch.

16. The German Centre Party was a Christian democratic and Catholic political party, formed in 1870. It took a middle position on most issues (between the Social Democrats and the conservatives like those in the German Conservative Party and later the German National People's Party) and was very influential during the Imperial Period (1871–1918) and the Weimar Republic when it was the third largest party in the Reichstag. See Blackbourn, "The Political Alignment of Centre Party in Wilhelmine Germany," 822–25.

17. The intent of Article 48 was to allow the president to avoid what could be a slow legislative process in order "to take decisive action in times of crisis." Presidents Ebert and Hindenburg both used it regularly; Hindenburg often abused it when no consensus in the Reichstag could be reached. See "Article 48," *Holocaust Encyclopedia*, United States Holocaust Memorial Museum, https://encyclopedia.ushmm.org/content/en/article/article-48.

18. Ibid.

19. "Hindenburg invoked Article 48 sixty times in 1932 alone." Ibid.

20. The Weimar Constitution permitted the president to appoint or remove the chancellor.

21. For more on the elections of the Weimar Republic, see a Historical Exhibition Presented by the German Bundestag: Deutscher Bundestag, "Elections in the Weimar Republic," published March 2006, https://www.bundestag.de/resource/blob/189774/7c6dd629f4afff7bf4f962a45c110b5f/elections_weimar_republic-data.pdf.

22. The DNVP was a conservative party that was formed in 1918 after the end of World War I. It rejected the republican Weimar Constitution and sought a restoration of the monarchy. The DNVP also repudiated the Treaty of Versailles, the peace treaty that Germany and the Allied powers signed after the First World War that required Germany to accept full responsibility for the war, disarm, make ample territorial concessions, and pay significant reparations to Britain and France. Several prominent Nazis began in the DNVP, which eventually lost most of their voters to the NSDAP after 1929. See Evans, *The Feminist Movement in Germany*, 244, 253.

23. Palmier, *Weimar in Exile*, 14. His introduction also covers the extensive historiography of German exiles dating from as far back as 1935–38.

24. Palmier, *Weimar in Exile*, 11, 664n38.

25. Gesellschaft für Exilforschung, http://www.exilforschung.de/index.php?p=3#english. Claus-Dieter Krohn, who served on the board of the Society for Exile Studies and as coeditor of the journal, has also published several important books on German exiles, including *Frauen und Exil* and *Handbuch der deutschsprachigen Emigration*.

26. Kienle, "Gotteszell," 83–4.

27. "Women Reds Held in Camp by Nazis: Wuerttemberg Detains Wives, Daughters, and Sweethearts of Political Prisoners. They Are an Unhappy Lot with Homes and Trades of Their Breadwinners Gone, They Await Release in Worried Mood," *New York Times*, June 21, 1933, 8.

28. White, "Moringen-Solling (Women)," 128–31.

29. Steinberg, "Should I Stay or Should I Go?" 83–4.

30. Palmier, *Weimar in Exile*, 137–8; Mann, *Ein Zeitalter wird besichtigt*, 472.

31. Seger, *The Reminiscences of Gerhart Henry Seger*, 80, https://dlc.library.columbia.edu/catalog/cul:mcvdncjw1g.

32. Seger wrote a chapter about this tour in his *Reisetagebuch*, pages 42–52, and Ilse described it in chapter 7. See also ibid., 80–1, for more on his European tour.

33. Braskén, "'Make Scandinavia a Bulwark against Fascism!'" 110.
34. Braskén, Copsey, and Featherstone, *Anti-Fascism in a Global Perspective*.
35. Braskén, "'Aid the Victims of German Fascism!'" 199. See also Rabinbach, "Paris."
36. Brauer had been a well-known SPD member and mayor of Altona during the Weimar Republic. On the day of the March 5, 1933, election, the police searched his apartment, and the SA occupied it the next day. He fled to Austria later that month, but the situation there became too dangerous with the German SA roaming free, so he escaped to Switzerland and then to France. With the help of French acquaintances and a French Socialist, he made his way to Paris, where he was living in exile in 1934. For more on his persecution and flight from Germany, see Schildt, *Max Brauer*, 43–8, and Fladhammer and Wildt, eds., *Max Brauer im Exil*, 24–31.
37. Kaplan, *Between Dignity and Despair*, 8.
38. Ibid., 7.
39. Sharp, "Dangerous Visionaries and Revolutionary Transformations." Sharp discusses the historiography of women's political participation in the 1918–19 German revolution on pages 409–11.
40. Ibid., 403.
41. Kramer, *Rebellin in München, Moskau, und Berlin*.
42. Haffner, *Defying Hitler*.
43. Sender became a member of the SPD when it reunited with the USPD in 1922, but a small faction of USPD members continued as an independent party without much significance until 1931, when they united with the Socialist Workers' Party of Germany (Sozialistische Arbeiterpartei Deutschland).
44. Sender, *The Autobiography of a German Rebel*.
45. Gellately, *Backing Hitler*, 58.
46. Gurewitsch, ed., *Mothers, Sisters, Resisters*; Stoltzfus, Paldiel, and Baumel-Schwartz, eds., *Women Defying Hitler*; Rittner and Roth, eds., *Different Voices*; Schad, *Frauen gegen Hitler*; Geyken, *Wir standen nichts abseits*; Stiefel, *Sie waren im Getriebe*.
47. Gurewitsch, ed., *Mothers, Sisters, Resisters*, xiv–xv.
48. Stoltzfus, Paldiel, and Baumel-Schwartz, "Women Defying Hitler," 6.
49. Gurewitsch, ed., *Mothers, Sisters, Resisters*, 221; ibid., 11.
50. Berghahn, "Defiance and Resistance to Nazism from the Perspective of Gender, Class, and Generation," 77–8.
51. Gurewitsch, ed., *Mothers, Sisters, Resisters*, 3.
52. Gellately, *Backing Hitler*, 2–5.
53. Fitzpatrick and Gellately, "Introduction to the Practices of Denunciation in Modern European History," 6.
54. Bergen, *War and Genocide*, 263. See also Gurewitsch, ed., *Mothers, Sisters, Resisters*, 221.
55. White, "Rosslau," 157–58.
56. Gurewitsch, ed., *Mothers, Sisters, Resisters*, 4.
57. Aycoberry, *The Social History of the Third Reich*; Bessel, *Life in the Third Reich*; Crew, ed., *Nazism and German Society*; Grunberger, *A Social History of the Third Reich*; Peukert, *Inside Nazi Germany*; Pine, *Hitler's 'National Community'*; Pine, ed., *Life and Times in Nazi Germany*. See also the forum on "Everyday Life in Nazi Germany."
58. Ringelheim, "Women and the Holocaust," 378–79; Gurewitsch, ed., *Mothers, Sisters, Resisters*, 5.
59. Gurewitsch, ed., *Mothers, Sisters, Resisters*, 8.
60. Kaplan, *Between Dignity and Despair*, 6.
61. Ibid., 10.

1

Becoming a Wife and Mother with Nazism on the Rise

Gerhart Seger was born on November 16, 1896, in Leipzig, Germany. His father, Johann Friedrich Seger, was a tailor who had cofounded a clothing workers' union and belonged to the SPD (Sozialdemokratische Partei Deutschlands; Social Democratic Party of Germany). Johann also became a political editor of the Social Democratic *Leipziger Volkszeitung*, one of the most well-respected workers' newspapers. He was elected to the city council in 1911, and after the First World War, he served as its head. From 1915 until 1918, he was a member of the state parliament of Saxony. In 1919–20, he was a member of the constituent national assembly in Weimar as a member of the Independent Social Democratic Party (Unabhängige Sozialdemokratische Partei Deutschlands; USPD), and from 1920 until his early death in 1928, he was a member of the SPD in the Reichstag. Gerhart's mother died of tuberculosis when he was very young, so the only mother he knew was his father's second wife, Hedwig Seger, who raised him.

Gerhart attended elementary school as well as a vocational school where he learned how to be a stone printer and graphic artist until the First World War. With his father's political influence, Gerhart became engaged in the Social Democratic worker youth movement. He held his first lecture for the group when he was only sixteen years old, thus beginning a long life of giving political speeches. From 1915 to 1918, during the First World War, he served in the cavalry, the infantry, and finally the air force. He was on the front in Russia, Italy, and France, including during the Battle of the Somme.

After the war, he attended the University of Leipzig, where he studied cultural history and journalism. He credited the Leipzig School of Journalism with making him into a capable journalist.[1] He started his work as a journalist in 1920 when he took over as editor for the USPD's *Die Freiheit* (*Freedom*) in Berlin. In 1922, when a significant portion of the USPD reunited with the SPD, Gerhart became a member of this party for the first time.[2] From 1920 to 1933, he worked as a journalist in Kiel, Berlin, and Plauen and as a foreign correspondent in most European capitals. From 1923 to 1928, he was the secretary general of the German Peace Society (Deutsche Friedensgesellschaft, DFG), a pacifist organization that had upward of thirty thousand members at the time.[3]

Because this is Ilse's memoir, the story below begins when she met Gerhart while he was working at the German Peace Society.

September 1970

Some time ago, your mother [Renate] mentioned that it might be quite interesting for you when you are older, and later on for your own children, to learn how it happened that she, your grandfather, and I, all three of us born in Germany, came over to this country, found a new home here, and finally became United States citizens. So I will try to tell you a little bit about it. Quite a few of the events that eventually made this happen you will learn in your school, when you study European history later on. So I will try to stick mostly to our own personal experiences.

Your grandfather and I got married after a very short courtship on June 16, 1928. At that time, Opi was secretary general of the Deutsche Friedensgesellschaft, a German peace organization that started in 1892 and to which many famous Germans belonged.[4] For this organization, he traveled throughout Germany quite often, lecturing to all sorts of audiences, and one day he came to Freiburg, Baden, the town in which my family and I had lived since the end of the war. He was the guest of very good friends of mine, and in their house, we saw each other for the first time.[5] I liked him very much, and I was fascinated by his conversations; just like all the other guests, I enjoyed his well-told jokes, mostly with political meanings—quite different from the kind of conversation I was used to. At home, for instance, since my father was an actor and director, the topics mostly had something to do with the theater, and of course Opi was quite different from the student groups with whom I spent most of my social life. Little did I know then about the great and most important part this man would play later on in my life. The next day after we met, he left again, and for me he was nothing more than the pleasant memory of a very nice, interesting evening, and pretty soon I had forgotten all about him.

But then at Christmas he came to visit my friends again, and I, too, was invited for that evening—as I heard later, as a special wish of his.

I enjoyed his company very much again, and later on he brought me home. We talked and talked that night, and I don't remember how many times we walked around the block. Two days later, we were engaged! My parents were quite upset; for them, he was a complete stranger, and my friends were a bit worried in the beginning too. But then everybody calmed down, and not quite half a year later, we married and moved to Berlin, where the headquarters of the Peace Society was.

But we stayed there for only a few months because Opi, who was looking for a job as a newspaperman again, the subject he had studied in Leipzig, where he was born, was offered a very good position as editor in chief in the town of Dessau/Anhalt, at a Social Democratic newspaper there.[6] And from there his political career started—and pretty soon our troubles too!

But before that, we had a very interesting and happy life there. We had a beautiful apartment, our first, since in Berlin we lived in two furnished rooms. Very quickly we made good friends. The famous Bauhaus had found its second home there.[7] The city had a very good theater, opera, and concert orchestra, and since Opi was the drama reviewer for his newspaper too, there was hardly a week in which we did not spend at least one evening at the theater.

But pretty soon the political atmosphere in Germany got more and more difficult. There was not, as is the case here [in the US], a two-party system in Germany, but there were at least ten big parties and I don't remember how many little ones—splinter parties, as they were called. Opi was elected as a candidate to become a member of the Reichstag, the German parliament, for the Social Democratic Party, and the campaigning time started. During this time, a new party was growing very fast, the so-called National Socialist German Workers' Party, whose leader was a man by the name of Adolf Hitler, the man who later became responsible for incredible tragedies throughout Europe and who finally started the Second World War. Opi had watched the rise of this party and the doctrine of its leader, had read his infamous book, *Mein Kampf*, and had seen the private army with which this man had surrounded himself—the *Sturmtruppen*, or the SS and SA, as they were called. Opi was one of those who recognized rather early the danger this man and his followers presented. He knew that if this man would ever gain the majority in the Reichstag, Germany would become a dictatorship.

Of course, other people realized that too, but a very great part of the German people were politically untrained. As a matter of fact, the name Workers' Party was completely misleading: very few workers ever became National Socialists, or Nazis, as they were called. Most of the followers came from the middle-income groups, the bourgeoisie, and later on, sad as it is, from groups of people who should have known better: teachers, scientists, physicians, etc. So, when Opi started his campaigning, his speeches were mainly directed against this party and what it stood for. He tried to tell his listeners about the danger the program of this party would pose to millions of people and to the future of Germany. Very often, wild debates developed and fights started, and the police had to interfere, and it ended with quite a few bloody heads.

I tried to be with Opi whenever I could because I was always afraid that someday something might happen to him. His own party members persuaded him to buy a revolver. He did that, finally, very reluctantly; the police gave him a permit right away, but most of the time, the revolver was somewhere in a closet at home; he just carried his permit. But we had good times just the same. We went to little villages on trucks with our banners flying and a little band that started playing as soon as we entered one of those villages and went to the marketplace; after a while of playing, when enough people were around us, Opi started his speech. It was a little bit more difficult at that time. There were no loudspeakers to carry the voice of the speaker all over the place. He had very much to rely on his own strong voice. That is fine if you do it once, but if you have to speak in five or six such places, you are not only quite tired when you finally get home, but your voice is quite hoarse too. Opi drank a lot of warm milk with honey during that time. After such a day was over, the whole group sometimes stopped in one of those little country inns for a cold beer, and after everyone had rested a little, the band started playing just for a few dances. I remember one of those evenings especially well, when someone called out, "And now a solo dance for our candidate and his beautiful wife!" Boy, did we put a waltz on the floor, having the whole place all for ourselves.

Finally, in September 1930, election day was here. We were all waiting excitedly for the results of the election with the leaders of the Social Democratic Party of Dessau and some friends. News came over the radio, and telephones were ringing. We all had counting sheets in front of us, and in the beginning, everybody was very happy. But as it got later into the night, the news started to become very serious as far as the success of the election of our party was concerned. It became pretty clear that the Nazis had made quite some inroads in nearly every party and so had won quite a substantial victory and could send at least 107 delegates to the Reichstag. In all that excitement and bitter disappointment, we completely forgot about our own interest in this special election, until suddenly one of Opi's coeditors came running into the room where we were counting and listening to the results and cried, "Gerhart, Gerhart, you are elected!" This was, of course, a proud moment, as you can imagine. Opi was at that time not quite thirty-four years old, which is certainly very young to become a member of parliament. Everybody came around and shook hands and congratulated us, but there was no real happiness; we were all too depressed about the tremendous force the Nazi Party had shown. It was of little consolation that our party had lost very few votes.

The gain of the Nazis came mostly from the right and far right side and from all those little parties that had not much meaning on their own as long as they were alone. When we went home, dead tired and depressed, around six o'clock in the morning—it was so typical for your grandfather—all of a sudden, he sat up straight in the taxi, took my hand, and said, "Well, that means we have to work harder; we have to go to their meetings too, and not only wait and let them come to us." He had already started to make plans and think about who he would confer with, etc. And since we were young and optimistic, we all of a sudden had the feeling it would work out—it somehow would be all right. The pride and joy over Opi's personal success made us forget the disappointment we had felt before.

Now quite a different life began for us. Opi had to be in Berlin very often when the Reichstag was in session. He soon was elected to the foreign affairs committee, and besides this there were many lecture trips all over Germany. So I had to be alone quite a lot. But, of course, we had many very good friends who came to me or whom I could go to visit, and when Opi had to go to Berlin, I very often went with him. We usually stayed in the same little hotel near Potsdamer Platz. I even remember the name: Hotel Askanischer Hof. Even if I usually spent the day alone unless I went to the Reichstag's meetings, where I could always get a seat in the gallery and listen in, Opi and I were, of course, always together in the evening, unless there was a night session in the Reichstag. When that happened, I usually went home by train in the evening because Opi could sometimes still catch a late train around two or so in the morning, so that after a few hours' sleep, he still could go to his newspaper job in the morning.

There were, of course, times when the Reichstag was not in session and things were a bit less hectic. But that was the case only in the first year. Then it got worse. The Nazis made more and more trouble, and the cabinet of the government was dissolved. There were new elections for the Reichstag every time this happened, and this meant new election campaigns. You see, the Weimar Constitution that Germany had at that time was quite different from our constitution here [in the US], and we had quite a few newly elected parliaments during that time. It meant hard work for everybody who was in politics, but Opi was reelected every time. One of these elections even brought a setback for the Nazi Party, but unfortunately that did not last very long.[8]

But then something very wonderful happened to us. I found out that I would have a baby, and we were looking forward with great excitement to our trip to Freiburg to spend Christmas with my parents and brothers and to surprise them with our good news. We amused ourselves on the trip by thinking about boys' and girls' names. If it would be a boy, I wanted to call him Peter. Opi had some other names that I don't recall anymore, but if it would be a girl, we both agreed right away on Renate. And Opi somehow was quite sure it would be a girl, maybe because he wished it so much. But of course we both knew, whatever it would be, the most important thing was that it would be a healthy child, and from the way I felt the whole time, I was quite sure of that.

We spent ten wonderful and, especially for Opi, restful days in Freiburg, and when we went back home, the usual routine started. Between Opi's work at his newspaper and his frequent trips to Berlin—if possible with me, but more often alone; there were quite a few meetings all over the country to which our party sent him—I had a lot of time for myself. So I read very much, and between all kinds of books, I started reading well-known American authors like Sinclair Lewis, Upton Sinclair, Theodore Dreiser, Jack London, and many others. So many things seemed strange and difficult to understand, but everything was quite exciting about this country [America]. Together with my reading and quite a few American movies, silent ones of course, I tried to get a picture of this land, and it interested me to no end. Opi and I spoke a lot about it; he was just as interested as I was, maybe even more so since his father had been on a lecture trip through America quite some years ago. We both wished that there would be a possibility for us sometime to go and see this country. But we both thought about it as a wish—one of those dreams one has. Such a trip would be terribly expensive, and besides, one didn't travel so easily in that time, especially to another continent.

During this year, life in Germany started to change. Hitler's private army, the SA and SS, had grown. His followers got more and more fanatical about his program, which appealed to the worst overly patriotic ideas, which are always a hindrance to political thinking and common sense. Another very important part in his program was his antisemitism, and his party symbol was a red flag with a swastika in a white circle in the middle of it, which later, when he became chancellor, was also made the official flag of Germany.[9]

For me, when I saw this flag, it was always as if a big spider was crawling over it. I had a real physical aversion to it. This swastika, which originally used to be an Indian luck sign, had become a sign for antisemitism.[10] People started to wear it like one wears campaign buttons during elections, only the meaning of it was not as harmless as that. It meant, of course, that they were all behind Hitler, but it meant too that they were in agreement with his program as far as his treatment of Jews was concerned. It is certainly true that quite a few of these people never really read Hitler's program. He blamed the Jews for everything that was wrong in Germany—for unemployment, which was very high at that time; for having international connections; and for being an inferior race.

As I have discovered now by trying to describe all this a little bit to you, I realize how difficult this is to understand, and I wonder if I make any sense to you. It is such a sad experience when one finds out that people are not only of different opinions, which would be all right, but that because they are of different opinions, they start to hate each other. That became more and more the case in Germany. Mistrust and fear grew. Our Jewish friends started to think about leaving the country. But that, of course, was not as easily done as said. They were Germans, had always felt like Germans, but now they were told that they didn't belong, they were strangers, inferior, and the battle cry started: "Jews out!" Of course, not all Germans thought like that, especially not the working class, the union people, and part of the middle class. But it meant more and more courage was needed now to hold on to their own beliefs. Not all people are fighters, and it is so much easier to go with the trend.

By now, very much against the convictions of most of them, but out of practical necessity, the anti-Hitler parties had founded a sort of protective association: the Reichsbanner, which had as its symbol three little arrows in a row, and whose members and sympathizers greeted each other with the word "liberty." One of the reasons behind the forming of the Reichsbanner was to give our speakers and meetings some protection. More and more frequently, political meetings became brawls started by the SA (without whom no Nazi speaker ever opened his mouth) when someone in the audience tried to argue with the speaker. Most of the time, the police, who were very often already partly on the side of the Nazis, made only halfhearted efforts to hold the crowd in order. For me, it was a good feeling when I knew the Reichsbanner had sent some of their people there when Opi had to speak. Because our baby was to be born soon, I went less and less with him, and it was always a very anxious evening until he finally came home.

Finally, the day we were so anxiously waiting for arrived. Opi brought me to the hospital early in the morning, and at 4:30 in the afternoon, we were the proud parents of a lovely little girl: Renate, your dear mother.[11] She was a long, slender little girl who looked very much like her father. She had dark hair and about ten long eyelashes, five on each eye. I counted them because they looked so funny, quite long and dark. My mother, who had of course come from Freiburg to be with us for the first weeks, as well as Opi, insisted that she had my mouth. After ten days, Opi brought us home. I would have liked to go earlier, but our doctor insisted on keeping me a little longer until I really had my strength back. After all, the agitation and the anxiety of the last few months had taken a bit more out of me than it would have in normal times.

The next few weeks I remember as very peaceful and happy. Opi had taken two weeks' vacation, so he was with us all the time, and one day, he insisted on giving the baby a bath. I had a good time looking at that performance, but Opi got so scared that the baby might slip in the little bathtub that I finally took pity on him and took over. But he learned to diaper the baby and loved to hold his daughter. Every Sunday for that first half year, there was picture-taking time, and no matter what else we wanted to do on those Sundays, this came first.

But as happy as we were, things around us had not changed—or, rather, they had gotten worse. The atmosphere in the country was something that is not so easy to describe. The Nazis, encouraged by their obvious success, had become more and more aggressive, and people were more and more scared. It is one thing to disagree about something, but if the other side is always the attacker, the more timid people finally give in, especially when they do not have very definite opinions of their own or strong political convictions. And that quite a lot of the German people did not have.

Most of them, particularly the so-called middle class, the bourgeoisie, were never really politically inclined, and all the noise, the parades, the talk about Germany's honor, the necessity of her becoming a world power again, etc., were very tempting and easy to believe. These people were completely caught in Hitler's demagoguery. They might even have believed what he and his party leaders were telling them because they heard what they wanted to hear; they did not have to think very much because he made up their minds for them. And on top of this, they started to become afraid. Since the Nazis were so aggressive, they had the feeling it would be better to be on their side to be safe.

Of course, not all Germans were like that. There was still a very strong opposition, but it required some courage to belong to it. Besides, the middle class never liked the Social Democrats, who were the strongest opponents of the Nazis. But one thing I will never understand is how it was possible to incite so many basically decent people all of a sudden to such a fanatic hatred of the Jews, who, in many cases, were their neighbors, their doctors, their lawyers—people they had known and trusted for many years. How could they follow a party that had quite openly proclaimed in its program the persecution and destruction of people who had lived there for generations, had done their citizens' duty in war and peace like everybody else? How could parents and teachers let their children sing a song, for instance, that started with the words *"Und wenn das Judenblut vom Messer spritzt,"* meaning "And when the Jewish blood is spurting from the knife"?

But back to us. It was again Christmastime, and we decided to go to Freiburg. Our little girl was now four months old, and the doctor didn't see any reason why she should not travel. Of course, that would be on a train, not in a nice car, as you all are used to traveling in. But the trains were well-heated and comfortable. I could get some milk warmed up any time in the dining car of the train, and besides, Renatchen, or Püppi, as we used to call her, loved to eat mashed bananas, which I could easily prepare on the train. Besides, she would be asleep most of the time.[12] I was very happy about this trip. In the first place, we liked to spend Christmas with my family, and of course, we were very anxious to present the youngest member of the family. But there was another reason too. Opi was not politically known in

Freiburg. We would have some privacy there, not like in Dessau, where nearly everybody knew him, friend and foe. More than once, SA troops passed us on the streets, waving their fists at us and shouting all sorts of threats and making obscene remarks.

When we arrived in Freiburg, the whole family was at the railway station, and since besides our luggage we had a collapsible baby carriage, we needed two taxis to get home. Quite a luxury in those days! When we arrived at the apartment, I put the baby on the sofa, and everybody was crowding around it to see and talk to the *"wunderkind."* But that finally became a little bit too much for Püppi, and all of a sudden, her big, blue eyes filled with tears and she started to cry bitterly, the first time on that long trip. So I chased the family out of the room and carried her around for a little while until she quieted down and I could put her in the little baby basket my mother had prepared for her where she fell asleep right away.

The next day, she adjusted herself very quickly to the new surroundings and the new faces and smiled very happily at everybody who talked to her. And the Christmas tree was a big success. She wanted to touch all the lights and was not a bit afraid. I remember that all so vividly because this was such a beautiful Christmas. We felt so relaxed and so far away from reality. At least, I tried to close my eyes and not look when I saw Nazis in their uniforms or the hated swastika on the lapels of other people. Things as a whole were much quieter in Freiburg at that time than they were in Dessau. Besides, in 1932, nobody had a television set. There was radio, of course, which by no means everybody had either, but that transmitted mostly music and theater plays—no news. Of course, Opi bought his newspapers every day, but I don't remember that we talked about politics very much during the time we were there. I think this was the last real good time we had in Germany before Hitler finally became chancellor.

But eventually we had to go home again and face the everyday responsibilities. Shortly after the Christmas recess was over, the Reichstag was dissolved again, and a new election period started. Again, that meant a lot of campaigning for Opi, and I was grateful when it was only in and around Dessau so he could at least be home at night. But our nights were not always very peaceful. Very often at one or two o'clock in the morning, our phone rang, and when Opi or I answered, somebody at the other end started to make threatening remarks or just laughed and hung up. After an especially unpleasant night, we even considered having our phone disconnected, but of course, that was impossible. We needed the phone. Opi had to be reached by our own people.

One night when the phone rang again and again, we decided not to answer it and turned the bell of our bedroom phone completely off. The next morning, we found out that someone in our own party had wanted to reach Opi and tell him about a fight between the SA and some Reichsbanner people, which had happened in our own neighborhood. One Reichsbanner man, whom we knew very well, had been stabbed by the Nazis very badly and had to be brought to the hospital in serious condition. The caller had wanted some advice from Opi. I don't quite remember any more what he wanted Opi to do. It had something to do with the police, and besides, he wanted to give Opi the story for his paper. But I know that from that night on, we never turned the bell of the phone off again. A long trial developed out of this incident, but of course, the culprit was never convicted due to a lack of proof. Luckily, the wounded man recovered.

One night, Opi came home very late, dead tired from campaigning in the villages around Dessau; one of the drivers who worked for the newspaper drove him in a car that belonged to the newspaper. We went to bed soon afterward, and Opi was asleep even before I could turn off the lights. I had just fallen half asleep myself when I heard loud noises in the street (our bedroom was at the front of the house). There was singing and shouting, the way people very often behave when they have had too much to drink. I thought they would walk by and tried to fall asleep again. But when the group had reached our house, they started shouting Opi's name, hammering against the two iron garden doors, which were on each side of the house and which were always locked at night, and calling, "Seger, you traitor, come down, you pig."

I looked over to Opi's bed, but he was fast asleep; he hadn't heard anything. First, I lay very still, hoping, since there was no light on in the whole house and since all the neighbors were already in bed, the rowdies would give up and march on. But no such luck. They got noisier and noisier. Finally, I became so furious because I was afraid that they would wake Opi up that I got out of bed, opened the sliding door that led to a terrace in front of our bedroom, and looked down over the railing where I saw a group of about twenty Nazis in their SA uniforms standing in the street. When they saw me, they roared even louder and shouted again, "We want Seger; we want that pig. Send him out!" Furiously I shouted back at them, "You are drunk. You'd better go home, or I will call the police!"

I know this was not a very clever thing to do, but I was so angry by then that I didn't think very clearly at that moment. All of a sudden, I saw a bluish flame and heard a loud detonation, and something passed the right side of my head and entered the bedroom. Someone shouted a loud command, and the group ran away in all directions, some of them even climbing over the garden fence of the house across the street. At the same time, Opi came running over to me, grasped my arm, and pulled me inside the room. I was sort of numb for a moment—someone had really shot at me; it was so unbelievable. As Opi found out a minute later, the bullet had passed about five inches away from my head, had splintered the wood frame of the terrace door a little bit, and then disappeared somewhere in the bedroom. Opi called the police, and I went to see if the baby was all right. Thank God, she had slept through all this. Everything was quiet now. Opi got dressed, and we waited for the police. One of our neighbors, who lived with her mother next door, knocked at our door and wanted to know if everything was all right, which I thought was very nice of her, since she belonged to a party that had formed a coalition with the NSDAP (Nazi Party), the Deutschnationale Volkspartei [German National People's Party], one of the oldest conservative parties in Germany. Finally we heard the police sirens, about half an hour after Opi's call—of course, Opi had described all that had happened to us—and our neighbor disappeared. Opi went down and opened one of the garden doors and let the four policemen in. He and I had to describe again what had happened. They listened, but nobody took any notes, and finally they went up to our bedroom. They looked at the door, and when Opi showed them the spot where the bullet had entered, they didn't say a word. When Opi showed them the bullet, which we had not touched and which was still in the same spot where it had fallen, one of the men picked it up quickly and put it in his pocket, and then they left. When Opi led them out, he remarked that they should try to find the Nazis, to which one of the policemen murmured that there was not much sense in that and that they would have disappeared by then anyhow.

When Opi came upstairs again, we tried to decide what to do. From the way the police had handled our complaint, we knew that we could not expect much cooperation from them. We found out a few days later that we were right when Opi met a plainclothes policeman, a member of our party, who told him that nobody had even reported the incident. While we were still trying to make up our minds about what to do, our neighbor came over again. She was of the opinion that the best thing to do would be for Opi to try to get out of the house and for Renatchen and I to spend the rest of the night in her apartment, so if the Nazis returned, our apartment would be empty. Of course, Opi did not want to do that at first, but I convinced him that this was the best thing to do. We quickly packed an overnight bag and called a twenty-four-hour taxi service we had used quite often. Of course, this would be a risk, but since the Nazis had not seen Opi, they really did not know if he was in the house or not. The taxi arrived very quickly. The driver held the door open and drove away even before Opi had closed the door completely. I locked the garden door and felt very lonely for a moment, to tell the truth. But then I went quickly upstairs and picked up Renatchen, who woke up, of course, and looked at me with big, serious eyes but did not cry at all. The moment I entered the apartment of my neighbor, I heard shouting and hammering at the garden door; they really had come back. And then my neighbor did something very courageous. She opened a window and called down, "Please go home. I belong to the Black-White-Red block, and I assure you Mr. Seger is not here, only his wife and baby. My mother is sick, and if you don't stop that noise, I have to call my party warden."[13]

That somehow did the trick. They certainly were on a rampage of their own and did not want any trouble with their headquarters. They finally left, just shouting a few "Heil Hitlers!" and my neighbor closed the window and sat down with a deep sigh. By then I was really glad that Opi was out of the house. I am sure my neighbor would have said the same thing, but since it was the truth, it had made it a little easier. By then it was about four o'clock in the morning. Renatchen had fallen asleep on the couch where I had put her, and I convinced my neighbor to go to bed again, which she finally did. I couldn't sleep; my thoughts were with Opi. Had he made it? Was the driver trustworthy, or was he one of them? Of course, he would have recognized Opi.

The hours between when I finally went back into our apartment and the phone rang at seven o'clock were endless! Opi had made it to the next town, was still in a little hotel there, and would go from there by train back to Dessau and right away to his office. He told me that the driver of the car had been the owner of that taxi outfit, and he had suspected something was wrong when Opi's call came through and had decided to come himself. He told Opi that he was not a Nazi, did not belong to any party, but that his son was a member of the Reichsbanner. So we were really lucky there too.

Telling you about this episode, another event comes to my mind, a much less dramatic one but exciting enough for me just the same. And I believe it has a little bit to do with my dislike for guns for quite another reason than that they are mostly used for killing people.

The Reichsbanner organization had decided it was time to demonstrate that there was still quite some opposition to the Nazi doctrine in Dessau. Our young people especially wanted to do something, and so all the leaders agreed on a march through the main streets of Dessau that would end with a speech from Opi at a big garden restaurant, the Tivoli, which was mostly frequented by workers and party members. Everybody was enthusiastic about it with the exception of a few overanxious people who were afraid some trouble might occur, but they were outvoted. After the police granted permission for the march, it was widely advertised by Opi's newspaper and handbills, which young boys distributed in the streets. And somehow, we all were looking forward to it. Opi was only a bit unhappy about one thing: he had to wear the Reichsbanner uniform. He had sworn to himself that he would never wear a uniform again after the First World War was over. But since he belonged to the leadership of the Reichsbanner group of Dessau, he could not very well say no at an occasion like this. As a matter of fact, this was the only time I ever saw him in a uniform. He looked well enough in it, but just the same, I liked him better in his civilian clothes.

When the marching day came, of course he had to be at the gathering spot early to help organize the march. I was supposed to come later, after I had brought our baby over to friends for the time that we would be away. Just when I wanted to leave, the phone rang, and one of our party members, whom I knew quite well, asked me if Opi had his gun with him. He had been one of those who had insisted he should have one. I wasn't sure so I looked, and of course he had his permit with him as always, but the gun was still in the usual spot in his desk. When I told this to the caller, he persuaded me to bring the gun with me so that I could give it to Opi before the march started because there were all kinds of rumors in town that the Nazis had planned some trouble after the march was over, and the police were gone. Reluctantly, I promised to do so. I still remember the navy blue handbag in which I carried the gun. When I sat in the bus to get to the city, I didn't dare to look at any of the other passengers.

I had the feeling that only by looking at me, people would find out what I was carrying in my bag! In other words, I was quite scared because I knew only too well that I wasn't allowed to carry a gun without a permit.

When I finally arrived at the place where the march was supposed to start, everybody was already in line; Opi was in the first row of the Reichsbanner men. He saw me and smiled at me, but of course I had no chance to give him the gun. So I could do nothing but line up with the other marchers at the end of the parade, holding my handbag with that awful gun in it with both hands in front of me. The march seemed to be a success. Many people lined the sidewalk; some greeted us loudly and friendly, many with the word "liberty." Some gave the Hitler salute and shouted obscenities. But truthfully, I did not hear and see very much around me. I sang our worker songs with all the other people and marched to the rhythm of the band, but all I could really think was if only the march would be over and I could get rid of the gun!

Finally, we reached the Tivoli without any incident. Opi gave a marvelous speech, and everybody was enjoying themselves. I was waiting for him in the corner of the garden, next to the house, and after he had spoken to a lot of people and had shaken a lot of hands, he came over to me and gave me a kiss. I whispered into his ear what I was carrying in my handbag, and instead of saying "thank you" to me, he nearly shouted at me, "Are you crazy? What on earth gave you that silly idea?"

Now a little angry myself, I told him what had happened and that I got worried about him when the man on the telephone told me about all these rumors. Then, Opi told me the police had demanded that none of the participants were allowed to carry any kind of weapon during the march, and the leaders would be fully responsible for any disobedience if any weapon should be discovered. This rule had been repeated in all the meetings preceding the march. Now I could understand why Opi was angry for a moment. It really had not so much to do with me as with the man who told me to bring the gun, who should have known better. Later on, Opi had quite a discussion with him. The man admitted that he had known about the order but insisted that he had only been worried about Opi's safety. Now, so many years later, I am not quite so sure any more about his motives. What if some trouble had started? Wouldn't it have made quite a story if a leader of the Social Democratic Party and a member of the Reichstag would have broken his pledge? There were traitors and provocateurs in our ranks too.

Well, I am glad to tell you, nothing really happened. The rumors, if there were any, were just rumors, and when we went home in the evening, Opi put the gun, which he had, of course, taken out of my bag long ago, back in the drawer of his desk where it stayed most of the time. I saw it only once again, much later, when the police confiscated it. By that time, Opi was already in a concentration camp, and it didn't matter anymore.

Soon Opi had to go again on a lot of campaign trips, and Renatchen and I had to keep each other company. Sometimes friends visited us, or we went to visit them. But most of our Jewish friends were terribly depressed and occupied with plans for their future and what best to do. No one really wanted to leave Germany, but it became more and more difficult for them, and to leave the country seemed the only way out. Those who made their decision as early as that were lucky, as difficult as it seemed at the moment! For most of them, it saved their lives!

Much of what Ilse covers in this chapter is not covered in Gerhart's memoir, *Oranienburg*, which begins with his transport from a Dessau prison to Oranienburg concentration camp in June 1933. This includes the personal information about how she met Gerhart, their courtship and marriage, and the birth of their first child, as well as the election cycle between 1930 and 1932, the growing tensions between the Nazi Party and the SPD, and how this affected their lives. Her recollections of these very personal affairs demonstrate how memories can be gendered; she chose to retell the more domestic elements of their story while her husband did not. But even more importantly, Ilse's memoir offers readers a crucial lens into everyday life right prior to the Nazis coming to power that Gerhart's memoir does not.

The same year Gerhart and Ilse got married—1928—he became the chief editor of *Volksblatt für Anhalt*, a Social Democratic newspaper in Dessau, which Ilse alluded to above. While she claimed that this was when Gerhart's political career, and thus their troubles, began, she also suggested that they had a nice life, even while he was campaigning for a seat in the German Reichstag.

Ilse provides us an outside, gendered perspective of the political chaos of the last years of the Weimar Republic, in particular the constant cycle of dissolving the Reichstag, campaigning, and new elections that affected her and Gerhart's life from the summer of 1930 until 1932. As Toni Sender, a member of the Reichstag, remembered, "Most of the legislative work was accomplished by decree," and "the lack of a normally functioning parliament was felt more and more as the economic crisis became more acute and the number of unemployed increased." After all, as Sender said, the Nazis were creating chaos in order "to prevent constructive parliamentary labor."[14] Ilse also mentioned how she felt about the stronger presence of the Nazi Party in Germany—seeing the swastika flag more often, the rise of antisemitism, and how difficult it became to resist the party's growing momentum. She admitted a strong aversion to the flag and to Hitler's supporters and the followers of this growing movement.

She also reflected on why people came to support Hitler. Although the Nazi Party came to be very broadly based, the single biggest group of early supporters were workers. But then, as Ilse pointed out, many members of the middle class—small-business people, tradespeople, civil service employees, and farmers—turned toward the Nazis after the Great Depression because they feared losing their income and status. They were drawn to the heightened sense of nationalism the party offered and Hitler's promise to make Germany great again.

Ilse also spoke about the tensions between the Nazi Party—namely, between the SA—and the Reichsbanner. The SA was the NSDAP's paramilitary force, which primarily provided protection at Nazi rallies or assemblies, disrupted the meetings of opposition parties, and intimidated Hitler's opponents, primarily Communists. SA members would often get involved in street fights with members of the KPD (Kommunistische Partei Deutschlands; Communist Party of Germany) throughout the 1920s and early 1930s. These street skirmishes became so common that members of the SPD, the Centre Party, and German Democratic Party (Deutsche Demokratische Partei; DDP) formed the Reichsbanner Schwarz-Rot-Gold (Black-Red-Gold Banner of the Reich) in February 1924 in order to defend parliamentary democracy against the extremist parties on the political right (the NSDAP) and political left (the KPD).[15] The Reichsbanner also taught the population to respect the Weimar Republic and its constitution. They claimed some three million members by their first anniversary, many of them veterans.[16] Initially a nonpartisan organization that protected and fostered the republic, the organization increasingly became associated with the SPD, sought to create a social democracy, and served as their paramilitary force. According to Roger Chickering, it is debatable whether the Reichsbanner "worked to the benefit or the detriment of republican institutions in Germany." On the one hand, the organization reflected the active and healthy activism of those in defense of the Republic, but on the other hand, "a case can be made that by resorting to extra-legal means to combat the threat from the right, the Reichsbanner undermined the respect for constituted law that is essential to viable popular government." Contemporary observers often pointed out the similarities between the Reichsbanner and the SA; after all, both exacerbated political unrest and caused violence.[17] Toni Sender, who was even closer to this violence than Ilse, recalled how a growing number of Nazis, flaunting swastikas, in addition to Communists interrupted her speeches and shouted her down with their chants of "Red Front" and "Heil Hitler" whenever she addressed meetings.[18] Ilse recounted how some of this violence was targeted at her family.

Between all the campaigning, the growing presence of the Nazi Party, and the mounting violence, a lot of what Ilse remembered was becoming Gerhart's wife and a new mother to Renate. Her identities as a wife and mother become even more essential throughout her story and are crucial to understanding her memory of her time in Germany. At times, these roles were reflected in the joy, happiness, and anxiety that spring from having a new child. At other times, they were reflected in the loyalty she showed to her husband, even nervously carrying a gun in her handbag to give to him at a rally, for example. Such a defiant act likely drew less attention because she was a woman and slipped through crowds unnoticed and without arousing suspicion.[19] And a lot of the time, she simply conveyed the tedious routines of everyday life.

Notes

1. Seger, *Reminiscences*, 2–5, 9, https://dlc.library.columbia.edu/catalog/cul:mcvdncjw1g.
2. Sagner, *Gerhart Seger*, 14.
3. The DFG was founded in 1892 in Berlin and still exists to this day. Historically, it consistently stood against militarism and imperialism and called for disarmament and abolishing conscription, including during periods when it was not particularly popular to do so in Germany. For more on the DFG, see Holl, *Pazifismus in Deutschland*.
4. Since this memoir was written for her grandchildren, Ilse used the German term for grandfather, *Opi*, to refer to Gerhart.
5. During the Weimar Republic, Freiburg was part of the German state Baden. It is now part of Baden-Württemberg.
6. Anhalt, where Dessau is located, was an independent state and SPD stronghold during the Weimar Republic.
7. Bauhaus was a school of art, handcrafts, and architecture that would eventually become an artistic movement focused on a modern, functional aesthetic. It was founded by Walter Gropius in 1919 in Weimar and existed there as well as in Dessau and Berlin until it was it was closed in 1933 due to pressure from the Nazis. See Edwards, "Lessons of the Bauhaus," 135–36.
8. Here, she is referring to the slight setback the Nazis experienced in the November 1932 election, when they lost 4.3 percent of the vote from their high of 37.4 percent in July 1932.
9. On September 15, 1935, Hitler signed the *Reichsflaggengesetz* (Reich Flag Law) as part of the Nuremberg Laws. Article 2 of this law named the swastika flag as the national flag. The Reich minister of the interior, Wilhelm Frick, and the Reich minister of war, Werner von

Blomberg, signed this law. See a copy in the National Archives: https://catalog.archives.gov/id/128214796.

10. For more on the origins of the swastika, see "The History of the Swastika," *Holocaust Encyclopedia*, United States Holocaust Memorial Museum, https://encyclopedia.ushmm.org/content/en/article/history-of-the-swastika.

11. Renate Seger was born on August 16, 1932.

12. These were nicknames Ilse used for Renate and appear throughout the memoir.

13. The Black-White-Red block referred to supporters of the NSDAP.

14. Sender, *The Autobiography of a German Rebel*, 278–79, 289.

15. The SPD, Centre Party, and DDP were the political parties that remained the most committed to maintaining Germany's democratic system throughout the Weimar Republic. Together, they formed the Weimar Coalition, which had the majority of delegates at the constituent assembly in Weimar in 1919 and was responsible for forming the constitution of the Weimar Republic. See Deutscher Bundestag, "Elections in the Weimar Republic," published March 2006, https://www.bundestag.de/resource/blob/189774/7c6dd629f4afff7bf4f962a45c110b5f/elections_weimar_republic-data.pdf.

16. See Chickering, "The Reichsbanner and the Weimar Republic," 525–26.

17. Ibid., 528–33.

18. Sender, *The Autobiography of a German Rebel*, 281.

19. Stoltzfus, Paldiel, and Baumel-Schwartz, "Women Defying Hitler," 11.

2

The Reichstag Fire and Gerhart's Arrest

Ilse breezed through the details of President Paul von Hindenburg appointing Hitler as chancellor on January 30, 1933. The significance of the event was hardly known when it happened. Ilse remembered being hopeful that although Hitler was in power, the Nazis still did not have the majority in the Reichstag, and as she stated, they needed to change the constitution to suit their fantasies of dictatorship. She would soon find out that Hitler never needed to change the Weimar Constitution and instead relied on the Reichstag Fire Decree and later the Enabling Act to rule by decree.

Hitler immediately asked President Hindenburg to dissolve the Reichstag and call for new elections, which were set for March 5, 1933. Days before the election, on February 27, 1933, a fire broke out at the Reichstag building, the seat of the German Parliament, which is how Ilse begins the following chapter.

Although it is unclear to this day who set the Reichstag fire, Hitler blamed the KPD (Kommunistische Partei Deutschlands; Communist Party of Germany) and capitalized on the fire to further consolidate his power. Hitler convinced Hindenburg to invoke Article 48 of the Weimar Constitution and sign an emergency decree, the Reichstag Fire Decree, under the pretense of a purported Communist uprising. The decree indefinitely suspended all civil liberties that had been guaranteed in the Weimar Constitution, including habeas corpus, the right to public assembly, freedom of expression, and freedom of the press. It allowed police to exceed the previous legal limits on house searches, to intercept mail, and to tap telephones.[1] It also gave the federal government the ability to assume power over the state governments if they failed to maintain order.

Because the police could arrest and detain anyone they saw fit, they arrested hundreds of Communists and Social Democrats in the days and weeks after the fire—so many, in fact, that Gerhart's friends and colleagues tried to persuade him to leave the country or go into hiding. As Ilse mentioned, some of the leading members of the party managed to escape, and the SPD (Sozialdemokratische Partei Deutschlands; Social Democratic Party of Germany) leadership built a new party apparatus from Prague in the summer of 1933.[2] Ilse suggested at the time that they still believed in some sense of law and order, which, in hindsight, she maintained, was a naive way to think. But even so, Gerhart was not interested in leaving, insisting that someone had to stay and fight.

The elections planned for March 5, 1933, went on as scheduled, but they can hardly be seen as democratic because of numerous irregularities and infringements of rights.[3] The Reichstag Fire Decree already had serious ramifications on the outcome of the election because it heavily suppressed the KPD, essentially banning it in all but name. Hitler chose to treat them as criminals, rather than incite a violent reaction by outlawing the party altogether. In addition to the KPD, the Nazis also restricted the actions of the SPD, sending the SA to break up their meetings, loot their offices and homes, ban their newspapers, and commit violence against and arrest and imprison thousands of their members.[4] The Nazis also used the SA and SS to monitor the elections. The NSDAP (Nazi Party) picked up 92 seats in the election, increasing their total to 288 (out of 647), but they still did not hold a majority in the Reichstag with only 43.9 percent of the vote. Gerhart Seger won his seat, as did 119 other Social Democrats and 81 Communists.

The Social Democrats and Communists were allowed to run in the election, even though some were under arrest or had fled the country. But none of that mattered because within a week after the election, the police used the stipulations of the Reichstag Fire Decree to arrest all eighty-one Communists and a few dozen Social Democrats, Gerhart Seger included. Gerhart was taken into "protective custody" (*Schutzhaft*) on March 12, 1933, without cause even though he had left Dessau for Leipzig.[5] As Ilse noted, the local police in Leipzig, with the help of the SA, arrested Seger and initially held him at the police precinct in Leipzig before transferring him to the city prison in Dessau. It was not uncommon for the local police to work alongside the SA. Most police easily adjusted to the approach of the Nazis and welcomed the opportunity to fight crime and possess more power.[6] As historian Jane Caplan noted, local and state agencies explicitly collaborated in the opening of detention centers and camps from March 1933 onward.[7]

With all of these members of the Reichstag missing, Hitler was able to pass the Enabling Act through the Reichstag with a two-thirds majority (444 in favor) on March 23, 1933. The remaining 94 Social Democrats in the Reichstag all voted against it. This law gave Hitler the authority to enact laws without the approval of the Reichstag or President Hindenburg, thus creating a de facto dictatorship.[8]

And then came the 27th of February 1933! It was late in the evening, and I was just thinking of going to bed when the phone rang. At first, I hesitated a little, as it was too late for friends to call, and I had told you about those annoying calls we used to get sometimes. But then I answered and was so happy to hear Opi's voice. He seemed very excited and quickly asked if everything was all right. When I said yes and started to ask him when he would be coming home, he interrupted me: "Did you hear about the Reichstag?" I had not. And then he told me that the Reichstag was on fire. He would try to catch the next train home and would be in Dessau as quickly as possible. When I started to ask questions, he only said, "Not over the phone. Darling, let me go now. Maybe I can still make the night train." Then the phone clicked, and he was gone.

And here I was, all alone with this terrible, exciting, and somehow unbelievable news! I ran over to our little radio, but as happened every so often, I had forgotten to check the batteries for some time, and they had run dry and the radio was dead. I went downstairs and into the street and looked up to the windows of my neighbors, but they were all dark. And the only friends who lived in our neighborhood whom I could have gone to see in the middle of the night were visiting relatives and staying overnight, and I knew there was no phone in the house. I finally went to bed and tried to get some sleep, which was not quite as easy as it sounds, but I finally managed. Luckily, I did not know at that moment how that Reichstag fire would later influence our lives. I got a little inkling of it the next morning, when Opi arrived very early, and we talked and talked endlessly at the breakfast table. He had, of course, bought every newspaper he could lay his hands on. One thing seemed to be sure: the fire did not just happen; that was impossible in a building like that. It was arson, but by whom and for what purpose?

I should have mentioned before that the last election campaign already took place under the chancellorship of Adolf Hitler, who had finally received this post from the old German president, Field Marshall von Hindenburg. This was some achievement for Hitler, but just the same, he and his party leaders knew that not even that would give the Nazi Party the absolute majority they needed to go through with changing the constitution, with all their plans to build the kind of Germany they dreamed of under the dictatorship of Adolf Hitler.

Election day was only a few days away. Something very drastic was needed, and then the Reichstag went up in flames! "A sign from heaven," Hitler is supposed to have exclaimed when he overlooked the smoking ruins.

In our library, we have an excellent book, written by a special correspondent of the London *Times*, Douglas Reed, who was stationed in Berlin at that time.[9] Driving home through the Tiergarten near the Brandenburg Gate, which is very near the Reichstag, he heard the sirens of fire engines and saw them racing in the direction of the Reichstag. Stopping his car and looking out of the window, he saw that big, gray building "surmounted by a ball of fire." He described not only this night but also the immediate happenings in the following weeks; later on, he covered the trial of the five people who allegedly had started this fire, which in turn started the most terrible and tragic times for so many people in Germany and, later on, in nearly all of Europe.

The days that followed the fire were quite difficult and filled with anxiety. There were arrests of Social Democrats and thousands of Communists all over the country. Friends and party members tried to persuade Opi to go away, to leave the country, to at least go into hiding somewhere until the Reichstag would be in session again and his immunity as a member would be valid again. It really is pathetic, thinking back now, how one still believed in some kind of law and order—even Opi, who had seen the danger of the Nazis and what they stood for at such an early stage. At that time, nobody could have convinced him that he should leave the country. His answer was, "Not everybody can just leave. The workers have to stay too. Somehow we have to fight this through." He finally agreed to go away from Dessau at least for the few days until the new Reichstag was in session and his immunity was established again. A police officer who was a member of our party warned that the Nazis had planned quite a list of arrests within the next few days, which helped him make the decision rather quickly. We would go to Leipzig and stay there with Opi's mother until the 25th of March, the opening session of the newly elected Reichstag.

We would leave very early in the morning on Sunday, and one of the drivers of Opi's newspaper would drive us instead of taking the train because this seemed to be the safest way. We packed a few necessary things for the three of us. We even took the baby carriage with us. Fortunately, it was a collapsible one. Everything was ready when the driver arrived. It was still dark outside, and everybody in the neighborhood was asleep. Out of precaution, nobody so far had told the driver where we were going, only that it would be out of town and that he should have a full tank of gas. Now, we told him where we wanted to go, and when we passed the newspaper building on our way out of the city, he stopped and asked if he could quickly call his wife and tell her that he would probably be away all day so that she would not worry. We told him just to hurry, which he did, and then we drove on to Leipzig.

One of Opi's colleagues, the assistant editor of the paper, who was a good friend of ours, had decided to make the trip with us so he and Opi could discuss the next edition of the newspaper. Opi wanted to commute by train a few times but be back at night until we all could go home again. I didn't listen too closely. Renatchen was sleeping quite content in my arms, and I guess I dozed off for a little while too.

We arrived in Leipzig shortly before noon. Since we had written to my mother-in-law only a day or so before and just made some vague remarks about a short visit sometime in the near future, we worried a bit that she might be upset about this unexpected invasion. But I must say, she took everything in stride. Being the wife of an active politician—Opi's father had been a member of the Reichstag too, until shortly before his death in 1928—and a Social Democrat herself, she was, of course, aware of what was going on in Germany and had worried about her son for quite some time. She quickly fixed us something to eat, and after lunch, our friend and the driver left for their return trip to Dessau.

As I remember, we spent a very nice afternoon in a beautiful park in my mother-in-law's neighborhood, and everything was quiet and peaceful. It stayed that way for a few days. In the evening, I went to the railroad station to pick up Opi, and of course there were a few anxious moments—would he be on the train? Luckily, he was, already waving his newspapers at me before he was hardly out of the train.

But then came Sunday, March 12. It was a warm, sunny spring day, and I decided to take a little walk with Renatchen in the park. Opi wanted to stay home and do a little work for his paper. His mother was preparing lunch, and in the afternoon, we all wanted to go to the Palmgarten, a beautiful restaurant in a park that got its name from three big hothouses connected with it that were filled with exotic palm trees of every kind imaginable, to have coffee and cake, an old German custom for family entertainment on Sunday afternoons.

Well, it worked out quite differently! When I came back with Renatchen, my mother-in-law was standing in the open apartment door;

she had watched for me from the window. Before I could say anything, she burst into tears. "They took Gerhart away!" There it was: something that had always been on our minds but that we had tried to suppress. I couldn't say anything. I tried to control myself and to help her to the couch, and to put Renatchen down there too. Finally, after she had calmed down a little and I had enough hold of myself, I tried to find out what and how it had happened. There was not much to tell; everything had happened so fast. A few minutes before I had come home, the doorbell rang, and Opi, thinking it would be Renatchen and me, opened the door. But instead of us, three Leipzig policemen and some storm troopers were standing out there. One of the policemen asked if he was Gerhart Seger, a member of the Reichstag. When Opi said yes, the policeman told him that he was under arrest and had to come with them to police headquarters. When he asked under what charge, the policeman said that he would be told later. They let him take his hat and coat, and, flanking him from both sides, they took him downstairs to their cars and went off. There was nothing rough so far, and as my mother-in-law told me, the two policemen were even polite and called him Herr Abgeordneter, which gave us hope that at least these two were not Nazis.[10] I could not help thinking that if he only would have gone with us [Renatchen and me], then we would have seen the police cars and just have gone to the other side of the street. They did not know us in Leipzig, and there were enough young couples with baby carriages on the street on a nice Sunday. But then, what would it have helped? Where could we go? One did not leave the country on the spur of the moment. Besides, we would not have had enough money with us at that moment to buy train tickets to the next city, much less to the border.

At first, I wanted to run over to the police precinct, to find out if Opi was really there and if there was anything I could do. But then, I could not leave my mother-in-law alone with Renatchen at the moment. She was too upset still to take care of a seven-month-old baby. Hoping against hope, she was saying again and again, "Maybe they will let him go. He will come back tonight. They did not tell him to take his night things!" I did not have the heart to destroy her little self-delusion. I knew myself that at the moment, there was really nothing I could do but take care of Renatchen, who was quietly playing with some baby toy and, thank God, had no idea of what was going on around her. I just had to wait until the next morning. As you can imagine, none of us slept very much that night. There was that terrible fear: would I find him the next morning? Did they really take him to the police, or had they taken him to some Nazi headquarters? My only hope was these two policemen and that none of the Nazis who were with them had known Opi, so there was no personal triumph in capturing him, as there would have been in Dessau. I tried very hard to convince myself of that.

Early the next morning, I fed Renatchen and gave her a bath and prepared bottles and some solid food for her for the entire day, so it only had to be warmed up. Since she still slept a lot during the day, she would not be too much work for my mother-in-law, who had given me the telephone number of her best friend, who did not live very far from her. I promised to call there as soon as I knew something so that the friend could go over and give her the message. Then I left. I did not know my way too well around Leipzig, but luckily the trolley car that went by the street in which Opi's mother lived passed the police headquarters, and I would be there in a short time.

The police precinct was an impressive building, connected directly to the city prison, and I felt quite cold when I entered it to start my search. And it certainly was not easy! I no longer remember how many officials and policemen I asked where I could get some information about Opi. Most of them said that they knew nothing about political prisoners. One of them looked me up and down and said, "If they brought him here, then he deserves it. Heil Hitler." I got more desperate by the minute. At that point, I was there for nearly two hours and had not found out anything! It was harder and harder to tell my story and not break out in tears.

Coming out of one of those offices without anything to go on again, I saw a policeman in uniform coming out of a room; looking through the open door, I saw only one man sitting behind a desk and some bookshelves along the wall. I presumed this man might be a higher official than those I had seen so far, and as soon as the policeman had turned around the corner, I knocked on the door. A rather friendly voice said, "Come in." The elderly man behind the desk looked up and gave me a surprised look. "I am afraid you are in the wrong room, Miss," he said. But when I told him that I was looking for some information that nobody seemed to be in the position to give me, he asked me to sit down. He was the first friendly person I had met since I had entered that terrible building. I told him my story. He stood up and said, "You mean Gerhart Seger, Fritz Seger's son? They have him too?" When I nodded, he came over to me, put his hand on my shoulder, and told me that he was an old friend of Opi's late father and that he had known Opi as a little boy. He promised he would try everything to find out for me what he could. He asked me to wait in his room for him and to try to relax a little if possible, and then he left.

I really felt a little better for a moment. At least there was some reaction, and I was sure if anybody could, he would find out where Opi was. But that good feeling did not last long. I waited and waited, and he did not come back. The phone rang a few times, which made me jump, but nobody came into the room. Finally—it must have been more than an hour or so—the door opened, and he stepped quickly inside and closed the door. Before I could ask him anything, he said, "Don't worry. I found him. He is all right!" And then he told me that Opi had spent the night in a prison cell alone, and nobody had harmed him. He had also found out that the police department of Dessau had asked for his transfer back there and that two detectives would come to Leipzig the next day to pick him up. I asked if I could see him now for a moment, but he told me that this was not possible. But he suggested that I should come back the next day before two o'clock, when the Dessau policemen would arrive, and stand in front of the prison. I was disappointed, of course, but relieved to know that so far, Opi was all right. I thanked him very much for his help and left. I found a telephone somewhere in the hall, called my mother-in-law's friend, and asked her to go over there and just tell her, "It is all right." She did not ask any questions—everybody had become very careful during these days—and she promised to run right away. When I came home, she was there already. Now I could fill in the details. My mother-in-law even remembered the man who had helped me; he really was a high official in the police detective department, but she thought he had retired long ago.

The next day, long before the time I had been told, I went to the entrance of the prison, where our friend had told me to go. After waiting for some time, I saw a taxi drive up, and two men stepped out of it. One of them was the detective I mentioned before, the one who was a member of our party. The other was an elderly man I did not know. I had no idea then how many times I would confront him some months later! I quickly went over to them, told them who I was, and asked if I could see my husband at least for a few minutes before they took him to the railway station. They looked at each other, and the one I knew said he did not see any reason why not and that I should wait where I was. Then, they went inside, and a short time later, the door opened again, and they came out with Opi between them! He looked a little pale, and his suit was a bit rumpled, but otherwise he seemed all right. Before we could touch each other, the elder policeman said, "If you promise not to try anything foolish, we will walk to the station, and you can talk with each other, but I warn you we will be right behind you." Then he saw the little suitcase that I was carrying. I had brought some fresh shirts and underwear and Opi's toiletries kit. He took it from me, opened it, and looked through its contents; satisfied that nothing dangerous was in it, he gave it to Opi to carry. Then we started out for the railway station arm in arm, and we finally could talk to each other.

Opi told me what had happened to him. It was not much; he had hardly seen anybody. They had given him some food, and the guard even gave him his own evening paper so he at least had something to read. In the morning, he was told that the Dessau police would pick him up. When he had asked if he could get in touch with me somehow, he was told he could do that when he was back in Dessau. Then I reported my story and how it had happened that I was at the prison gate to meet him. We also discussed what I should do next. Of course, I wanted to go back to Dessau the next day with Renatchen, but Opi, who was still convinced that he would be free for the first Reichstag session, did not want me to come to Dessau before that time and stay there alone. I should stay with his mother until then. I should just come once or twice to see him, bring him some fresh clothes and books, and go right back to Leipzig. I saw his reasons and reluctantly promised to do as he said.

And then we were at the railway station. I must admit that our two guards had behaved quite decently. They stayed so far behind us that we knew they were not even trying to listen to our conversation. But now they came over to us. We could just give each other a kiss, and then they took him between them and went through the gate with him. He looked back once and waved, and then they were gone.

I turned around, feeling quite lonely, and slowly started my way back to my mother-in-law's home. At least Renatchen would be there, and all of a sudden, I had a terrible longing for her, and I nearly ran the last part of the way. The big smile she gave me when she saw me helped a lot to make me feel less lonely!

The next day, I traveled to Dessau, and from the railway station, I went directly to the city jail. I was allowed to see Opi for an hour, but a police officer was sitting with us at the table the whole time. So our visit and conversation were rather formal. But at least I could see him and convince myself that he was all right. He told me that the district attorney had visited him in his cell shortly after he had arrived. They knew each other from some social occasions. He was a very conservative man and affiliated with the Deutschnationale Volkspartei [German National People's Party], and a very decent man. He told Opi that he regretted seeing him under these circumstances, with which, of course, he had nothing to do, and that he would try whatever he could to make the situation bearable. He asked Opi if he wanted to have his food brought in from a nearby restaurant, for which he would have to pay, of course. He could have a newspaper every morning and books and writing materials. Opi declined the food offer but asked instead if he could have a cell of his own. This was granted, and he was even allowed to have his light on in the evening as long as he wanted. Opi still looked pale, but I felt that somehow, he had already adjusted himself to the situation a little. The hour was over very quickly, and when we had to say goodbye, the police officer turned to look out of the window, which I thought was very decent of him.

Before I left the prison, I asked if I could see the district attorney, who let me come into his office right away. I had never met him before. He was a tall, good-looking man, about fifty years old and very polite. He told me not to worry and assured me that he would do what he could to make things a little easier for Opi. "My political views are different from those of your husband, but I certainly do not agree with many things that are going on now," he told me quite frankly.

I left and went to our home to pack some fresh clothing and a few books that Opi wanted, and then I dropped in to see our friends who lived in the same house and who were very anxious to know how everything was. They already knew that Opi was in jail. It was really amazing how news spread through the grapevine in those times; the newspapers had reported nothing so far.

On the way back to the railway station, I went to the prison once more and left the things I had packed for Opi with the guard, who promised me that they would be delivered to him as soon as possible. Then I took the train back to Leipzig.

I visited Opi two more times from Leipzig, and then came the fateful Reichstag session of March 23, and nothing changed! Opi had received, by registered mail, his credentials as a reelected member of the new Reichstag, which for a moment made him hopeful again that he might be free as soon as the Reichstag was in session. But of course, nothing of the sort happened.

As soon as the first session was over, Hitler now had the majority and was in absolute power after throwing all the Communist members as well as a great number of the Social Democrats into jail; he did not lose any time in starting his Third Reich. He never would have made it by the mandate of the whole German people but accomplished it only through these unlawful acts.

Luckily, some of the leading members of the Social Democratic Party had managed to escape to Prague, the capital of Czechoslovakia, which at that time, of course, was not a Communist country, and whose prime minister in 1933 was Edvard Beneš, whose political convictions were very much like ours. He offered them [Social Democratic leaders] asylum and protection so that they could start working from there against the Nazis, to try to inform other countries about what was happening in Germany.[11] Hitler had ordered strong censorship of all news reports, and so only the kind of news that the Nazis wanted to be printed came out of the country.

During my stay in Leipzig, I distinctly remember two things that showed another part of the course that the new regime would take. One was a radio transmission of a concert conducted by Bruno Walter, one of Germany's world-famous conductors. We [my mother-in-law and I] were very much looking forward to that broadcast. We hoped that it would help us take our minds away from our worries, at least for a short time. We settled down long before it was to start, so as not to miss anything. Finally, it was eight o'clock, and nothing happened. The announcer had given the time, and instead of the tuning of instruments, we could hear only some indistinguishable noises. And then another voice came over the air and said, "We are sorry to announce that tonight's concert has been canceled and you will hear instead . . ." And then some sort of march music started. We turned the radio off, very disappointed, and speculated what the reason for the cancellation could have been. Maybe a sudden indisposition of the conductor? But that would have been announced. And then I remembered, Bruno Walter was Jewish!

That was the beginning. Pretty soon, the music of composers of Jewish descent, even if they had died long ago, was not allowed to be played, nor were their records allowed to be sold, and Jewish artists were not allowed to perform anywhere.

The second incident that I remember from that time in Leipzig was the book burning. It was on a late afternoon, and the window and the door to the terrace, which Renatchen's baby carriage was standing on, were open. All of sudden, small parts of half-burned paper and ashes came flying into the room. Renatchen's carriage cover was sprinkled with paper and ashes. We quickly took her inside and closed the window and the door. We thought there must be a fire in the neighborhood and expected to hear the sirens of the fire engines. Instead, the doorbell rang, and one of the neighbors came inside quickly when I opened the door. Still very excited from what she had seen, she told us that she had passed a large crowd of people, mostly SA and Hitler Youth, carrying little swastika flags and all sorts of signs. They had made a bonfire out of thousands of books that they had taken from libraries, schools, bookstores, and private homes. They were shouting and dancing around that tremendous fire like people possessed. That was where the ashes had come from! As we learned the next day, these fires had sprung up "spontaneously" all over the country, and a tremendous wealth of books, quite a few of them irreplaceable, first editions or out-of-print books, were destroyed this way. The idea was to "stamp out dangerous literature" written by Jews, "Vaterland's Verraeter" (traitors of the country), or any other author they disliked at the moment. It was very depressing and frightening to see what senseless acts fanatics are capable of.

As I said before, the first session of the Reichstag had passed, and we knew now that Opi's status would hardly change in the near future. I returned to Dessau with Renate so that at least I could see Opi more often. Quite often, I took Renatchen with me so that she would not forget her father, but for him, it was always very hard to see her leave again. Otherwise, he kept himself well occupied. He had started to learn English through a self-teaching method in book form, which I had to buy for him. And with his tremendous energy—he worked eight to ten hours a day on it—he mastered the language so well that after only two months, he could read both books without a dictionary and the London *Times*, which the district attorney had allowed him to receive in the prison. As he later often said, he was better informed during his time in jail than most of the Germans outside.

Of course, I had the privilege to visit Opi every second day for an hour. But, as I said before, we were never alone with each other. Our conversation sometimes became a bit strained. We could not talk about things that really occupied our minds. We tried to avoid mentioning the names of friends and what they were doing. We had no idea how much of our conversation would be reported to the Nazi headquarters. Both of us were nervous and depressed. We were happy to see each other, yes, but when I had to leave again, everything seemed so empty and senseless. I remember one visit in which we were especially depressed. After all, this was going on now for nine weeks. When I had to leave, Opi said a little bitterly, "At least you can walk out of here." I was a bit hurt. Of course, I could go home, but my thoughts were there all the time just the same. I did not feel freer than he. How could he say such a thing? But, many months later, I found out myself what it means to be imprisoned, to have the door locked behind you, and to see the visitor leave! But this really did not mean anything. We both were waiting anxiously every second day for that short hour to see each other. Just holding hands for a little while felt good!

My life during that time was mostly occupied with taking care of Renate and trying to keep informed about what was going on in the country. One thing I found out rather soon—the value of people as friends, or so-called friends. Since we were very ardent theater lovers, we had never missed a new play, a premiere or first performance. The municipal theater of Dessau was what is called a repertory theater here [in the US]. We had plays, opera, musicals, and, once a week, a symphony concert. Besides, Opi had written the drama reviews for his newspaper. We had met nearly all the actors, especially the young ones who were more or less in our own age group. They liked to come to our house, and when our baby was born, they brought flowers and gifts. We always had a good time together, and very often we met in a very nice restaurant near the theater after a performance. Now, I found out that these same people, all of a sudden, became very interested in a store window or even crossed to the other side of the street when they saw me coming. Nobody was interested in that "beautiful child" anymore, and what hurt even more, nobody inquired about the man [Opi] to whom they had come with a lot of problems, asking for advice about this or that, even if they had been his guest quite often. They were all afraid! They wanted to be on the safe side, and everybody felt watched! After the first disappointment, I got used to it; they were not important, but their behavior was a symptom of the time. But later on, I found out that even people who were really good friends started to feel uneasy to be seen with me on the street. They did not mind so much my visiting them, but they would rather not come to our place and used all sorts of excuses. And one day, when I passed their house—it was some kind of a holiday the Nazis had announced—I saw a flag with the swastika hanging out of their window. And that, of course, was the end of our friendship as far as I was concerned. Later, when Opi was already in the concentration camp, they did send me some money through a third party "to help me a little," which, of course, I did not accept.

But, of course, there were other friends and some people whom I had never considered as friends, just acquaintances, party members, or workers, who stood by me as long as I was in Germany. They were a great help to me, and we were very grateful for their friendship.

May 1, the workers' holiday, used to be a real holiday in Germany. The factories and workshops were closed, and there were parades in the streets. Those restaurants that mostly catered to the working class were decorated with Maiengrün, mostly birch branches and twigs, and the biergartens had hired little bands for dance music in the evening. But, this year, there was an uneasy feeling about this usually happy day. The Nazis had ordered the workers to come for the May Day parade, which, of course, they would lead in full uniform with swastika flags, banners, and all sorts of Nazi slogans. There was little else the men could do in order not to lose their jobs since, in nearly every factory, the foremen were already Nazis, or a Nazi commissar was put there as overseer.[12] The number of unemployed in the country at that time was about seven million, which meant a lot in a heavily industrialized state the size of Germany. Whoever lost his job—and he would have if he refused to march—could easily be replaced. And all for the glory of Hitler! So there was little choice but to march.

This was a great disappointment for Opi. Somehow, he had hoped for at least some sort of resistance. He was quite depressed when I visited him that afternoon and became even more depressed when I told him that a group of Nazi storm troopers had forced their entry into the house of the workers' union, had easily overwhelmed the few men who were left in charge there, had hit and mistreated them terribly, and finally had chased them out into the street. They had destroyed a lot of documents, files, and furniture and then raised the Nazi flag. The seizure of nearly all the unions in Germany took place that day—another step forward into complete dictatorship.

But in spite of all this, something nice happened to Opi too. He had found out that people had not forgotten him. Quite a few had come to the prison gate very early in the morning and left flowers for him. Of course, they had not given their names to the guard at the prison gate, just saying, "These flowers are for Gerhart Seger." One guard had even found an old vase somewhere and brought it to Opi with some of the flowers so that he could at least have some in his cell. Something like this was still possible at that time. Even the Nazis couldn't change the whole population overnight!

But, of course, by and by the whole way of life changed for the population. Those who followed the new regime, either by conviction or because they wanted to be on the winning side, became bolder and more conceited every day, and the other part became quieter and more reticent. Rumors sprang up everywhere, and it was more and more difficult to find out what was the truth and what was not. One of the most persistent rumors was that the Nazis had opened up concentration camps for their political opponents and Jews. So far, nobody really knew where these camps were situated, but these rumors were consistent enough to make everybody afraid and tense.

Hitler further consolidated his power throughout the spring and summer of 1933. Nazis took control of state governments. They took over the civil service after the passage of the Law for the Restoration of the Professional Civil Service on April 7, which excluded non-Aryans, particularly those of Jewish descent, and political opponents from their civil service positions. On May 2, the Nazis seized the offices, banks, and newspapers of the free trade unions and arrested the leaders—an event Ilse recalled here. This was when the Nazis abolished the Social Democratic trade unions; ransacked the SPD offices; and arrested, assaulted, or murdered many of their officials.[13] Ilse also remembered the book burning that took place in Leipzig, which happened in conjunction with book burnings all over Germany and Austria on May 10. Organized by the German Students' Association, university students burned the books of Jews, pacifists, liberals, anarchists, Communists, Socialists, sexologists, and foreigners—some twenty-five thousand volumes of "un-German" books.[14] A July 14 law made any other political party outside of the NSDAP in Germany illegal.

The Nazis also opened a number of different detention sites in the first years they were in power. Historians at the United States Holocaust Memorial Museum have categorized these into three broad categories: protective custody camps (wings or blocks of existing prisons, penitentiaries, or detention centers that were separated from other criminals); concentration camps created on an ad hoc basis when the prisons became overwhelmed and space became available; and torture sites.[15] Robert Gellately has demonstrated that the public was informed regularly about the thousands of arrests, and there was "no attempt to hide the fact that those arrested were sent without trial to concentration camps."[16] Caplan has suggested that the German public accepted the political detention of Communists, whom many already thought of as "subversives and rabble-rousers," due to the exceptional circumstances—a kind of permanent state of emergency initiated by the Reichstag fire. There were also precedents dating back to the late nineteenth century and continuing through the Weimar era of housing convicted vagrants, prostitutes, the "workshy," and even Communists (after the 1919 revolution and several times between 1920 and 1923). Generally, they would be temporarily held in a type of workhouse or camp in order to be disciplined through labor. These older practices, then, made the opening of various types of detention sites in 1933 more legitimate and blurred the boundaries between normal and abnormal. As Caplan said, "Though specious, this linkage of disciplined work and ideological re-education became a staple of Nazi propaganda. It established the terms in which the camps were represented to the German public, and masked the vicious and systematic regimes of harsh and often economically useless labour, brutal mistreatment and deliberate humiliation to which inmates were in reality subjected."[17]

Ilse's memories of the Reichstag fire and the immediate aftermath of the escapes and arrests of KPD and SPD members, including Gerhart's, is not something he covers in *Oranienburg*. Nor does he cover his time in the Dessau prison or the actions of the Nazis in the early months of 1933, including the book burning or early persecution of the Jews. Ilse's account, then, offers us a rare look at everyday life and how average citizens perceived the early arrests, violence, and antisemitism of the Nazis. Certainly, she felt the impact more than most, considering her husband and the father of her child was arrested without cause, and she spent much of her time trying to determine how to see him or how to get him help. She was also more attuned to these changes because of her circle of acquaintances and friends who kept her abreast of the political news.

Notes

1. Gellately, *Backing Hitler*, 19.
2. Buchholz and Rother, *Der Parteivorstand der SPD im Exil*, xxx.
3. Deutscher Bundestag, "Elections in the Weimar Republic," published March 2006, https://www.bundestag.de/resource/blob/189774/7c6dd629f4afff7bf4f962a45c110b5f/elections_weimar_republic-data.pdf.
4. Evans, *The Coming of the Third Reich*, 335–37.
5. The Nazis transformed the previous German practice of protective custody (*Schutzhaft*), dating back to the German Revolution of 1848. "On the one hand, Schutzhaft signified arrest for personal protection. On the other hand, it meant taking seditious elements into custody during emergencies." The Nazis understood protective custody as the political detainment of people (like members of the KPD) due to the political setting; in this case, the justification came from the Reichstag Fire Decree. In other words, it was "a temporary and acceptable remedy for dealing with the supposed leftist threat." See White, "Introduction to the Early

Camps," 3–5, and Caplan, "Political Detention and the Origin of the Concentration Camps in Nazi Germany," 23, 27–8.

6. Gellately, *Backing Hitler*, 18.

7. Caplan, "Political Detention," 29.

8. For more on the Enabling Act, see "The Enabling Act," *Holocaust Encyclopedia*, United States Holocaust Memorial Museum, https://encyclopedia.ushmm.org/content/en/article/the-enabling-act.

9. Ilse is referring to Reed, *The Burning of the Reichstag*.

10. They were referring to him in a formal manner as a member of the Reichstag.

11. Tomáš Masaryk was actually the president of Czechoslovakia in 1933. He did have a liberal asylum policy toward German refugees. See Steinberg, "Should I Stay or Should I Go?" 83. Edvard Beneš was not president of Czechoslovakia until 1935, having served as the foreign minister of Czechoslovakia in 1933 (when all this was taking place) and as the prime minister from 1921 to 1922. Ilse was correct to mention that Beneš's political leanings were similar to Social Democrats in Germany. He was a member of the Czech National Social Party, which was a civil nationalist political party that had a moderate and reformist Socialist view.

12. Here, Ilse mistakenly used commissar, used to refer to a government official in the Soviet Union, instead of commissioner.

13. Berger, *Social Democracy and the Working Class in Nineteenth and Twentieth Century Germany*, 139.

14. For more on the book burnings, see "Book Burning," *Holocaust Encyclopedia*, United States Holocaust Memorial Museum, https://encyclopedia.ushmm.org/content/en/article/book-burning.

15. White, "Introduction to the Early Camps," 5.

16. Gellately, *Backing Hitler*, 19.

17. Caplan, "Political Detention," 27–33, quote on 33.

3

Visiting Oranienburg and Resisting Nazism

Gerhart Seger arrived in Oranienburg on June 14, 1933, and spent the next six months there. Much of what we know about his life in Oranienburg appeared in *Oranienburg*, which was one of the first firsthand accounts of the conditions in a concentration camp. It was translated into several languages.

Oranienburg, one of the first concentration camps, opened on March 21, 1933, on a main road in the town of Oranienburg, accessible via the commuter train twenty kilometers from Berlin, on the grounds of an old brewery. A so-called wild camp, the SA ran the camp, and it was rather haphazard in terms of its structure, appearance, conditions, and policies; improvisation was common among these wild camps, and the fact that a brewery had been converted into a camp was not unheard of.[1] On June 14, 1933, the SA shipped Gerhart, thirty-nine Communists, and two other Social Democrats to Oranienburg after holding them in the Dessau prison.[2] Most of the working-class inmates were members of the KPD (Kommunistische Partei Deutschlands; Communist Party of Germany) or SPD (Sozialdemokratische Partei Deutschlands; Social Democratic Party of Germany) or other smaller left-wing organizations; Seger was one of the more well-known individuals imprisoned there because of his status in the Reichstag.[3] People in the surrounding area were well aware of the camp, as indicated by the fact that Ilse's hosts described it quite well below. Gerhart reported people going about their business and "rollicking youths" playing in the river as they arrived in town.[4] In fact, most people passing by could see into the camp, and because of its location within the town, it was a "transparent concentration camp." The SA camp commander invited German and foreign journalists to tour the camp, the local press wrote extensively about it, and a radio program reported from the camp.[5] Robert Gellately has confirmed the press's extensive and positive coverage of the opening of Oranienburg, depicting it as a camp that was teaching discipline and obedience.[6] What we know, however, is that in this camp, the Nazis forced prisoners to perform communal labor for the town, mistreated them, tortured them, and dehumanized them by shaving their heads—a sight that resulted in shock for Ilse and caused Gerhart to feel utterly humiliated when she visited him the first time two days after he arrived. Although the Nazis did not intend to kill prisoners in Oranienburg, there were deaths, two of which Gerhart witnessed.[7] The SS took over the SA-run camp in July 1934 and dissolved it later, as was often the case with the early wild camps.[8] In July 1936, the SS opened another camp known as Sachsenhausen in the town of Oranienburg, which lasted through the end of the war.

Below, Ilse recounted her experiences of visiting Gerhart in the camp.

One morning, around six o'clock in June 1933, my phone rang, and when I answered, still half asleep, a man's voice said very quickly, "If you want to see your husband once more before they take him away with all the other political prisoners, come as quickly as possible to the prison gate," and then the man hung up. I was shaking all over, and it was very hard to get dressed. I raced over to my friends', rang the bell like mad until they came rushing to the door, gave them the key to our apartment so that they could take care of Renate, who was still asleep, explained with a few words what had happened, and rushed off to the prison. When I arrived there, a lot of people were standing on the sidewalk across the street from the prison. That was as close as the police let them get. I don't remember exactly how I managed it, but somehow I got through to the prison entrance, and the guards, who all knew me by now, let me in. Thinking back now, I am sure that the district attorney must have had something to do with the telephone call and must have given some instructions because one of them brought me through a side door into a small hallway with a staircase. He told me to wait there and went upstairs. After a few minutes, he came back with Opi! At first, neither of us could talk; we just held each other. Then, Opi told me quickly that he and all the other political prisoners would be brought to Oranienburg by train and that he would write to me as soon as he could. Then, the guard came over, took Opi by the arm, and led him away.

I rushed out of the hallway and through the prison gate into the street. Two big open trucks were now standing there with police all around, and the prisoners started to come out of the prison yard where they had been assembled and climbed into the trucks. The crowd on the other side of the street was very quiet, and some women cried. I went over there too, and suddenly someone put his arm around my shoulders. It was our city editor and friend, who somehow had also learned about the transport of the prisoners. And then at last, Opi came out. The crowd started to move, and the police quickly stood in front of the people, who raised their hands and shouted, "Goodbye, Comrade Seger. Goodbye, Gerhart. Come back soon. *Freiheit* (liberty)!" The police pushed the people back, and the trucks started moving. We all ran after them to the railway station, which was only a few minutes away from the prison. Of course, the prisoners got there before us, but the train was still standing there. I rushed through the gate to the platform, pushing away our friend, who wanted to hold me back. The railway official was shouting wildly after me—in Germany, you are not allowed to go through a station gate unless you have either your train ticket or at least a platform ticket. But I made it in time. There, I saw Opi sitting at one of the closed windows of the two cars that were reserved for the prisoners. He did not look out, and I had to shout loudly until he finally looked up and saw me. He smiled a little, waved too, and then the train left, and he was gone! I stood there for another minute to look after the train until one of the policemen on the platform told me rather sternly to leave. I went out through the gate I had rushed through a few minutes before and paid my ten pfennig, and the man who had shouted so angrily at me before did not say a word; he just looked at me.

When I came out of the station, most of the people who had followed the trucks like me had left, but the city editor had waited for me and brought me home. The friends I had given my apartment key to waited for me there. They had given Renatchen her bottle and had made me some coffee, which I badly needed. We all stayed together nearly the whole day, and though nobody could do anything or suggest anything helpful, it was good to have them around me. It kept me from breaking down completely. But we talked about everything over and over again, and suddenly, I remembered that a brother of another friend of ours, a physician, who lived not far from us, had a brother in Oranienburg who was a lawyer by profession. We had met him and his wife shortly before Opi was taken into "protective custody," when he had visited his brother in Dessau. Both families, being Jewish and Socialists, had made their decision to emigrate to Israel as soon as they could sell their houses (at that time this was still possible even for a Jew) and end their affairs in Germany.[9] We got the address from our friends in Dessau, and I decided to travel to Oranienburg on June 16, our fifth wedding anniversary. At first, everybody tried to talk me out of doing this and to wait until I had heard from Opi himself. But I could not wait. I had to find out where he was and how he was. I just had to go. So they promised me to take good care of Renatchen, which I knew they would. One good thing was that she still was such a little baby and, of course, my friends were not strangers to her. Luckily, she had no idea what was going on around her!

I again packed a suitcase with things I thought Opi would need, an English novel I had just bought for him to bring to the prison, and a warm blanket. I took a very early train to Berlin and from there, a commuter train to Oranienburg. The trip took about four hours, if I remember correctly. In Oranienburg, I took a taxi to the house of the brother of my friends from Dessau, who had called him up in the meantime to tell him that I was coming because I had a "mysterious problem." I hoped they would know where the concentration camp was. I stayed there for a little while, and they told me as much as they knew about the place. It was situated on the outskirts of that little city and used to be a brewery some time ago. It was surrounded by a high barbed wire fence and, of course, heavily guarded. It would be too far to walk there from my hosts' house, so they advised me to take a taxi. They owned a car, but of course, it would be too dangerous for them to bring me to that spot themselves, which of course, I understood perfectly well. I called for a taxi from their house, thanked them for their help, and waited there for a few minutes until the taxi arrived.

When I told the driver where I wanted to go, he hesitated for a moment but then drove off. We arrived there in about fifteen minutes. It was a big, dark, ugly-looking building. Through its high iron gate, one could look into a wide yard where a lot of storm troopers were walking around. On the rooftop of a side wing of the brewery, I could see guards standing next to machine guns, looking down into the yard. I also saw a few people in civilian clothes doing some work there and assumed that they were prisoners. It was too far away to recognize anyone from where I stood. I had asked the driver to wait for me, and he drove a little way from the entrance and stopped there. I stood there for a moment and tried very hard to keep from shaking before I moved over to the closed gate. Two storm troopers with rifles over their shoulders were slowly marching back and forth inside the gate. I called to one of them, and when he came over to the gate, I told him that I wanted to see Commandant Schäfer, whose name already was well known in Oranienburg for obvious reasons!¹⁰ He answered quite politely—of course, he did not know what I had come for, and since I had asked for Schäfer, it was none of his business—that the commandant was not in at the moment, and he didn't know when he would be back. So I asked for his deputy and said I would like to talk to him instead. The storm trooper finally opened the gate and let me come in. He led me into a sort of guardhouse next to the gate, which was furnished with a table and a few chairs and a small picture of Hitler on the wall as the only decoration, and he asked me to wait there. Then, he called another storm trooper and gave him an order. The man ran over to the main building, and after a while, he came back with another storm trooper who had quite a few insignia on his uniform. The two guards gave him a military salute, and one of them brought him over to me. Of course, he said, "Heil Hitler!" but I ignored that and answered with *"Guten Tag* [good day]." He also told me that Commandant Schäfer was not in at the moment and asked if he could help me instead. I told him who I was and that I had come to see my husband, who had been there since the 14th of June.

His face changed. He certainly had not expected anything like that. In a quite different tone, he informed me that there were no visiting hours that day and that I should come back at a later date (I think it was about a week or ten days later). But I was not to be that easily dismissed. I was not shaky anymore, and I had to see Opi. I told him very quietly that this was our wedding anniversary, that I had come a long way, and that I simply had to see my husband and give him a few things I had brought with me. Well, it worked. He sent the storm trooper who had brought him over to fetch Opi. And then something happened that nearly made me faint—he came back without Opi! For a second, I thought something terrible had happened, but then I heard the man say, "Seger does not want to see his wife." For a moment, I felt as if something had hit me. Before I could say anything, the officer shouted at the man to bring the prisoner over without delay. Thinking about it now, I would not have seen Opi on that day if the officer had not been so furious that a prisoner had dared not to follow an order. The storm trooper ran away again, and within a few moments I saw him coming back with a man. For a second, I was not quite sure: was it Opi? It was, but what had they done to him?! They had shaved his head completely—not just given him a crew cut but literally shaved it! Like a criminal, a murderer! I don't know if in this country [America] this regulation ever existed. But it did in Germany. If someone was convicted of a serious crime, like assault with a murderous weapon or murder, he was not kept in a simple jail or prison; he was sent to a penitentiary. And one of the most humiliating punishments was the shaving of the prisoner's head. And they had done that to Opi! He came into the room and did not even look at me. And then he said in a very low voice, "Do you understand that I did not want you to see me like this?" Of course, I understood now, but after all, he was alive, he did not seem to be physically hurt, and that was all that counted. I took his hands, and he finally gave me a quick kiss, but he still tried to avoid my eyes and just held my hand.

To help us both, I started to unpack the suitcase to give him the things I had brought with me. The guard looked over everything very carefully before he let Opi have it. The English novel he gave back to me right away, and the officer remarked, "He won't have much time for reading here." Opi rejected the blanket I had brought him right away. None of the other prisoners had a real blanket so far, and he did not want to have anything different from them. Then the officer told Opi to get back to his quarters, and after a short embrace, he left without looking back once.

I left too, feeling terribly empty and tired. I had no idea when I could see Opi again. I was very frightened too; what else would they do to him? This was not like the prison, which was bad enough, but, after all, there was still law and order. But here? Nobody controlled this place. They could do what they wanted with their prisoners.

Very reluctantly, I walked over to the taxi, grateful that the driver really had waited for me, and told him to bring me to the station. When I paid him, he refused the tip, just saying, "These are bad times—all the best for you," and he drove away. Sometimes you find sympathy where you least expect it!

After a week or so, I got my first short letter from Opi. It was, of course, censored, and even without the censor's stamp on the envelope, it was easy to recognize the way the letter was written. The one good news in it that the prisoners were allowed to write was that on one of the coming Sundays, there would be two hours of visiting time. Opi asked if I could come and bring a few marks for stamps and maybe something to eat, like hard salami or some tin cans with fish or anything that would not spoil so easily.

I remember this first visit very well. I was looking forward to it so much, but I was afraid at the same time; how would I find him? I did not sleep very much the night before the trip. In my little suitcase, I had put all sorts of things that I thought he might need: soap, toothpaste, some chocolate, sardines, a big piece of salami, and a box of cookies. I left early in the morning—Renatchen was already at my friend's home—and was at the station nearly half an hour before the train was to leave. The visiting hour was at 2:00 p.m., so I would have at least an hour between my arrival time in Oranienburg and the opening of the gate of the camp.

It was a beautiful summer day, and the long walk helped to quiet me down a bit. When I arrived at the gate, quite a few people, mostly women and children, were already there. Inside the gate, a lot of storm troopers were looking us over, some of them making obscene remarks, some of them plainly bored or disdainful. As Opi told me later, on visiting day, only a few got passes to leave, and, of course, they [the storm troopers] resented that.

Finally, the gates were opened, and we were let into the yard. At the end of it, long tables were standing with benches on either side. Behind it, the prisoners were standing. I saw Opi right away and tried to run over to him. But, of course, that was not allowed. We were told to sit down on one side of the table and to open our packages and suitcases. The guards looked very carefully through our things, and then, finally, the prisoners were allowed to sit down across the table from us, and we could at least hold hands. Of course, the guards walked back and forth on both sides of the tables, but for the moment, they simply did not exist; nobody around us really existed for this short precious time that we were together and could look at each other. Opi's hair had grown a little bit already. He told me that just a few hours before I had come on the 16th, they had shaved his head and that he had simply needed some time to overcome this feeling of being so humiliated, the more so since he'd had no idea that I was coming. But he was over it now, and so many things had happened in the meantime to other inmates that this didn't matter anymore.

He wanted to hear about Renate, our friends, and what was happening in the outside world. I had gotten him a subscription to the *Völkischer Beobachter*, the newspaper of the National Socialist movement, since that was the only newspaper that was permitted for the prisoners.[11] But that, of course, was only very one-sided news. And we, on the outside, did not know much more since by then all of the newspapers that were against the Nazis either were *gleich-geschaltet* (politically coordinated) or had ceased to exist.[12] Naturally, there were lots of rumors going on about this and that. But there was no way of finding out if these were only rumors or if they were real facts. One thing we found out very soon was that when it was a "good" rumor, something one tried to pin some hope on, one pretty soon found out that it was only just a rumor!

But to come back to this first visit, Opi told me about the conditions in the camp. They still had no real blankets, just old burlap sacks that hardly kept them warm and a second one filled with a bit of straw that served as mattresses. The food was terrible and certainly needed some supplementation from relatives since all the inmates had to do hard labor. Our conversation was not easy; we had to quickly change the subject when the guards were passing by since they interfered as soon as someone started to whisper or said something that seemed suspicious to them.

The two hours passed very quickly, and the visitors had to leave. We were told that the prisoners would write to us when the next visiting day was announced, and then the gates were closed behind us. I turned around to look through the gate, but the prisoners had already been marched out of sight. So I walked together with the other women who had come by train the long way to the railway station, tired, very worried, and discouraged.

Opi had asked me to go to the district attorney as soon as possible and tell him about the conditions in the camp and especially about the sleeping facilities. So I called the district attorney's office the next morning and got an appointment with him for the following day. When I told him about the burlap sacks, he became very furious. He said that they had sent blankets and even bedclothes from one of the state prisons to Oranienburg some weeks ago and naturally thought that the prisoners had received them promptly. He promised me that he would try everything to see that the blankets would get to the prisoners. And he kept his promise. As Opi told me later, the blankets had arrived, but they had landed on the beds of the storm troopers, and it had taken quite a few more weeks, and I am sure some clever and persistent action by the district attorney, for the blankets to finally be turned over to the prisoners.

These visits to Oranienburg were always a matter of chance. We never knew beforehand how long the visiting time would be. All the women lived as far away as we women from Anhalt did and naturally could not afford to make the trip on every visiting Sunday.[13] We were supposed to visit for two hours, but if the storm trooper in charge did not feel like it, the time could all of a sudden be only half an hour for all of us. Or for some reason or another, they were sometimes canceled all together, and we were lucky if the prisoners were told long enough beforehand so they could at least inform their relatives and save them the trip. Twice, they were canceled completely: once for two Sundays in a row and the second time for eight weeks. But not only that, the letter to tell their relatives this awful news was the last one they were allowed to write during this time, and they were not allowed to receive any mail either. During these endless eight weeks, all I received was a package with dirty laundry, without a word from him in it. I could see it was really sent by him only by the address on the package.

After the end of this eight-week period, I finally got a short letter from Opi. The punishment, whatever it was, was over, and the visiting date was set for the coming Sunday. I decided to take Renatchen with me this time—a decision that was made easier by the fact that the son of the mayor of a little neighboring town, whose father was also a prisoner in Oranienburg, owned a car and let me know that he could take us. I gladly accepted this offer, which made it so much easier to travel with the baby and all the things I would have to take with me: fresh laundry, some food for Opi, and whatever I needed for Renate.

This was the only time I took our little girl with me to that horrible place. She was now nearly one year old. She had last seen her father when I took her with me a few times to the prison in Dessau. I had written Opi to tell him that I would bring her this time, and he was looking forward so much to this visit, especially since, as I said before, it was the first one after the eight weeks of quarantine.

It was a nice, warm day, but I was a little worried as to how Renate would take this long ride in an open car, all the more so since she had never been in an automobile. I took her blanket with me and covered her up warmly. At the beginning of our trip, she looked around, very interested in the trees and houses we passed so quickly, but pretty soon she nestled herself deeper into my arms and slept peacefully nearly the whole trip.

When we arrived in Oranienburg, for once the gates were opened on time, and everybody ran over to the tables where the prisoners were already waiting on the other side. Opi looked a bit thinner but quite tan from all the outdoor work. Renatchen was sitting on my lap and looked astonished at the strange man who started to talk to her. I put her down on the table between us, and Opi stretched his arms out to take her on his lap. But that was too much; she started to cry loudly and turned with outstretched arms back to me. It was a heartbreaking moment for both of us! Naturally, it was understandable because the child had not seen her father for months, and his still very short hair made him look different too. There were also the strange surroundings and the long trip; all this came together. But just the same, it was a bitter disappointment for the father who had longed so much to see his little daughter. He was very nearly in tears for a moment. Certainly, he understood, but that did not make it easier. After a little while, Renatchen stopped crying, but I could not bring her to touch her father or even smile at him. When we had to leave, she just let him stroke her hand for a second but then turned her head away so he didn't even try to kiss her. He just told me not to bring her again because this made everything even more difficult for him.

That evening, when we got home and went to see our friends for a moment, it really hurt me to see how friendly she was when she greeted them and had no objection at all when they picked her up. But of course, they were not strangers to her; she had seen them nearly every day.

On top of all my anxiety and worries about Opi, something else started to trouble me, and that was our financial condition. I had told Opi when he inquired about it that it was all right. I had received his last Reichstag allowance and one or two salary payments from the newspaper. But since a few weeks back, the paper was edited by a so-called commissioner, a Nazi, and of course the payments were stopped. We had a little savings account, which I had closed already, following the good advice of my friends who were afraid it might be confiscated. I kept part of it, and I had sent a small amount to my parents in Freiburg for safekeeping. But our beautiful apartment was now too expensive, and I started to look around for a small one that I could afford. Quite reluctantly, I applied for welfare relief, which was granted to me, and in addition to that, I was supposed to get a small rent subsidy as soon as I had found a cheaper apartment. But that was easier said than done. I went all over town looking for something suitable. For one thing, there were very few small apartments in the price range that I could afford, or they were simply just too ugly. But additionally, as soon as I gave my name and explained a bit who I was, the landlords told me in more or less friendly tones that they did not want to rent the apartment to me for various reasons, and that was that.

Finally, I found a nice little apartment only two blocks away from where we lived. It was on a whole street of relatively new three-story apartment houses that belonged to a corporation. The manager was a young widow who told me quite honestly that all the tenants were National Socialists, including herself, but since they were all "nice" people, she didn't think there would be any difficulties. Well, this was not a very pleasant prospect, of course, but there was another reason that made me hesitate to sign the lease, and that was the rent was higher than I had expected, even when I added the small subsidy I was supposed to get from the welfare department. I told the manager that I had to think it over, and she promised to keep the apartment for me until the next day. I went home quite depressed. It would be a very tight budget. Renatchen and I would not need very much, but there were the trips to Oranienburg; the food packages that I simply had to send; and the few marks I always left for Opi when I was there, which he very seldom used only for himself because there was always some other inmate who was grateful for some cigarettes or some pipe tobacco, which he could not afford to buy, things like that. On the other hand, the apartment was so close to my friends, which was so important for me. I finally went over to see my friends to discuss my troubles. I don't think I've mentioned the name of these people so far. They were Otto and Leni Posse. He was a public school teacher. Both were longtime Social Democrats but never officially active in the party as such. They were the most good-hearted and helpful people I have ever met. I really don't know how I would have ever gotten through these difficult times without them! Since we lived in the same house, we got together every day, and they certainly shared all my problems as if they were their own.

I told them about the apartment and that I really did not think that I could afford it. They had a pleasant surprise for me. They had spoken with a few party workers, and together they had decided, since they still had their jobs, to collect a small amount between themselves that would make it possible for me to rent a decent apartment. As they said, that was the least they could do so that Opi would not have to worry about his family on top of everything else. The only condition was that I was not supposed to know who these comrades were. They would give the money to Otto Posse every month, and he would forward it to me so that nobody else would ever know about it. How cautious people had become about everything they did! I certainly was touched and very grateful. I had my suspicion who these people were, but since they wanted it that way, all I could do was to let Otto thank them for me and Opi, who was just as touched as I was when

I told him about this on my next visit. It made him feel good to know that he was not forgotten by his old friends and coworkers.

There was something else the Posses told me that afternoon before I went over to rent that little apartment, which was also a great relief to me. These same comrades had told him that they would do the moving for me. One of them owned a small truck they would use, so everything would work out all right. The carpenter who had made our four built-in bookcases, also a comrade, would come too and dismantle them for me. He rebuilt one of these four right away in the new apartment, and that is the one we still have in our living room here [in the US].

Another problem, of course, were our many books. Opi had inherited his father's whole library. He himself already had quite a number of books of his own when we got married, and we had bought quite a few more in the five years since then. But part of this problem seemed to be solved very luckily, at least so I thought at that time. I already had a young cleaning woman working for me before Renatchen was born. She loved Renatchen like her own baby, and when I told her that I simply could not afford her anymore, she broke into tears. Of course, she understood that I had to let her go, but she insisted that she would come at least once a week without pay as long as I was still in that big apartment, just to help me and to see the baby. Of course, I did not want to take advantage of her in accepting this nice offer, but she insisted, so I finally gave in. Naturally, I was grateful to her; she was a very nice person, and since she had already been with us for over three years, I would have missed her too. I spoke to her about my book problem also and pondered with her about what to do with them. When she came the following week, she told me she had a solution. She had talked with her husband and her mother, whose little house they lived in. The house had a big attic, and there was enough room for all the books that I could not take with me to the new apartment. She and her husband would come a few evenings with a little wagon and pick up as many books as possible and store them in her mother's house until I could take them back again. At first, I hesitated. It would be so much trouble for them. But this would be a wonderful solution, and I did not see any other possibility, so I accepted her offer. But this time, I insisted that I would pay her husband something for doing this, and finally she agreed. They came a few evenings and took quite a lot of our books with them, until I thought that I could take the rest with me. There was a small storage room for every apartment in the house I was moving into, and the books I could not get into the one bookcase I was going to keep could go into boxes and be stored there.

I felt quite relieved and certainly grateful to the young couple. Little did I know that we would never see these books again! As I heard much later, they had all landed in the paper mill of Dessau! What I will never know, of course, was whether these young people had something to do with it; was it all planned that way, or had some neighbor watched them and notified the Nazi headquarters? I am still inclined to believe the latter. But a few weeks later, when I was already in my new apartment and was coming home from shopping, a young SA man passed me on a bicycle. He did not see me, but I recognized him, and for a moment my heart stood still—he was the husband of my cleaning woman! But, as I said before, I still can't quite believe that they did not act in good faith, at least not as far as she was concerned.

Well, Renatchen and I got finally settled in that new apartment, and I tried very hard to feel at home there. But somehow it never worked. Our separation seemed even more difficult to endure there than in the old surroundings. My anxiety and worries grew. Would we ever really be together again? It all looked so hopeless. I tried very hard to overcome this deep depression by concentrating as much as I could on Renatchen, who could walk now and, being very proud of this new, exciting achievement, always wanted to go out. I still had to take her carriage when I wanted to go somewhere a little farther, but she had to walk quite a bit first until she settled down in that carriage again.

The way my new neighbors acted didn't help me feel better either. I was told they were all Nazis, mostly elderly people who lived on their retirement pensions. But I never expected so much hostility. The first time I saw some of them, I naturally said, "Good day." The answer was a stare and then a loud "Heil Hitler" with a high outstretched arm and a turn away from me as quickly as possible. That, of course, was the last time I ever spoke to them. On nice days, when they were sitting outside in the little backyard that belonged to the apartment house and where every tenant had a small spot assigned to them, big enough for a small table and a few chairs, I heard them talk loudly about the "reds" and all their bad deeds; all the big pensions that every member of the Reichstag received, even when he was there for only a few weeks; and how the Führer had put an end to all this outrage. This, of course, was not true at all. Members of the Reichstag never received a pension, no matter how long their terms were or how often they had been reelected.

I spoke to one of my neighbors only once, and that was to a young woman. She and her husband lived in the opposite apartment on my floor. This happened after I lived there about a week or so. I was coming up the stairs with Renatchen when she opened her door and quickly came over to me and told me in a very low voice that they had moved in only a few days before me. She just wanted to tell me that she knew who I was and that she was very sorry for me and warned me about the other neighbors who had already grumbled when they heard that "such a person" would move in. But when I wanted to say something, she quickly continued that her husband must not know that she had spoken to me. They were not Nazis, but he was afraid he might lose his job if someone reported that they had any contact with me. So that was that! We never spoke with each other again, just said "hello" when we sometimes met on the stairs and smiled at each other. I am quite sure these young people were not Nazis, at least not at that time. But it shows how scared people became.

But, of course, there were other people too. Sometimes I had three or four visitors, people who belonged to the Social Democratic Party, people I hardly knew other than having seen them in some meetings or having gone around with them during the election campaigns I told you about. They wanted to know how Opi was and wanted to be remembered by him. Very often, they brought a small salami or some candy, which I was supposed to take with me on my next visit to Oranienburg. Some of the men worked at the famous German airplane factory, the *Junkerswerke*, and since there were quite a lot of Nazis working there too, they heard a lot and knew quite a few things much earlier than anybody else.[14] They even knew when the Nazis planned new arrests.

During these days, I learned the true meaning of that beautiful word comrade. The German word for it is *Genosse*, at least in the more political sense, as it was used in the working class. I think it goes back to the beginning of the Socialist movement, which started in the middle of the nineteenth century. Until all this happened to us, I had used this word once in a while, but it did not mean much to me. As a matter of fact, I had always felt slightly funny when I used it. My upbringing had been very bourgeois. My first contact with the so-called working class came through Opi and our life in Dessau. But now I discovered the significance of this word, and I gladly used it. I felt good when they called me *Genossin*, the female form, instead of Frau Seger. I certainly was grateful for their visits, but in a way, they made me nervous too. I was always afraid for them. If one of my "good" neighbors were to call the Nazi block warden and tell him that they thought there was something suspicious going on in my apartment, they would certainly be in trouble. Luckily, nothing like that happened.

We had another kind of get-together in Leni and Otto Posse's house once a week with our city editor and his wife and a few other trustworthy friends. It gave us the feeling of belonging to each other. There was a necessity to talk about what was going on around us, even if we could not do anything to change things.

Part of our meetings we spent listening to the radio when the proceedings of the Reichstag fire trial were transmitted. This, of course, was very exciting, and we had long debates afterward. For us, there was no doubt at all that the Nazis had started the fire. There was certainly not any gain for the Communists in starting it. But how and when would there ever be any proof of that?

We were usually ten or twelve people. There was always the possibility, since Otto was a teacher, that a parent would look him up, wanting to know something about the school or the child, so we tried to be prepared for that. We always had cake and coffee on the table and some playing cards in front of us so that we could start playing as soon as the doorbell might ring. I know the whole idea sounds a bit silly now, but then none of us had training as a conspirator.

These evenings were good for our morale. They gave us the feeling of defying the evil atmosphere around us—some sort of resistance, if I may call it that, against all the distrust and hatred around us. We would stick together no matter what.

Most of our Jewish friends had left the country by now. Dr. Hess was in Shanghai, where he later married my good friend, Hilda, whom you have met at my home.[15] She had followed him into exile, knowing quite well that by marrying a Jew, she would never be able to go back to Germany as long as the Nazis were in power. Other Jewish friends went to Israel or England. I missed them, but this was the only solution for them, as much as most of them hated to leave. If only all of them had done that in time! The conditions for the Jews became more and more difficult, but even then, none of us could foresee what was in store for those who stayed!

There was one day in summer that I remember very vividly, and that was the first boycott day against the Jews.[16] All the newspapers bore big headlines about this day and asked the population not to buy in a Jewish store or to have any contact with Jews. Posters with big swastikas and the same slogan were all over the city.

The biggest department store in Dessau belonged to a concern.[17] The other one, Borchardt, a smaller one, belonged to a Jew. He was not a member of our party, but his sympathies were there, and whenever there was a collection for a special purpose—for instance, for the workmen's little recreation home, some sport outfit for the youth group, or the cultural fund of the party—one could count on his generous contributions. I liked the store and bought nearly all of my clothes there. I knew most of the salesladies in the dress department and also the buyer for this department. Sometimes I just went in to say "hello," and when the buyer was there and had something new, she showed it to me. Quite often, she asked me if I could try on one of these dresses, just to see how it looked on me. If I had the time, I obliged, and, of course, sometimes bought something I had not intended to at all. But if I did not buy, it was just as well.

On this boycott day, I had to think of these girls and how they must have felt. I had no idea who was Jewish and who was not, but the store was the biggest Jewish store in town. After thinking it over for a little while, I brought Renatchen over to the Posses' and asked them if they could keep her for an hour or so because I had to buy something that Opi had asked for and that I wanted to put in the laundry package I had to send to him. They warned me to be careful, and I promised to be back soon.

I was not quite sure what I wanted to do when I came to Cavalier Street, the Fifth Avenue of Dessau, where the Borchardt store was. As soon as I entered the street, I saw a lot of storm troopers milling around. I passed a small Jewish store that I knew well, but it was closed, and so were a few others. But Borchardt was open. In front of the entrance, there were quite a few storm troopers, standing to the right and left of the door, giving out pamphlets to every passer-by: "Don't buy from the Jews. Heil Hitler!" Most people passed quickly, not even looking at the store, took the pamphlet, and gave the Hitler salute.

I had gone over to the other side of the street and passed the store. But then I turned around, crossed the street, and quickly went into the store. Nobody had recognized me. They just shouted something like "She is one of them too" and something else that I did not quite understand.

I did not see any customers in the store, and most of the salesgirls were standing around in groups, talking to each other, or looking anxiously toward the door. Some of them recognized me and came rushing over. "Please tell us, what are they doing outside? Are there very many?" They were nervous and scared. None of them had anything to do with politics. They had their jobs, and they did not want to lose them. I could only tell them that so far everything was relatively quiet outside, and nothing violent had happened. I bought a small curtain rod, which I didn't need at all, but I just had to buy something. Before I left, the store manager came and told the personnel that Mr. Borchardt had phoned and that the store would be closed for the day. I was very glad to hear that the girls could go home, and I left too. When I came out of the store, one of the SA men recognized me; wild heckling and shouting started, and I don't care to repeat the names with which they showered me, waving their fists in my face. I walked through them, looking neither left nor right, proudly carrying my little bag with the curtain rod, and crossed the street to the other side. I won't deny that my heart did not stop beating wildly until I was away from Cavalier Street and much closer to home.

When the Posses found out my real reason for going into the city, they were a little angry with me. But I could not help it; I felt satisfied with myself. I had that same feeling, weeks later, when Hitler decided to leave the League of Nations. To make this more dramatic, knowing very well how this would turn out, he ordered a plebiscite on November 12, 1933, and challenged the German people to vote either "yes" or "no" for his action in a supposedly secret vote.[18] Very cunningly, he had ordered millions of little pins with the word "yes" on them, which his storm troopers offered to everyone who came out of the voting booth, which most of the time was just a table behind a curtain that most people didn't even bother to close.

I was on my way to Blumberg, where the Nazis had a small branch of the Oranienburg Camp.[19] Opi, together with a small group of other prisoners, had to work on a special job there. I think it was the demolishing of an old factory. Some other women and I drove together again in the car of the mayor's son, whom I mentioned before. During the trip, we stopped somewhere in front of a village inn that was marked as a voting place. Needless to say, I voted "no." When we came out of the voting booth, the storm troopers offered everyone a "yes" pin, which I refused. There was a snicker, but that was all. To my dismay, I saw that all the other women and the mayor's son had these "yes" pins on their coat lapels. When we were in the car again, I asked them why they had taken the pins, knowing very well their anti-Hitler feelings. Their reasoning was that it might make trouble for the prisoners if they came to the camp without these pins. I saw their point, but I just could not have done it. Anyhow, who would believe that we would give a vote of confidence to a man who had put our men behind bars because they happened not to agree with him? Quite ironically, it was just the opposite when we arrived at the concentration camp. The guards made fun of these women and called them cheats and liars, so it did not help at all.

As Opi told me that day, the prisoners had long debated how to vote, and most of them had decided to give a "yes" vote. They hoped to show the outside world that their vote was under duress. Who would voluntarily vote for his own jailer? Well, the whole world didn't see and didn't care very much either. No matter, yes or no, Hitler would have won anyhow. I knew quite a few people in Dessau who voted "no," but when the results in their various districts were released, they found out that their "no" votes had disappeared. Over the whole country, there were only 5 percent counted officially![20]

I went once more to Blumberg before Opi was back in the Oranienburg camp. At that time, I met Dr. Munzer and his wife, who was visiting him. Dr. Munzer had been brought to the camp just a few days before Opi had his first gall bladder attack and had helped him during that painful attack. Opi had written to me about it, and I was certainly glad to know that there was a doctor near him. The two men became good friends there, and that friendship was renewed when we met the Munzers here in the United States three and a half years later.[21]

Every time I visited Opi now, I found him more and more depressed. Everything seemed so hopeless. Many of the prisoners who had come with him were released again, and many new ones had come. But, of course, all the other members of the Reichstag or people who had played a more important role in either the Social Democratic or Communist Parties were still there or taken to other concentration camps. That was something we both were very much afraid of because in the meantime, the Nazis had opened up quite a few more camps much farther away from Dessau, meaning the possibility of seeing each other would have been very difficult or even impossible. But the worst part of it was the terrible uncertainty. If somebody has to go to jail for whatever he might have done, there is a term set for his release, and if he behaves well, he might even be released before the end of this set time. But in our case, as well as in thousands of others, nothing like that existed. There was always the terrifying thought on our minds: will we ever really be together again? We never mentioned it to each other, but we knew that thought was there. That was the time when my hair all of a sudden started to show the first gray in it.

One good thing happened to me during these terrible months. One day in September, I got a telegram from Freiburg in which my mother announced she was coming the next day! My parents wanted me to come to Freiburg with Renate and stay there for few weeks. Naturally, that was impossible; I could not go that far away even for only a few weeks. Of course, they were worried, and so they finally decided that Mother should come to Dessau for two weeks instead.

Those two weeks with my mother—your great-grandmother— are some of the nicest memories I have of that trying time. It was so good to have someone around who cared, who was always there, especially in the long, lonely evenings so that one could talk about all those worries and anxieties. I was very grateful for those two weeks. I still remember one Sunday evening coming home from Oranienburg, seeing a light in the window of my apartment, and knowing that she would be waiting there for me. It helped a lot!

I also remember a little episode that happened a few weeks before Mother came. One morning, a policeman delivered a small package to me with the message that I had to come to the police headquarters the following day at such and such a time. The new police commissioner, who had come from Berlin a few months ago, wanted to see me. I did not know this man in person. His name was Heisig; I knew only that he had played a part in the trial of the Reichstag fire.[22] The papers mentioned this when he took over his assignment in Dessau. I did not have the faintest idea what this man wanted from me. I was a little nervous, and so were my friends when I told them about it. We had heard through the grapevine about a few wives of Communist prisoners who had been summoned, but nobody had found out why. Even being in the same boat, there was very little contact between our two parties.

The next morning, I put on my most elegant dress, which I had not worn since Opi was imprisoned, and then went with Renatchen in her carriage to the police headquarters. When we arrived there, I left the carriage outside and went to the desk sergeant with Renatchen in my arms. When I gave my name, he called another policeman who took me up to the commissioner's room. He went in and after a minute came out again, held the door open for me, and told me to go right in. It was a typical office with a big desk in front of a large window. A relatively young man, at least for a police commissioner, was sitting behind it. He gave me the Hitler salute and asked me to sit down on the chair in front of the desk. I did and took Renatchen on my lap. She was a little subdued by the strange surroundings and sat quite still. He looked at me for a moment, and then in a rather stern voice, he asked me, "What are your connections with France?" At first, I did not understand the meaning of that question. But then it dawned on me. I forgot to mention that the little package the policeman had delivered to me the day before with the order to come to police headquarters had been sent to me by a friend of ours who lived in Paris. It contained a sweet little jacket for Renate, and that was all. No note or anything. But since it was coming from France, the post office had delivered it to the police, and they had opened it, of course, before it was forwarded to me. So that was it! Some time ago, the Nazi newspapers had printed some articles about connections that the Social Democrats had with the French Social Democrats for the purpose of overthrowing the Nazi regime.[23] Nothing of that was true, but it served its purpose to convince some more naive people of the necessity of the concentration camps. I really had to smile. I was not nervous at all any more. I explained my connections very easily, and I don't think he found any reason not to believe me.

I do not recall our whole conversation that morning. I remember only that I finally asked him what the chances were for the release of a man in Opi's position. It was a silly question, I know. He said something like eventually everybody would be discharged, but it takes time and so on. I really had not expected a clear answer to my question, but, after all, he was one of the highest Nazi officials I had met so far. And at least he said "eventually everybody" would be discharged. That did not sound quite as hopeless to me, and in a situation like ours, one tries to grasp at every straw.

Renatchen, who until then had sat quietly on my lap, wanted to get down now, and when I let her, she went right over to the big filing cabinet and started to open the drawers. It was time to go. It never occurred to me to ask if he was through with me—the whole visit after the first stern question was really more like a social call. When I said goodbye, he stood up, came around his desk, saluted, and said, "Mrs. Seger, do not forget, we National Socialists can be gentlemen too." Well, I don't know how much of a gentleman he really was. All I can say is as long as I was in Dessau, he behaved quite decently toward me, but more of that later.

It was November now, and Mother had gone back to Freiburg. There was talk about an amnesty that Hitler would proclaim shortly before Christmas. It was to concern several hundred prisoners, a cross section of every concentration camp. Would Opi be one of them? I remember how much the Posses and I talked about it. I harbored the silly hope that all those who were taken into custody first should now certainly be the ones who would fall under the amnesty too. My friends were less convinced about that, but then, of course, they did not want to discourage me too much. They knew that only talking and thinking about such a possibility already helped a little.

When I visited Opi again, he told me that nearly every prisoner was contemplating the amnesty. But he told me quite honestly that he did not think that the length of stay would have anything to do with it even if there was one. He became more and more depressed and even wrote about that quite openly in his letters. There was one letter I especially remember in which he wrote, "*Ich kann das nicht mehr lange mitmachen. Du musst das verstehen.*" (I cannot go on with this much longer. You have to understand this.) I was quite scared when I got this letter. As I said somewhere before, all our mail was censored. This remark was open to all kinds of conclusions. It could lead to harsh punishment. But somehow it went through. The SA man who did the censoring either did not read the letter very carefully, or they were so sure of themselves that they did not bother.

One evening, a week before I could go to Oranienburg again, my bell rang rather late. I pressed the buzzer that opened the front door downstairs and looked over the railing. A man slowly came up the stairs, and when he arrived at the last landing, I recognized him. He was the mayor of the little town not far from Dessau whose son had taken me twice in his car to Oranienburg. I let him into the apartment quickly. There, he told me that he had been discharged all of a sudden, that some people in his town had vouched for him or something like that, and that now he was on his way home. But he had promised Opi that he would come to me first, since he had to stay in Dessau overnight anyhow until his son could pick him up the next morning. I thanked him very much for coming. I knew it took some courage for someone just discharged from a concentration camp to come and visit me.

But then he told me the real reason why he had come. Opi planned to escape. At first, I was completely stunned! How could he do that, the way the camp was guarded? He would be shot right away! I had to fight hard not to break into tears. My visitor waited for a moment, then he told me that Opi had a plan. He and a whole group of men had to work outside of the camp, and there might be a possibility. It all had to be decided on the spur of the moment. It might be soon or much later, but he wanted to be prepared for it. I could be of help if I could bring one hundred Reichsmarks with me next Sunday, and he would somehow find a way to slip the money over to him.

When the mayor had left, I walked back and forth endlessly in my little living room. What was the right thing to do? Should I try to talk Opi out of this frightening attempt? Was there the slightest chance of success? Did I have the right to do that?

Much later, when my stove had gone cold, I went to bed just to get warm again. I don't think I slept at all that night, and I was grateful when the sun finally came up. But I had made my decision—I think it was the most difficult one I'd ever had to make in my whole life. There was no way out. I knew Opi. When he had set his mind on something, he would try to go through with it. I had no part in this decision anyhow, other than to be of as much help as possible. I would bring him the money.

When I had withdrawn our savings account from the bank some time ago, I had sent part of it to my parents for safekeeping, and I had kept three hundred marks in one-hundred-mark bills for any emergency that might arise. The mayor had told me that Opi wanted the money in twenty-mark bills if possible. So I had to change the hundred-mark bill. I did not dare go to the bank to do that; somebody might recognize me there and get suspicious. This sounds farfetched, I know, but one was thinking of many things in Nazi Germany that would have never occurred to anybody before that time. So I asked Otto Posse if he would do this for me, since I might need some of the money for Christmas. One-hundred-mark bills were just as difficult to exchange in a store in Germany as hundred-dollar bills are here [in the US]. I will never know if he believed me or not, but he did not ask any questions; he just did it.

A few days before the mayor had come to see me, I had written to Käthe Kupsch, Opi's secretary when he worked for the German Peace Society some years ago, that on one of my next visits to Oranienburg, I would like to see her. Opi had told me that she had a friend who was an American Quaker who lived in Berlin at the time. I thought there might be a small chance that when this man heard about the conditions in the concentration camp, he would bring it out into the open. Maybe, as an American, he might have some influence somewhere. I could have asked her about that in a letter, of course, but I had no way of knowing if my mail was opened by the police. She had answered right away that I was welcome any time. I should just call her when I was in Oranienburg so that she would be home. I would tell Opi that, and maybe that would influence him not to do anything rash for the time being.

The next Saturday, I brought Renatchen over to the Posses', packed some fresh laundry and some food for Opi, and tried to figure out what to do with the money. And then I had an idea. I had intended to bring Opi some photos of Renatchen that Otto Posse had taken of her. I folded the five twenty-mark bills twice (the German bills are much smaller than our [American] twenty-dollar bills), slipped a rubber band around them, and put them on top of the last picture in the pile, and then put another rubber band around the whole package so that the bills could not slip out.

Sunday morning was very cold and windy. The train was not very well heated either, and I was already half-frozen when I arrived at the gate of the concentration camp, as usual, half an hour early. Everybody stood as close as possible to the gates so that we could rush in the minute they opened. Since the beginning of winter, the tables for the visiting hours had been inside a sort of a wide corridor. There was a big potbelly stove that the prisoners kept as hot as possible so there would be at least some warmth awaiting us there.

But when it was two o'clock, the beginning of the visiting time, a storm trooper came over and shouted, "The gates will be opened half an hour later today." We all shouted at him, but he just turned around, and we stood there trembling helplessly in that icy wind. We were scared too; maybe they would not let us in at all—it had happened before. But then, after more than half an hour, he came back and gave the order to open the gates.

Finally, I sat opposite Opi at that long table. My hands were so cold that I could hardly open my travel bag for the guard when he came to inspect what we had brought for the prisoners. We were not allowed to give anything to them before the guards had seen it.

Opi took my hands into his to warm them up. How rough his hands were from the hard outdoor work he'd had to do these last few weeks! He looked pale and tired. His hair had grown again, but he looked changed just the same. He told me that the delay in opening the gates was a punishment for something one of the prisoners had done that morning. I don't remember what anymore, but everyone else had to be punished too!

And then he pleaded with me to understand him, that he could not live like this much longer. This way of life was impossible for both of us. He thought he had a chance to escape. He did not know exactly when this chance would occur; it would have to be on the spur of the moment. That was all he would tell me. "The less you know, the better it will be for you."

Most of the things I wanted to say, I left unsaid. I knew in my heart that nothing would change his mind. The whole conversation was rather difficult anyhow. We had to change the subject constantly the minute the guards passed behind us. Finally, I told him that I had brought the money and had put it between some photos I still had in my handbag, and how I had done it. He thought it over for a moment, and then he told me to slip off the outer rubber band when I took the pictures out of my bag and to slide them over to him the minute he had taken out his handkerchief, taken off his glasses, and started to wipe them. We both watched out for the guards passing behind us, and when their backs were turned, I quickly slipped the rubber band off the pictures, passed them over to Opi the moment he had his glasses and his handkerchief in his hands, and watched him anxiously. He swiftly dropped the handkerchief on the pictures, grabbed the whole package with it, and bent down under the table for a second. When he came up again, he grinned at me; he put the pictures in front of him, put his handkerchief back in his pocket, put on his glasses, and started to look at the photos. The guard behind his side of the table had turned around now, saw the pictures, took them away from Opi, and looked them over carefully. Finally, he gave them back to Opi and grumbled at me, "You know you have to show everything to us before you give it to the prisoners!" I muttered something about forgetting about the pictures before, and he let it go with that.

When the guard was again out of earshot, Opi told me that he had hidden the money in one of his shoes when he ducked under the table. We had only a few more minutes, then a whistle blew, and the visiting hour was over. We held hands for a moment, and then the guards ordered the prisoners back to their quarters, and everybody had to leave. I saw Opi turning around and waving at me, and then he disappeared through the door at the end of the corridor.

Ilse's recollections of visiting Oranienburg and her conversations with Gerhart while he was in the camp coincide with his own account of Oranienburg in his book. In *A Nation Terrorized*, Gerhart reported sleeping on the cement floor in straw sacks that would rot from underneath in the damp and cold brewery. He also relayed this to Ilse on one of her first visits and asked her to call the authorities to report it—a sign that initially, prisoners and their families had some leverage. Ilse also recounted above how Gerhart told her that when authorities from Anhalt, who had visited the camp to check on the food and accommodations, sent sheets and blankets along, the SA used them for their own beds. There were no washing facilities initially, and then, after July, there was only one washroom for some 1,100 prisoners. Gerhart described the food as "vile beyond imagination," and many prisoners threw the food away or went hungry rather than eat it. Families could supplement this wretched diet with food they brought for the prisoners on visits, but as Ilse mentioned above, these happened very irregularly. Gerhart talked about performing hard outdoor labor—a fact Ilse confirmed just by seeing his hands—on various town projects from seven a.m. to five p.m., including sometimes hours-long marches to the place of operations. Torture was a regular part of interrogations in room 16, and the SA frequently used blows to bully the prisoners or standing cells to arbitrarily punish them.[24]

While he was imprisoned, the Nazis confiscated Gerhart's books and papers, which Ilse discussed above. The SA or SS often ransacked and destroyed the contents of Social Democratic Party offices and trade union offices or committed violence in members' homes.[25] Gerhart had access to a newspaper every morning, books, and writing materials when he was being held in the city prison in Dessau. He also enjoyed the privilege of having Ilse visit him every other day for an hour, which she discussed in the previous chapter. However, once he was sent to Oranienburg, she could visit him only irregularly, and he had access only to the *Völkischer Beobachter*, the Nazi Party's newspaper, which Ilse bought him a subscription to. Gerhart confirmed what Ilse experienced—visiting hours were very arbitrary but usually took place on Sundays, although there were also lengthy bans on visitors.[26] Some cultural activities, such as the setting up of libraries, existed in the early camps. These libraries were stockpiled with Nazi publications, which served the dual purpose of reeducating political dissidents and filling their idle time.[27]

As 1933 progressed, more and more people became afraid of losing their jobs or facing other punishment(s) if they associated with SPD members or others who were considered opponents of the regime. This was certainly the case for Ilse's neighbor, who lived across the hall from her in the new apartment building she moved into. While she initially had spoken with Ilse after she moved in, she then would barely acknowledge her—a sign that indicated that people, even if they were not Nazis, were becoming more and more fearful of what might happen to them if they associated with Hitler's so-called enemies.

Meanwhile, SPD members and allies continued to meet in informal settings, often at one another's homes, and openly shared their opinions about the Nazi regime and its abuses. Ilse (and even Gerhart) benefited from many gestures of kindness, humanity, and solidarity from this local, national, and eventually international network. In the previous chapter, fellow comrades had left flowers for Gerhart outside of the Dessau prison. And in this chapter, SPD members donated money for Ilse to rent a new apartment in Dessau and helped her move, demonstrating the importance and effectiveness of clandestine networks of resistance under a repressive regime.

Ilse talked about how she and her friends discussed the Reichstag fire, which they suspected the Nazis had started. Her comments in this chapter show that even in 1933, responsibility for the Reichstag fire was a topic of debate among Germans themselves. Historian Ian Kershaw has confirmed this, noting that at the time, "critical observers" widely disbelieved the Nazi version that the fire was a Communist crime, and diplomats, foreign journalists, and liberal circles (including Ilse and her friends) immediately gave weight to the idea that the Nazis had started it.[28] By August 1933, a small group of exiled Communists, led by Willi Münzenberg and living in Paris, which was quickly becoming the antifascist capital of Europe, produced a book called *The Brown Book of the Hitler Terror*, claiming that the Reichstag fire "was the well-planned culminating act of terror that the Nazis used to secure total control over Germany."[29] The identity of who set the fire remains an ongoing topic of debate among historians today.[30] Although Germans in the 1930s and historians today debate the issue, the consequences of the Reichstag fire were far more important, especially for people like Gerhart Seger and other KPD and SPD members.

These days and nights of sitting around with comrades and friends discussing the Reichstag fire and the new Nazi regime provided Ilse and other members a way to release their confusion and anger about what was going on around them, especially while some of their partners were imprisoned for no other reason than being opposed to Hitler. She claimed such discussions were good for morale, and she also viewed them as a form of resistance. Ilse's view of resistance fits with the historian Doris Bergen's broad definition of resistance because at the time, even Ilse's seemingly innocuous conversations against the regime could have resulted in punishment from Nazi authorities.[31]

Many of Ilse's actions were antithetical to the culture of isolation and denunciation the Nazis propagated. Gathering with friends to discuss verboten topics certainly undermined Nazi strategy. At times, Ilse's home served as a space of resistance—a stark contrast to the women in Wendy Lower's *Hitler's Furies* who turned their homes into a space of violence on the Eastern front.[32] Ilse's story demonstrates that people could and did subtly resist in their domestic and everyday lives.

However, her resistance to the Nazi regime moved beyond closed-door conversations and became much more overt. During the April 1, 1933, Nazi boycott of Jewish stores and businesses, Ilse openly admitted to resisting the boycott by leaving her daughter with her friends and going into Dessau with the sole purpose of shopping at the Jewish-owned Borchardt's. Her gender likely informed the form of protest she took—shopping; being a woman out shopping in the middle of the day certainly aroused less suspicion than if she were a man operating in the female realm of a department store.[33] Not only did she walk through crowds of SA men heckling and shouting at her, but she also purposefully bought something she did not need in order to show her support of the salesladies, owner, and store. Admittedly, she recognized how such an action could have brought disapproval, and her heart furiously pounded as she left the store. While neither Ilse nor her Jewish friends, as she admits above, knew in 1933 what was coming, even these small, everyday acts of resistance early on were significant. After all, many of her Jewish friends had already left Germany; she was still there and thus could still fight, demonstrating non-Jewish solidarity with them.

Later, in November 1933, when Hitler called a referendum to gain approval for his decision to withdraw Germany from the League of Nations, she resisted pressure from SA men who were at the polling station where she stopped on her way to visit Gerhart in Blumberg, and peer pressure from the women she was traveling with, by voting against Hitler's decision. All of the women she was with had voted yes, or at least had taken one of the "yes" pins from the SA men to put on their lapels. Meanwhile, the SA men shamed her for her refusal to take one of these pins.

Most significantly, Ilse resisted the Nazi regime by smuggling one hundred marks into the Oranienburg concentration camp, which Gerhart had requested of her while he was planning his escape. This act could have potentially led to some type of severe punishment, such as a revocation of her privileges to visit her husband, or potentially something worse for him inside the camp or for her and her daughter outside of the camp. Additionally, it took serious consideration and clever planning on her part to figure out a way to smuggle the money past the SA guards and over to her husband during their visit.

Based on Ilse's account, Gerhart made the decision to attempt an escape because he was getting more and more depressed, and the situation was seemingly more and more hopeless for him. The beginning of political detention had been very chaotic with a "continuous cycle of arrests and releases." In fact, usually the prisoners at Oranienburg were imprisoned for only two or three months in order to stifle the workers' movement and "neutralize political opposition while the Nazis took over."[34] Thousands of opponents had been detained and sent to camps by the end of 1933. Historians estimate that between 30,000 and 80,000 opponents had been arrested and sent to camps. Nikolaus Wachsmann estimates that the number of those temporarily detained in 1933 probably reached 150,00 or even 200,000. The estimates are so wide-ranging because some people spent only a very short amount of time in "protective custody" or were arrested and released repeatedly.[35]

The Nazis started to release some early prisoners who had been arrested in the fall and winter of 1933. The Christmas Amnesty that year resulted in the release of several hundred Communist and Social Democratic prisoners and the shrinking or closure of several concentration camps.[36] As Robert Gellately argues, "for a brief moment at the end of 1933, especially after the November election, the new regime was so firmly in control, that the Nazis considered getting rid of both the Gestapo and the camps."[37] Even Heisig reassured Ilse that everyone would eventually be discharged—something he may have been led to believe at the end of 1933. But he may have also been trying to assuage Ilse, and the reality was different for members of the Reichstag, whom the Nazis likely feared had too much power. Historians estimate that 241 former members of the Reichstag (including 93 Communists and 98 Social Democrats) had been arrested by the end of 1933.[38] There was always the threat that they could be sent to different camps—something Gerhart sought to avoid. And thus, he made the decision to escape—a decision Gerhart claimed he made when he found himself in a state where he felt the only choices were suicide or escape.[39]

Notes

1. The first Gestapo chief, Rudolf Diels, coined the term "wild camps" to refer to the hundreds of early camps that were set up from spring 1933 with no central coordination. See Diels, *Lucifer Ante Portas*, 257; Goeschel and Wachsmann, "Before Auschwitz," 522; "The Nazi Camp System: Terminology," *Holocaust Encyclopedia*, United States Holocaust Memorial Museum, https://encyclopedia.ushmm.org/content/en/article/the-nazi-camp-system-terminology.
2. Seger, *A Nation Terrorized*, 26.
3. Dörner, "Oranienburg," 148.
4. Seger, *A Nation Terrorized*, 27.
5. Ibid., 147–48.
6. Gellately, *Backing Hitler*, 55–56.

7. Seger, *A Nation Terrorized*, 38; "Oranienburg," *Holocaust Encyclopedia*, United States Holocaust Memorial Museum, https://encyclopedia.ushmm.org/content/en/article/oranienburg-1.

8. Goeschel and Wachsmann, "Before Auschwitz," 522.

9. Israel did not exist until 1947; in 1933, they would have emigrated to Palestine.

10. SA-Sturmbannführer Werner Schäfer was the commander of Oranienburg. See "Oranienburg," *Holocaust Encyclopedia*, United States Holocaust Memorial Museum, https://encyclopedia.ushmm.org/content/en/article/oranienburg-1.

11. The *Völkischer Beobachter* (*People's Observer*), the newspaper of the Nazi Party, first appeared in December 1920 and was printed weekly and then daily after 1923 until late April 1945. From November 1923, when Hitler was arrested for the Beer Hall Putsch, until February 1925, when Hitler was out of prison and relaunched the Nazi Party, the paper was banned and ceased publication. For more on news under the Nazis, see "Writing the News," *Holocaust Encyclopedia*, United States Holocaust Memorial Museum, https://encyclopedia.ushmm.org/content/en/article/writing-the-news.

12. The *Gleichschaltung*, or coordination, meant the elimination or Nazification of social and political institutions throughout Germany. This included all political parties; state governments; bureaucracies; trade unions, which would now be controlled by the central government; and all elements of education, the economy, the media, and culture. For more on the Gleichschaltung, see "Gleichschaltung: Coordinating the Nazi State," *Holocaust Encyclopedia*, United States Holocaust Memorial Museum, https://encyclopedia.ushmm.org/content/en/article/gleichschaltung-coordinating-the-nazi-state.

13. Anhalt is about two hours by train from Oranienburg.

14. *Junkers Flugzeug- und Motorenwerke* AG (Junkers Aircraft and Motor Works) was a German aircraft and aircraft engine manufacturer based in Dessau. For more on the company, see Kay, *Junkers Aircraft and Engines*.

15. Approximately 17,000 German and Austrian Jews emigrated to Shanghai during the first years of Nazi persecution. As other countries limited or denied entry to Jews, Shanghai became a refuge; no visas were required to enter Shanghai until August 1939. See "German and Austrian Jewish Refugees in Shanghai," *Holocaust Encyclopedia*, United Stated Holocaust Memorial Museum, https://encyclopedia.ushmm.org/content/en/article/german-and-austrian-jewish-refugees-in-shanghai.

16. This boycott against Jewish-owned businesses took place on April 1, 1933, so it would have been spring, rather than summer.

17. A concern is an organization or establishment for business.

18. Germany withdrew from the League of Nations in October 1933, citing the Western powers' refusal to allow her demands for military, and thus international, parity. Hitler had often criticized the disarmament clause of the Treaty of Versailles, which severely limited Germany's military. He then called for a referendum on withdrawing Germany from the League of Nations alongside Reichstag elections for November 12, 1933. The Nazis purposefully planned the election to coincide with the fifteenth anniversary of the armistice that ended the First World War in order to whip up nationalist sentiment since the Versailles Treaty was unpopular among many Germans. There was 96 percent voter turnout, and 95 percent of the people approved the referendum. There was certainly a lot of governmental pressure to vote yes but probably very little coercion or intimidation at the polls. See Zurcher, "The Hitler Referenda."

19. From September 1933, the Nazis had established a subcamp to Oranienburg at the Elisenau Manor in Blumberg. See Dörner, "Oranienburg," 147.

20. It is unclear what evidence Ilse had for votes disappearing. At this stage in the Nazi regime, it was still possible to vote "no" or to invalidate one's ballot or to not vote at all without great personal risk. See Winkler, *Germany*, 31.

21. Mark confirmed that the Munzer's were friends of his grandparents in New York, and that Dr. Munzer was Gerhart's doctor. Personal correspondence with Mark Brandt, June 14, 2024.

22. Helmut Heisig, a police detective in Breslau and Berlin, was one of the first officials to be accepted into the German Secret State Police (the Gestapo) a few weeks after the Nazis came to power. He had worked with Rudolf Diels, the first head of the Gestapo, when he was working in Berlin in the political police division. Heisig was one of the members of the special commission set up by Hermann Göring to investigate the Reichstag fire. He was the first to interrogate the alleged arsonist, Marinus van der Lubbe. He joined the NSDAP (Nazi Party) in May 1933, and he was transferred to Dessau to become head of the police and criminal investigation department. For more on Heisig's involvement in the Reichstag fire investigation, see Hett, "'This Story Is About Something Fundamental.'"

23. For more on how the contacts and networks that Social Democrats created in German border regions (such as France, Austria until 1934, and the Saar region until 1935) helped German SPD members after March 1933, see Steinberg, "Should I Stay or Should I Go?" 83–84.

24. Seger, *A Nation Terrorized*, 29–65, 159–65, quote on 52. A standing cell was so small that a prisoner could do nothing else but stand.

25. Evans, *The Coming of the Third Reich*, 340–42.

26. Seger, *A Nation Terrorized*, 147–50.

27. White, "Introduction to the Early Camps," 10.

28. Kershaw, *Hitler*, 731–32.

29. Rabinbach, "Paris," 186.

30. On the night of the fire, the Nazis arrested Marinus van der Lubbe, a Dutch Communist who claimed to be acting alone. The Nazis later tried and convicted van der Lubbe, who was sentenced to death and beheaded by guillotine in January 1934. William Shirer claimed in 1960 that the Nazis had goaded van der Lubbe into setting the fire and that "there is enough evidence to establish beyond a reasonable doubt that it was the Nazis who planned the arson and carried it out for their own political ends." According to Kershaw, the general consensus of historians at the time of his book (in 1998) was that van der Lubbe had set the fire. See Shirer, *The Rise and Fall of the Third Reich*, 192–93; Kershaw, *Hitler*, 456–58, 731–32.

31. Bergen, *War and Genocide*, 263.

32. See Lower, *Hitler's Furies*, especially chapter 5.

33. Stoltzfus, Paldiel, and Baumel-Schwartz, "Women Defying Hitler," 11.

34. Quotes from Caplan, "Political Detention," 21, 26, respectively; Dörner, "Oranienburg," 148; Wachsmann, "The Dynamic of Destruction," 18–19.

35. White, "Introduction to Early Camps," 5; Caplan, "Political Detention," 23; Wachsmann, "The Dynamic of Destruction," 18.

36. See White, "Introduction to the Early Camps," 8; Wachsmann, "The Dynamic of Destruction," 20.

37. Gellately, *Backing Hitler*, 61.

38. White, "Introduction to the Early Camps," 9.

39. Seger, *Oranienburg*, 65.

4

Under House Arrest

In this chapter, Ilse discusses what happened to her and Renate after she saw Gerhart in Oranienburg for the last time.

I felt kind of numb and still very cold. When I was back in Berlin, I decided to call Käthe Kupsch. She was home, and after getting directions how to get to her, I got on a bus that took me near the street where she lived. In a way, I was glad that I did not have to go home immediately. I knew that Renatchen was in good hands. I had told the Posses that I might stay in Berlin that night so they would not worry.

One hour later, I was in the nice warm apartment of Käthe Kupsch, a bowl of steaming hot soup in front of me, and finally getting warm again. We talked about that Quaker friend of hers. She had some doubts that he really could do something, but she promised to talk to him and somehow to let me know the results in some disguised way on an open postcard.

The next morning, I left for Dessau and first went to the Posses' house. I still remember the moment when Leni Posse opened the door. Renatchen, wearing a little white pullover and a red jumper that my mother had made for her during her visit, saw me and came rushing over to me. She threw her little arms around me and shouted with joy, "Mutti, Mutti!" It made me feel so good that I forgot all my worries for a moment.

I stayed for a short time at the Posses'. I told them about the shortened visiting time and about my stay with Käthe Kupsch, but of course I could not tell them what was most on my mind. Then, leaving Renate with them a little while longer, I went home to start the fires in my two stoves to get the ice-cold apartment a bit warmed up before I would pick her up.

Just when I wanted to leave again, my bell rang. When I opened the door, a man I did not know stood in front of it. Before I could say anything, he showed me a police identification card and asked to come in. When I asked him what he wanted, he told me he had to make some inquiries of families who had relatives in the Oranienburg concentration camp. He wanted to know when I had seen Opi last. I told him that I had just come back from my last visit the day before but had stayed in Berlin for the night. He asked me if I always stayed overnight after my visits. I told him I usually did not. The reason was the way we had been treated in Oranienburg this time—between the long delay in letting us in and the cold, I had needed some rest before traveling home. He left it at that and continued quite harmlessly, saying, "I have heard that the prisoners have to do some work outside of the camp. Do they get paid for it?"

I nearly laughed. Paid? But I was quite nervous by then. What did he really want? And then something came to my mind. I had forgotten to leave Opi the usual three marks; he had only the twenty-mark bills, which naturally he could not use. I told the man that as soon as he left, I would write to Opi and send him some money so he would have it in a few days. Finally, I asked him if all these inquiries had anything to do with the Christmas amnesty that was so much on my mind. He said he really did not know. Maybe he had just been ordered to question some families, and I was on that list. Then he left.

When he was gone, I went over the whole conversation in my mind. What was the real reason for it? Somehow, I convinced myself that it could only be the amnesty. I had to tell Opi about this visit; maybe it would make him consider everything once more. This all sounds quite naive today, but the condition I was in by then let me grasp at the tiniest bit of hope. I sat down and wrote a short letter telling Opi about my visitor and my hopes, put the money in the letter, and mailed it on my way to the Posses' to pick up Renatchen. I told them too what had happened. They seemed to agree with me that it might have something to do with the amnesty, but they warned me at the same time not to build my hopes too high.

We had dinner at the Posses', and when we came home, I put Renatchen to bed right away. It was still not very warm in the apartment, and I decided to go to bed early and try to read a little. Maybe that would make me sleepy.

It was around nine o'clock when I heard the siren of a police car. It stopped in front of my house. A few seconds later, my bell rang a few times. I got out of bed, put on a robe, ran into the hall, and pressed the downstairs buzzer.

Two men came rushing up the stairs, and when they came around the last landing, I recognized one of them. He was the policeman who had been here that afternoon. Before, he had been quite friendly. Now he and his companion saluted me with a loud "Heil Hitler" and without a further word passed me and went into the apartment. They opened the door to Renatchen's room, looked around there, then went into my bedroom, where they looked under the beds, opened the wardrobe, and pushed the clothes aside. They then went into the living room, looked around there, and turned to me with stern faces.

The new man said, "Your husband did something very foolish: he escaped from Oranienburg."

I shouted back at him, "Have they caught him?"

"No. That is why we are here. But he won't get very far. They will get him, and you know what will happen to him then!"

I sat down quickly because the room started to sway around me. *They don't have him*—that was all I could think of at the moment. Finally, I realized that the policeman had asked me something.

"Did you know anything about your husband's escape, that he planned to do this?"

I knew that I had to pull myself together and be very careful with my answers. "Of course not. If he would have told me something like that, I never would have let him do that."

Then I remembered the letter I had written, and I told them about it and what I had written. During all this questioning and talking, the policemen had started to look around, taking books out of the bookcase, looking behind them, opening the bottom compartment of the bookcase, and looking at the odds and ends I had in there. Then the one who had been here in the afternoon went over to Opi's desk. He sat down and started to open all the drawers and look through them casually. He did the same with all the papers on the blotter. Then he asked me, "Don't you have any letters from your husband?"

My heart sank. The letters were all neatly piled up on one side of the desk. If he read the last few letters, it would not be difficult for a trained policeman to read between the lines. He would find out that I was not quite so ignorant of what was going on in Opi's mind even without him mentioning any thoughts of escape directly.

So I did something on impulse. Without answering his question, I pushed the letters over to him and said, "Here are all his letters. You can read them yourself. As you can see by the stamps on the back of the envelopes, they were all censored."

He took the letters, turned them over one by one, and said, "I see, but since they are censored already, I don't have to read them." I certainly was relieved!

He got up, looked at his watch, and said to his colleague, "I think you should drive over to the post office and retrieve that letter Frau Seger said she wrote this afternoon." Then he turned to me. "You did send that letter?"

I felt I was on safe ground now, and my answer was quite assured. "Of course. Why would I lie? You would find out anyhow."

The other policeman left, and my afternoon visitor turned to me again and said, "It is good that you mailed that letter. It will help you. I have been with the criminal police force for quite some time and have a lot of experience. I can tell most of the time when people are lying, but you are not the type. I believe you. I had that feeling this afternoon when I was talking to you."

I nearly smiled. His self-confidence, of course, was my gain. Naturally, in a way, he was right. I hate to lie, but these were extraordinary circumstances, and the end justified the means.

All of a sudden, it occurred to me that when the policeman had been here earlier in the afternoon, he must have already known about Opi's flight, so that meant hours had passed since the escape was discovered, and they still had not captured him! This was a tiny ray of hope that he might make it after all!

Then, the other policeman came back with the letter and gave it to his colleague, who opened it and read it. He gave the three marks to me and passed the letter on to his companion and said, "I think Frau Seger is in the clear."

I took a deep breath. Maybe they would leave now! But then the other policeman said he had talked with headquarters when he was out, and so far there was no news. "But they will get him. We have found that there is a spot at the Schleswig-Holstein border to Denmark where some people have smuggled out political traitors, and we are sure your husband is headed there. The whole border is closed now, and we will catch him there!"

I looked at this man, and for the first time I saw that he wore a big silver swastika on his coat lapel. So that was where he belonged!

Then, he turned to his companion and told him they had been ordered to stay with me overnight, until they were notified that Opi had been captured. And without another word, he sat down, took out the *Völkischer Beobachter*, which he had in his coat pocket, and started to read. The other man turned to me and said, "Frau Seger, you can go to bed whenever you want to. We have to leave the living room door open." And then in a sterner voice, "Don't try anything. It would be useless."

I went into Renatchen's room. Luckily, she had slept through all this commotion. I picked her up, took her with me into my bedroom, and put her into Opi's bed. I wanted her next to me, wanted to hear her breathing. When I started to close my door, I was told to leave it open, and when I had to go to the bathroom, the policeman with the swastika came quickly out of the living room and told me not to lock the door, and he stood in front of it until I came out again. I don't know what they thought I might do—kill myself and leave my child alone?

I did not sleep very much that night. Most of the time I was listening, afraid I might hear the awful whistle of a police car, or that someone would bring the terrible news that they had caught Opi! Sometimes I dozed off for a short time just to wake up with a start again, and all the anxiety was back.

Finally, that endless night ended. Renatchen was still asleep. I heard the two men talking in the other room. So, nothing had changed! I dressed quickly, went out into the hall, and looked into the living room. The men had taken off their coats and loosened their ties; one of them was poking in the stove and put some coal on. When they saw me, they put their coats on hastily, and one of them came over to me. He told me they would be relieved in a little while, unless something had happened during the night. He asked me for the address of the friend I had stayed with overnight in Berlin, to check up on my story.

Then I heard the dreaded whistle of the police car. I got very tense—what would the news be?

One of my guards opened the door, and two other policemen came in. They told their colleagues they would take over, nothing else. I took a deep breath—that meant Opi was still free! But for how long?

Three endless days and nights passed. During the daytime my guards changed twice; at eight o'clock in the evening, the night watch came and stayed until eight o'clock in the morning. There were always two men, mostly elderly, plain-clothed men who had been with the police force for a long time. They were not politically interested in anything. For them, this was just a job they were ordered to do, and that was it.

Twice, the second guard was an SS man in uniform. As one of the police officers explained to me, sort of apologizing, they just did not have enough men to spare for this daily guard business. He told me this when he had to escort me to do some food shopping in our Konsum-Verein, a sort of cooperative shop that was a combination of a butcher and a grocery store where most of the workers' families bought their supplies. Every time I went there with Renatchen and my bodyguard, the other shoppers, mostly women of course, whispered to each other, and the looks they gave my escort were certainly not friendly! Quite a few times, the salesclerk, who of course knew me since I had been a customer there as long as we had lived in that neighborhood, put some things in my bag that I had not bought—half a pound of butter, a piece of sausage, or some cookies. At first I thought it was a mistake, and I told him so. But he shook his head and whispered that this or that woman had told him to do so and had paid for it. I could never thank these women. They had forbidden the clerk to point them out to me. What a difference between these warm-hearted women and the people who lived in my house!

But all this happened later. The first three days, I did not try to get out or even ask if it was possible. I was much too scared that something might happen, that there might be some news about Opi—I don't know, just something. The only person besides my guards I saw during those days was the woman who brought the milk every morning. And I could see her only under the watchful eyes of one of my guardians who came to the door with me every morning.

I don't remember very much about those first three days. I could hardly eat; everything seemed to get stuck in my throat. The nights seemed to never end. The little bit of conversation I had with the two policemen was not of much help either. They seemed to be convinced that Opi would eventually come home to us, and then they could catch him. And I, of course, was deadly afraid that he might do just that if he was still in Germany. If he was not, where could he be? I told myself that every hour these policemen stayed here was a good sign. But when I got that far with my thoughts, I started all over again—they still could pick him up somewhere! I longed to be alone with my worries or to talk to my friends about it. But there were always these strangers around me. In the daytime, I was mostly in my little kitchen or in Renatchen's room. But in the evening, I had to sit with them since my bedroom had no stove and was quite cold. I went to bed very early with some books, but I really did not read very much. I could not concentrate; after a few minutes I realized that I was just going through the motion of reading, and my thoughts were elsewhere.

On the fourth day, in the early afternoon, my bell rang. It went through me like an electric shock! A quick look out of the kitchen window did not show any police car or bicycle on the street below. I pressed the buzzer and opened the apartment door, one of the policemen standing right behind me. I heard speaking downstairs and recognized the voices of my mother-in-law and Otti Posse, the son of my friends. I liked my mother-in-law very much; she had been very good to me, but I had no idea how she would react in a situation like this. I really did not feel like seeing anybody, especially with the policemen in the same room. What could we talk about? I could not understand why the Posses had sent her over to me. But here she was, and since Otti had brought her over, the Posses must have told her about the situation here and that she had to be careful about what she was saying. Thank God, at least they [the authorities] had left her alone in Leipzig, I thought!

I heard her say goodbye to Otti, and then she slowly came up the stairs. When she came around the last landing, I quickly ran down the few steps to take the little suitcase she was carrying. When I bent over to kiss her, she whispered three words in my ear—the most beautiful words—"*er ist sicher*" (he is safe). This was a moment I can hardly describe. I felt like laughing and crying at the same time, and I needed all the strength and self-control I could muster so that the policemen who were watching us would not get suspicious. It was not easy, but we both managed and slowly went up the rest of the stairs. I introduced her to the two policemen—the other had come out of the living room—and we went inside. And, I must say, she played her part marvelously. When we were finally settled down inside, she leaned back in her chair and said, "I might not have come if I had known that you were not alone. But I know how you must feel about this terrible thing with Gerhart, and I wanted to be with you. I hoped that you might have heard something by now. I nearly fainted when I read about his escape in the newspaper the other day. How could he do such a thing?" And then she started to lament about what she'd had to go through in her old days and so on and so forth. I just let her talk, happy that I did not have to say much. This was the only way not to reveal what was going on inside of me. I was bursting to hear more about Opi and how she could be sure he was really safe! Yet there was nothing I could do about it but wait until we could go to bed and be alone in my room.

When Renatchen woke up from her afternoon nap, it took me a little while to get her acquainted with her grandmother. The last time my mother-in-law had seen the child was in March in Leipzig, when all of our troubles had started. To her [Renatchen], she was a stranger. But after a little while of being in her own surroundings, she finally lost her shyness, and the box of chocolates that her grandmother brought for her certainly helped.

I went into the kitchen to prepare something to eat. The two policemen seemed to feel a little awkward, but when my mother-in-law mentioned that she had come all the way from Leipzig, one of them said that he knew Leipzig quite well, and they started talking about the famous Palmengarten and all the other sights of the town.[1]

At eight o'clock, the two men were replaced for the night. The new men were a bit astonished to see my mother-in-law, but after we told them why she had come, they seemed to be satisfied.

Shortly after the first policemen left, one of them came back and talked for a moment with one of my new guardians who had let him into the hall. They spoke for a moment in low voices, and then the one policeman left again. Time passed very slowly. Finally it was about nine o'clock, and I could not stand it any longer. I looked at my mother-in-law and insisted she must be very tired after the excitement of the trip, and I thought we should go to bed. She reacted beautifully, with a nod and a big yawn, and started to get up. But the policeman who had answered the door a little while earlier got up too. In a very polite voice, he told us that my mother-in-law could stay here as long as she wanted as long as we all stayed in the same room, but she could not stay overnight. These were his orders from headquarters, which his colleague had told him half an hour earlier.

I was stunned. How could I find out where Opi was, and how she knew about him, if we could not be alone together? I had to hear more! An idea crossed my mind; it might not work, but I could try. I told him in a very determined tone that I could not let my mother-in-law go to the city alone at night, even if she could take a bus only a few blocks away from my street. She did not know her way around Dessau, and the whole idea was impossible! But he only shrugged his shoulders and said that he was sorry, but these were his orders. Then I explained my idea. I told him the only way to get out of this dilemma would be to bring my mother-in-law over to the house of my friends, the Posses, where she could spend the night. My last hope was that somehow on the way over, there might be a possibility to talk. I really couldn't see how, but as long as we were together, there still might be a chance.

He talked this over for a moment with his colleague, who did not see any harm in this, but of course one of them had to go with us. My hope sank, and my half-hearted objection that this would not be necessary since it was only a few minutes' walk and that they certainly did not think I would try to escape and leave my child behind, naturally did not change anything. I could just as well have saved my breath, but I was not thinking very rationally at the moment. I tried to get hold of myself so as not to say something that might antagonize the policemen, who, after all, were doing me a favor; they might change their minds, and this was my last chance.

I quickly helped my mother-in-law into her coat and got dressed myself, and after taking a quick look into Renatchen's room to see if everything was all right, we left. The policeman was really quite nice. When we were out in the street, he even took her little overnight case to carry it. He tried to make some conversation about the cold winter we were having and so on. I let my mother-in-law do the talking. I was thinking and thinking about what to do so I could hear more about Opi.

Finally, we reached the Posses' house. There was no light in the front window, but they could have already been in their bedroom, which was in the back of the house. The big iron garden doors one had to pass through to get to the entrance of the house were always locked at night. I rang the bell four times, a little agreement the Posses had with all their friends to be on the safe side. At first, there was no answer. Afraid that nobody was home, I rang again in the same way. Finally, after the third try, the lights went on in the front room, and a window was opened. Wrapped in a blanket, Otto Posse leaned out of the window and asked in an unfriendly tone, "Who is there?"

I went over to the lantern in front of the house so that he could recognize me. I quickly explained the situation and asked if my mother-in-law could stay overnight with them. Of course that would be all right, but there was one problem. He did not have a key for the garden door. Leni, his wife, was visiting with friends, and Otti was out bowling. He had stayed home because he had a miserable cold, and there was no third key. But luckily he remembered the name of the bowling alley, and he suggested calling Otti there. He had his bicycle with him, and it would not take more than ten or fifteen minutes for him to get home. There was a little restaurant just across the street that was still open where I could make the telephone call. With that remark, he closed the window, and we went over to that little coffeehouse, glad to get out of the cold.

And then one of those unbelievable things happened! While I was looking up the telephone number of the bowling alley, all of a sudden it dawned on me: this was the opportunity I had been hoping for! I turned to our guardian with a pleading smile and said, "Don't you think it would be much better if you called? If you tell them that you are a police officer, they will certainly look for young Posse right away. I think this would work so much better than if I would do it, don't you agree?"

He hesitated for a moment, and then, getting up, he remarked, "I guess you are right." With this, he went to the back of the restaurant where the telephone booth was, and we were alone!

We looked at each other for a moment, and then she bent forward a little and told me that Opi was safe and well in Prague. He had written a picture postcard to an old friend he had gone to school with and who was well known to my mother-in-law too. This young man had a tailor shop in Leipzig. Opi wrote that he was on vacation in Prague, and since he knew that his friend was always interested in men's fashion, gray seemed to be the color most asked for in men's suits at the moment. He was enjoying his vacation very much and hoped that everybody was well. Quite harmless and uninteresting. It was signed, "Your old friend G." For a moment, the young man wondered who this "old friend" was. He did not know anyone who might be on vacation in Prague. Of course, he knew that Opi was in a concentration camp. He also knew that he had escaped. By then, it had been in the newspapers. All of a sudden it dawned on him: this card signed "G" could mean only one thing. It was a message from his friend Gerhart Seger. For some reason, he [Opi] had not wanted his whereabouts to be known, so instead of writing to me or my mother-in-law directly, he had chosen this roundabout way, knowing he could trust his old school friend. And, of course, he was right. The young man had rushed over to my mother-in-law's right away with the card, and she had recognized her son's handwriting. They had burned the card as a precaution, naturally, and she had decided to make the trip to Dessau the next day to bring me the good news. Since she did not know where my new apartment was, she had gone to the Posses' first, and they had told her about my house arrest. They were not quite sure if the police would let her see me, but she tried anyhow, and luckily it worked!

That was her exciting story! After she had finished, she leaned back in her chair, smiled a little, and remarked, "Now I really could go back to Leipzig tonight."

I cannot describe what went on inside of me. He had really made it! It was like a dream! I did not have to be afraid any longer because he was out of the country, and he was safe!

At that moment, the policeman came back. He told us that he had spoken to the young Posse and that he would be here in a short while. Then he invited us for a cup of coffee. I don't think I have ever enjoyed any coffee more than that one! I occupied myself with it and let my mother-in-law do the talking. Pretty soon Otti came, and after a little tearful goodbye—after all, it had been quite a strain on the old lady too—she and Otti Posse went into the house, and my escort and I went home. That night I slept beautifully!

The next week was quite uneventful. So far, it seemed that the news of Opi's whereabouts had not reached the authorities. I was still as guarded as before. I think I met the whole detective force during that time.

One evening, one of the policemen told me he had been a Social Democratic voter for as long as he had been able to vote. He had managed to get rid of his companion for a little while so that he could talk to me; he'd pretended that he had forgotten his cigarettes and sent the younger man to buy some in the neighborhood. Since he was higher in rank than the other, it seemed quite harmless instead of going himself. During the short time we were alone, he told me how furious the Nazi Gauleiter Colonel Loeper, one of Opi's most hostile political opponents, had been and still was when he was told about Opi's escape.[2] Loeper had contemplated taking Renate away from me and putting her in a children's home somewhere without letting me know where because that might bring Opi back. Commissioner Heisig had prevented that and convinced him [Loeper] that if an action like that became known outside of Germany, it could only do harm without guaranteeing the desired effect. To make this clearer, I should mention that at that time, at the end of 1933, Germany—or, rather, Hitler—tried very hard to gain Great Britain's friendship, and news like this would certainly not have helped.[3] He then said that he personally hoped very much that Opi's escape would be successful and that he might be out of the country by then.

It felt very good to know that his wish had been fulfilled, but of course I did not tell him so. I had learned by this time not to trust anybody. Then his colleague came back with the cigarettes, and that ended our conversation. The two men started to play cards, and I went to bed pretty soon with a book. I finally could read again!

I remember another conversation. On one of the last days of my house arrest, one of my guards was a well-known Nazi. I had never seen him before but had heard enough about him and his cruelty as an interrogator of political prisoners. He was on a daytime shift, and when I was doing some laundry in the kitchen, he came to the door and started a conversation. He remarked that he could not understand why a man with such a good-looking woman like me would try a silly thing like escaping, which, of course, would never succeed. He said he [Opi] would be caught sooner or later and that naturally would mean severe punishment, and if he tried to resist—he did not finish his sentence, which, of course, was not necessary. I knew exactly what he meant! I let him talk and just continued with my work. It was easy for me to listen to this, knowing what I did, and since he could not see my face, I did not even have to pretend anything. Getting little response from me, he went into the living room again, and I was relieved. But not for long. Pretty soon, he came back to the kitchen. This time he started praising Opi. "Your husband is a highly intelligent man, you know. The only trouble is that he bet on the wrong horse. A man like him could have reached the highest places in our party; we can use people like him!"

Well, this was too much! Furiously, I turned around and, not very diplomatically I admit, nearly shouted at him, "There is something like conviction that one cannot change just because it would be convenient at the moment! Some people can, but never my husband!"

He looked a little surprised for a moment at my sudden outburst, but then he laughed and said, "You are not only pretty, you have a temper too." And then he asked a quick question: "Maybe you do know where your husband is?"

That brought me back to my senses; I knew remarks like these only made things worse. "I wish I knew," I said and quickly turned back to my laundry. He stood behind me for a moment without saying anything and then went back to his colleague. Soon afterward, his relief came, and I was certainly glad to see him go!

And then one morning after about ten days or so, I heard the police siren and a car stopping in front of the house. My bell rang, and one of the policemen—it was the one who had told me that he always voted Social Democrat—went downstairs. After a few minutes, he came up again with a big grin on his face. "Mrs. Seger, we just received news at headquarters that your husband is in Prague!" Then, as he entered the apartment, his face became very official, and he announced, "Your house arrest is over for the time being. But you have to sign this paper that you agree not to leave Dessau unless you have the permission of the authorities."

Well, this was a happy moment! I gladly signed the paper and took a deep breath when I could finally close the door behind the two policemen. For a moment, I just stood there, enjoying the feeling of being on my own again! Then, I went over to my gramophone and put on the record of the beautiful love song of the Lehár operetta *The Land of Smiles*, "*Dein ist mein ganzes Herz*" ("Yours Is All My Heart"). I picked up Renate and danced with her through my little apartment, singing together with Richard Tauber at the top of my lungs.[4] Finally, I had the possibility to unwind and feel normal again.

Then, I took Renatchen to the Posses', and we talked and talked about all that had happened since we had seen each other last. It felt so good to be with my friends again, knowing that Opi was safe. For the moment, that was all that counted. I did not even try to think beyond that.

One thing we could not understand was why it had taken so long for the news about Opi's arrival in Prague to reach the German authorities. Why had it not been in all the newspapers? Opi told me the reasons for this many months later, when we were finally together again. The executive committee of the Social Democratic Party had migrated to Prague and established its immigration headquarters there with the permission of the Czechoslovakian government. This, of course, was the first place Opi visited when he arrived in Prague. His friends there had thought it was safer for him to stay in hiding until he was granted political asylum.

A few days later, I got a telegram from my father saying that he would come to Dessau for two days. This was an answer to a long letter I had written to my parents the first night I was alone again. I certainly was looking forward to his visit, and I took Renate to pick him up at the railway station the next day. We were not home for long when I heard the dreaded police sirens again, and sure enough, a car stopped in front of our house. This time a policeman in uniform came up the stairs when I buzzed the door after the bell rang. "Are you Mrs. Seger?" he asked quite sternly. When I nodded, he said, "You have been seen coming home with a man; was that your husband?" Without saying anything, I let him come in.

My father was sitting on the couch, grinning a little. The policeman looked at him, then at me. A little embarrassed, he told us that there had been an anonymous telephone call at headquarters, that I had been seen coming home with a man who was still in my apartment, and it might be Gerhart Seger! My father quietly took out his passport and showed it to him. Then, he said quite sarcastically—I still remember that little scene quite vividly—"I will be here for two days only, but I can leave quite satisfied that the police watch so well over the morals of my daughter." The officer murmured something about orders and left. My father and I had a good laugh when I had closed the door behind him. I was quite sure that one of my "friendly" fellow tenants was the anonymous caller. He might have watched us coming home a little while ago. My father tried to persuade me to go home with him to Freiburg, which, of course, I could not do, and even if I could get permission, I had the feeling I must stay in Dessau so Opi knew where I was. My father was not happy about this, but he could understand it.

Two days later, my father had to leave again. He took some books with him, the *Propylaen World History* and two books on the discovery of the tomb of King Tutankhamun by Howard Carter. I mention this only because these were the only worthwhile books out of our beautiful library that were saved. All the others were confiscated and destroyed by the Nazis later on.

There was something I had not told my father or the Posses. When I saw Opi the last time in Oranienburg, he had advised me that if his escape was successful to start divorce proceedings right away; he thought that would protect me from any prosecution by the Nazis. I thought and thought about this but simply could not bring myself to do it. I am sure that if I had followed his advice, things might have been easier later on. But "no one can jump over his own shadow," as an old German expression says; everything in me was against it, even knowing perfectly well the reason for it and that we would remarry as soon as we were together again.[5] Months later, when he found out that we were in the concentration camp in Rosslau, he tried to do it from Prague, but it never worked out.

Everything was a little quieter for a while. I was anxiously waiting to hear from Opi, but I knew only too well that there was not a chance. His letters would never have reached me. I was sure that he was just as impatient as I was to be together again, but how? Christmas had passed. I had trimmed a tiny little tree for Renatchen with candles that frightened her a little at first, but later on, she had a lot of fun trying to blow them out. But for me, it was a very lonely Christmas, and only the thought that Opi was free made it a little easier.

One day, we heard through the grapevine—this kind of news was never in the newspapers—that the Nazis had opened a new concentration camp in a nearby city of Rosslau, which was connected to Dessau by trolley. They had confiscated a restaurant that was owned by members of our party and then converted it into a concentration camp. They used the big dance hall in the backyard as a dormitory for the prisoners and the restaurant in front as the guardroom and sleeping quarters for the guards, who were SS troopers, not the SA as in Oranienburg.[6] They kept around one hundred prisoners there, mostly Communists. Some had been in Oranienburg before and had been transferred there for reasons known only to the Nazis themselves. People who passed by that concentration camp had reported that quite often, one could hear the screams of the prisoners, especially when new ones had been brought in. Sometimes people were discharged, but they never talked about what was going on in there. The former prisoners were too afraid of being picked up again.

I found that out one day myself. I was in the city and recognized a Communist on the other side of the street who had been in Oranienburg with Opi. Happy to see him discharged, I went over to greet him. But he passed me by as if he had never seen me before. His wife, with whom I had waited many times before the prison gates in Oranienburg, and who was walking a few steps behind him, only gave me a shy little wave with her hand, but she did not stop either.

One day, my mother-in-law wrote that she would come from Leipzig to see us, and this time I was really looking forward to her visit. Besides, I had a little hope that she might have heard from Opi again—and she had hoped I might have some news. But, we both disappointed one another.

We had just eaten our lunch when Leni Posse came by. She looked pale and nervous and was in a great hurry to get home again. When she had told us why she had come, I easily understood why! She'd had a visitor, a woman who came directly from Prague, whom Opi had sent. I was supposed to go to a certain restaurant on the Elbe River and meet her there as soon as possible. She would wait for me there. She had a message for me from Opi that she was instructed to give only to me. Then, Leni quickly described the woman for me as a small, dark-haired person, wearing a dark coat and a white felt hat with a black ribbon. To recognize me, Opi had given her a small photograph of me that she had used as her introduction at the Posses' house. As soon as Leni finished telling me this, she wished me luck and left.

We were both stunned for a moment, but then we got very excited; finally, there would be some news we both were very much waiting for! I decided to leave Renatchen with my mother-in-law and run over to the restaurant, which luckily was not very far. I was just going to put my coat on when the bell rang again. I got quite a shock when I opened the door. The same detective who had come the day of Opi's escape and had asked me so many questions stood outside the door. My first thought was, of course, that he had somehow found out about the Czech woman who was waiting for me in the Elbhaus, which was the name of the restaurant. But this was not the reason why he had come. Someone had called police headquarters and told them that Gerhart Seger would speak over the Dutch radio station, Hilversum, which was known to send anti-Hitler propaganda and speeches via refugees, sometimes under cover names for safety reasons, to Germany.[7] It was punishable to listen to this station, but of course, many people listened to it secretly. The speech was supposed to be that night! And I was supposed to come to police headquarters to identify Opi's voice. This was ridiculous! Did they really think that I would do that? But that was not important. I would simply say that I couldn't tell; radio was not that good in 1934. But I had to get rid of him so that I could leave.

So I looked at my mother-in-law, hoping that she would understand, and then turned to the detective and explained to him that we had just decided to go the Elbhaus for coffee and cake before he arrived, but of course, we would be home long before the time the speech was supposed to take place, so he could pick me up. I wanted to get out of the house because I was afraid that the woman might get impatient and decide to come to my house after all. He told me that he was sorry, but that was not possible because he had orders to stay with me until we would be picked up in the evening. Not very hopeful, I tried something else. I reminded him of the terrible time my mother-in-law had when she was here the last time, and I had the idea that he could come with us. It would not make any difference as long as he stayed with us. It worked! He hesitated for a moment, and then he said he could not see any harm in that. After all, his responsibility was only that I was available when needed. I was not under any kind of arrest, so to speak.

I quickly dressed Renatchen, who was happy to hear that we were going out, and then we left. I breathed easier when we were out of the house. I was convinced that if the woman saw me come into the restaurant with two people, she would not dare make a move and would try again the next day. If only the detective had worn a uniform or something, that would have made him recognizable for what he was! It was really one of these unbelievable situations again. Why did all this have to happen on the same day?

The restaurant was nearly empty. There were only two couples sitting on one side of the room. On the other side, I saw a woman sitting with her back to the entrance, and she wore a white felt hat with a black ribbon! But why on earth was she not facing the door so that she could have seen us right away?

We sat down and ordered. I was quite tense but tried very hard not to show it. The woman, who sat about four tables away from us on the other side of the room, had not made a move or turned around. I still did not know whether she had seen us or not. I let Renatchen run around a little in the hope that the woman might see her. But Renatchen did not venture farther than the next table. It all seemed quite hopeless. Then I saw the woman get up and disappear into the ladies' room.

This was my opportunity! I grabbed Renatchen, excused myself, and went into the ladies' room too. The woman was waiting for me there. Luckily, nobody else was around. I quickly explained to her who the man with us was and what had happened. Then she gave me the message from Opi. He wanted us to come to Prague as quickly as possible, and this was how: he had worked out a plan with Czech Social Democratic comrades who worked with German comrades in an underground fashion, bringing anti-Hitler literature across the border and helping political refugees whenever they could. On a certain day the next week, she would be back with a Czech comrade who would drive a car. I was supposed to ride with this man, who would bring a forged passport for me, and she would travel with Renate by train back to Prague. Opi had described a certain spot in the park in my neighborhood where I should meet her and give her the child, and then I would walk over to the car, which would be parked near a seldom-used exit on a small side street. The time should be five o'clock in the evening, since, this being January, it would be nearly dark by then, and nobody would be in the park. I tried to tell her this would not be possible because I had given my word not to leave. I could not do this to my parents and friends who would certainly all be under suspicion of having helped me and would have to suffer the consequences.

The woman looked at me as if she had not understood what I had said and then remarked in her heavy Czech accent, "Your husband is awaiting you!" Then she left.

I waited for a moment to calm down a bit, then I picked up Renatchen, who had stood quietly next to me the whole time, just looking at that strange woman. Luckily, she could not talk yet.

When we entered the restaurant again, I saw that the woman had not returned to her table. I was glad to see that she evidently had left. A little while later, we also left and went home.

Around seven o'clock, another detective came to pick up our companion. The whole thing about Opi's speech seemed to have been a hoax. There was only music and some unimportant news during the time the speech was supposed to be broadcast, and that was all. I had the feeling that both detectives did not think very much of the whole business. Maybe somebody at police headquarters had been overzealous.

Naturally, I did not tell my mother-in-law about this fantastic plan Opi had figured out. I just told her that he was fine, that he wanted to know how we were, and I even told her a little about the divorce idea and that he wanted to know if I had done anything about it. After all, I had to tell her something. She was not very happy about this either, but she could see some sense in it. But then she said she hoped that this would not be necessary. We both should have some patience. Maybe the whole Hitler spook would be over soon, and things might become more normal again, and Opi would come back. I did not argue with her, but I certainly did not see things so naively, and why should I make it more difficult for her than it already was?

The next day, she went back to Leipzig, and I was alone with my thoughts. It was a terrible week. I could not talk with anybody about my problems, not even with the Posses. I had given them the same thin story I had told my mother-in-law, but I was quite sure they guessed that there was more to it. Nevertheless, they did not ask any questions, and I was glad about that. My thoughts went in circles. I wanted so much to be with Opi again, and here was a chance! On the other hand, what would the Nazis do to my family and my friends? Could I really go and endanger all of them? To whom was I more obligated: them or my husband? But then, were they really in danger? There was no proof whatsoever that they had helped me. Neither my family nor my friends in Dessau had any connections with Czechoslovakia. I knew that was not a very logical argument, but I could not think very logically at that point.

Finally, the day I was supposed to meet these people came around. During a sleepless night, I had convinced myself nothing would happen—I just had to go! So I packed a little overnight suitcase with a few necessary things for Renatchen and me and hid it under the little mattress in Renatchen's baby carriage. When I put her into the carriage, I had the feeling that everybody must have seen that something was wrong. She was sitting about ten inches higher than normal. Certainly, nobody but me would have seen anything strange in that, but in the state of mind I was in, I couldn't think normally anymore.

There were only a few people in the street, and nobody seemed to look at us. I had just crossed the street when I heard a man's voice behind me saying, "Good evening, Mrs. Seger." I nearly fainted when the man passed me, and I recognized him as one of the detectives who had been on guard duty one day in my apartment. I could hardly return his greeting. But he just smiled at Renate and continued his walk without looking back. Evidently his being there was just a coincidence and had nothing whatsoever to do with me. I walked a little slower, and when I reached the entrance of the park, he was already out of sight.

I went to the place the Czech woman had mentioned and waited. The park was completely empty, and it was getting dark by now. More than half an hour from the set time had passed, and nobody had shown up. Something must have gone wrong. The whole plan suddenly seemed unreal to me. I would not wait any longer. I would go home. When I had made that decision, a strange sense of relief came over me. I had no explanation for it, but somehow deep down in my heart, I must have had the feeling all along that this could not have worked—it was too fantastic. If it went wrong, the Nazis certainly would take Renate away from me! When I reached our little apartment and closed the door behind me, I experienced for the first time since I lived there that good feeling of really coming home!

But when I woke up early the next morning, this good feeling was gone. Maybe there would have been a chance? Maybe I should have waited a little longer in the park; I might be together with Opi by now, and then again, what would have happened here?

Well, I had no time to think about this much longer. My bell rang, and, hoping very much it might be my good friend Leni Posse, I pressed the buzzer and opened the door. But instead of my friend, two other familiar figures appeared on the last landing of the stairs: two detectives, one of them the same man who had been with us in the restaurant where I met the Czech woman. And now I found out why the flight plan had not worked out! I did not even have to ask the men what they came for this time. They were so full of what had happened that they started talking the minute that they were in the apartment. Last night, shortly before dark, a car with a Czech license plate had parked in front of the police headquarters with a man and a woman inside the car. When the policeman who was on guard duty in front of the building inquired what they wanted, the man demanded to see the officer in charge. And now came a strange story that is hard to believe.

As I learned much later from Opi, the Czech comrade who had offered to drive the car that was to pick us up had become ill a day before the set date. So at the last moment, they had rented a car with a driver, telling him some story and offering him good money, and he agreed to do the job. But what the Czech friends did not know was that this man was a convinced Nazi who knew who Gerhart Seger was. (There were quite a few [Nazi sympathizers] at that time in Czechoslovakia. It became a Communist state much later, around 1946, after the end of World War II.) Instead of doing what he had been paid for, he went straight to the Dessau police and told them the whole plan. The woman evidently had said nothing, pretending not to understand any German. When the detective started speaking about her, I waited anxiously—had he recognized her as the woman who had passed our table in the restaurant? Evidently not, otherwise he might have put two and two together. I breathed a little easier and uttered something that all this seems hard to believe. Then, I asked where these people were now, and I was told that they'd had to stay in prison overnight, but they [the detectives] thought that they would be released soon and sent home. I finally asked the detectives why they came to see me since I had nothing to do with these people. I quite convincingly lied. They told me then that they were sent here to stay with me until Commissioner Heisig arrived, who wanted to talk with me.

I left the room quite puzzled. Why would Heisig come to me? What did he want? Was there more than the two detectives had told me? I began to feel quite uneasy and a little scared.

Escaping from Oranienburg in 1933 would have certainly weighed seriously on someone like Gerhart since it essentially meant becoming a stateless person. However, it would have been easier than later on in the regime since most of the seventy camps formed that year used whatever space was available to them and lacked barbed wire, barracks, and guard towers.[8] Gerhart's time at this early wild camp, not being completely secluded from society and working outside the camp, closely resembled the later experiences of Nazi prisoners of war.[9] Gerhart managed to escape while he was working outside the camp on December 4, 1933, after he had some money smuggled to him in Oranienburg, including from Ilse. As he recounted later in *Oranienburg* and in an interview with the *New Yorker*, he was not wearing a prison uniform, rather his own clothes, which meant escaping was easier. Very early one winter morning, as he was performing hard labor hollowing out the bed of a canal about an hour northwest of Oranienburg, he used the embankment they had created from their work as cover as he ran through the otherwise open fields. Neither the SA guards nor the other prisoners noticed, and he made his way to a restaurant in town where he called a taxi. He traveled via taxi, tram, and streetcar through Berlin, even stopping at a bathhouse for his first warm bath in nine months. He stayed away from the center of town and used local trains and buses rather than express trains, which were more closely monitored, to reach the countryside near the Czechoslovakian border. He then walked eight hours through the mountains over the border to Prague in below freezing weather. The whole trip took him twenty-two hours.[10]

Ilse's resistance to the Nazi regime continued while she was under house arrest. Whether Ilse consciously thought of her actions as resistance is unclear here; after her mother-in-law arrived in Dessau to deliver news, she desperately wanted to know whether her husband was safe. But she certainly recognized that she could get in trouble with the guards if she were to discuss Gerhart's escape and his whereabouts with her mother-in-law, and thus she fulfilled Bergen's definition of resistance discussed above because her act carried a risk of punishment. This is presumably why Ilse concocted a plan to talk to her mother-in-law in private when they were on their way to the Posses' house, where her mother-in-law would be staying the night. While Gerhart's escape from Oranienburg was very bold and well known, even being reported in the newspapers at the time, Ilse and her mother-in-law carried out smaller but nevertheless personally significant acts to resist Nazism. Ilse also mentioned the women who left anonymous donations for her while she was shopping, which demonstrated tremendous moral courage and solidarity and gave Ilse hope during an otherwise isolating and uncertain time. Ilse also gained hope from one of the police officers who was guarding her; he was part of the SPD and showed his own type of early defiance to the regime by talking with Ilse privately about Gerhart. This officer was also an example of how men, who were in need of work, found it working for the Nazi regime but also simultaneously showed defiance.

The police finally got word that Gerhart had made it to Prague, where some other members of the SPD had escaped to, although Ilse and her mother-in-law already knew this. After this, Ilse was no longer under house arrest, but she continued to receive secret messages from her husband via SPD members. As Ilse recounted above, a Czech contact delivered a message to her at a restaurant about an escape plan for her and Renate. Gerhart had created the plan with the help of Czech Social Democratic comrades who worked underground with German comrades. Swen Steinberg's research on political networks in the German-Czechoslovakian borderland shows that an incident like this was likely common. As he says, "The cross-border cooperation of political parties and organizations (e.g. workers' sports, hiking and climbing and youth organizations) as well as the cooperation of social democratic or communist newspapers in Saxony and in the German-speaking northern part of Czechoslovakia had also made these borderlands a place of encounter and cooperation—and thus the border virtually invisible."[11] In other words, "the contacts and networks that were created in the 1920s helped to save lives from March 1933 on." It also helped that the President of Czechoslovakia, Tomáš G. Masaryk, had a liberal asylum policy with regard to German refugees.[12] Starting in the summer of 1933, the SPD leadership working out of Prague established a network of "border secretaries" and tried to install an illegal "Reich leadership" and six secretaries outside of Berlin.[13] There was even a system of "border offices, houses of the workers' hiker and sports movement, party offices and trade union houses or publishing and printing houses" that were used to provide refugees like Gerhart (although it is unclear if he actually used any of them) with accommodations, clothing, and food.[14] Presumably, Ilse would have used this network too if she had decided to escape.

Whether to escape to Prague or not was clearly something that weighed very heavily on her. The conflict she felt about leaving was revealed in the very tense moments when she went to meet the Czech contact at a restaurant (with a policeman in tow) and when she was on the way to a park to potentially follow through with the escape plan. She even feared at one point that the Nazis might take her daughter away from her—a very real possibility. For Ilse, it was a choice between putting her family, her friends, herself, and her daughter in danger to see her husband again or potentially never seeing him again. It is difficult to imagine the roller coaster of emotions that people like Ilse experienced, but she certainly had something in common with other refugees and their families who weighed the question of "should I stay or should I go?" quite heavily.[15]

Not every moment was anxiety-inducing and fraught for Ilse. At times, life was quite uneventful and filled with the monotony of caring for a toddler; at others, she even celebrated small triumphs like finding out that Gerhart had made it to Prague.

Ilse's outlook about the situation in Germany had clearly changed by early 1934. After the Nazis came to power, she still had a lot of hope that they would not be able to create the type of dictatorship they wanted because they did not have a majority in the Reichstag and would have had to change the constitution. After the Reichstag fire, she believed in a sense of justice when hundreds of Communists and Social Democrats were arrested.[16] Even upon seeing Gerhart in Oranienburg for the first time, she still suggested that there might be a sense of law and order, and she certainly acted like it when, for example, she unapologetically demanded to speak to the commandant of Oranienburg, Werner Schäfer. Even after Gerhart told her about his planned escape, she still held out a lot of hope. But when her mother-in-law visited in early 1934, Ilse viewed her as naive for believing that "the whole Hitler spook would soon be over" and that Gerhart would be returning to Germany.

Finally in this chapter, Ilse mentioned the opening of a new concentration camp, Rosslau. She claimed that the Nazis had confiscated the property to build Rosslau from SPD members, which was true; the SA converted a community center owned by a local trade union into a transitional concentration camp for "protective custody" detainees. The first twenty-five prisoners arrived in October 1933, and they were mostly Communists or other leftist opponents. Another forty detainees were transferred to the camp from Oranienburg because they were from Dessau.[17] Although she mentioned Rosslau only in passing here, Ilse would come to find out much more about the camp in the coming months.

Notes

1. The Palmengarten is a beautiful, large park in the center of Leipzig.
2. Wilhelm Friedrich Loeper was the Nazi Gauleiter of the Gau Magdeburg-Anhalt. The Nazis divided the country into thirty-three administrative regions known as *Gaue*.

Colonel was his military rank dating from the First World War. See Miller and Schulz, *Gauleiter*.

3. After 1933, Hitler's foreign policy aims included a type of Anglo-German partnership, and thus he praised the British Empire and the British people as their racial kin. See chapters 2 and 3 in Strobl, *The Germanic Isle*.

4. *The Land of Smiles* (*Das Land des Lächelns*) is an Austrian romantic operetta by Franz Lehár. "*Dein is mein ganzes Herz*" ("Yours Is My Heart Alone" is a better translation than the one Ilse provided) is an aria from the operetta. Richard Tauber, an Austrian tenor and film actor and a close friend of Lehár's, for whom the aria was written, sang it.

5. Ilse gave the literal translation of a German idiom. A better translation is "bringing oneself to do that which one would normally not do."

6. In August 1933, the SA had converted an old community center owned by a local trade union into a transitional concentration camp in order to relieve the overcrowded Anhalt prisons. Initially, SA guards oversaw the camp, but then the SS took control of the camp in January 1934, which is why Ilse would have noted that it was controlled by the SS and not the SA. It was fairly typical of the early wild camps to be established by various local, regional, state, and party agencies, often in collaboration and sometimes in competition with one another. The SA often played a leading role, and then after the Night of Long Knives especially, the SS took over. See White, "Rosslau," 157–58 and Goeschel and Wachsmann, "Before Auschwitz," 522.

7. Hilversum is a city in Northern Holland that is the center for radio and television broadcasting in the Netherlands. Although it is unclear which radio station Ilse was referring to here, there were a number of radio stations operating out of Hilversum in January 1934 that could have sent anti-Hitler speeches and propaganda. The Nazis referred to any radio station that enemies of the Reich broadcast or that broadcast anti-German materials as *Feindsender* (enemy radio stations).

8. White, "Introduction to the Early Camps," 5.

9. Scheck, *Love Between Enemies*, 17–19.

10. Seger, *Oranienburg*, 65–71; McKelway, "A Reporter at Large," 37–38.

11. Steinberg, "Should I Stay or Should I Go?" 83.

12. Ibid.

13. Buchholz and Rother, *Der Parteivorstand der SPD im Exil*, xxx–xxxi.

14. Steinberg, "Should I Stay or Should I Go?" 83–84.

15. Ibid., 91.

16. Nikolaus Wachsmann has suggested that, on the one hand, there was a rule of law that applied when thousands of political opponents were arrested. On the other hand, there was also mass detention that happened without any legal process. Wachsmann, "The Dynamics of Destruction," 18–19.

17. White, "Rosslau," 157–58.

Ilse Hart in about 1925, before she met Gerhart.

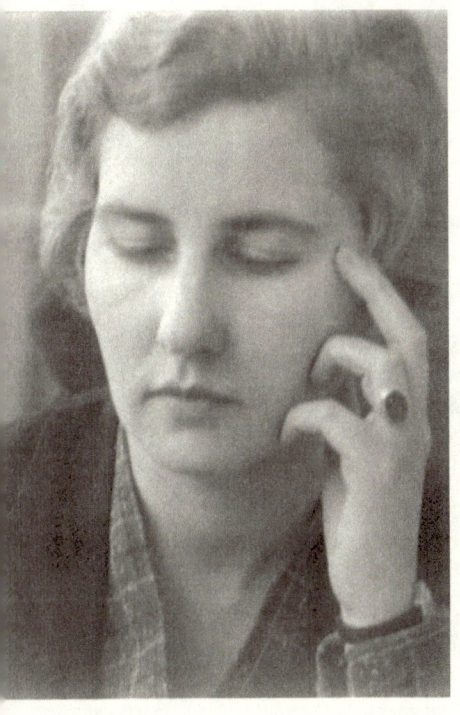

Ilse at about age thirty (left) and age seventy (right).

Ilse hiking in the Black Forest, about 1930.

Ilse's family, taken just after Ilse and Gerhart's marriage. *From left*, Ilse's father, Ernst Hart; Ilse's mother, Margaret Hart; Ilse's brother Wolfgang; Ilse; Gerhart; and Ilse's brother Joachim.

Ilse and Gerhart just after their marriage.

Ilse and Gerhart, about 1930.

Gerhart learned photography during his service with the *Luftstreitkräfte* (Imperial German Air Force) in World War I, and he remained an avid photographer for the rest of his life. Two of his favorite subjects were his wife and his daughter. Here is Ilse in about 1930.

Ilse in the living room of their apartment, after Gerhart's arrest.

Ilse and Renate while living in Switzerland, 1935.

Ilse and Renate reunited with Gerhart on their arrival in New York, December 19, 1935. This is essentially where Ilse's memoir ends.

Ilse and Gerhart, about 1955. Ilse liked to tell people that her hair went white overnight from the stress of the concentration camp. While she was exaggerating, her hair was completely white by her late thirties.

Renate and Richard Brandt on the day of their wedding, September 1956.

Ilse and Gerhart, about 1965.

Ilse's three grandchildren, Mark, Jennifer, and Andrew, 1968.

Ilse's last time in Germany in 1974.

5

A Hostage in Rosslau

In this chapter, we learn much more about the new concentration camp, Rosslau. The chapter opens with Commissioner Heisig letting Ilse know that she was being detained there. He claimed that Ilse had to move to Rosslau for safety concerns, but it became clear once she moved there that the whole reason for her being imprisoned was to entice Gerhart back to Germany; she became a hostage alongside her daughter. Ilse and Renate were not the only hostages of Nazi political prisoners, as discussed in the introduction. It was not an uncommon practice for the wives and children of Reichstag members who went into exile—or, as was the case with Gerhart, escaped into exile—to be taken hostage (*Geisel*) in camps. This was called "family arrest" (*Sippenhaft*), and it continued during the war years as well.[1] Ilse and Renate certainly became more well known than many other wives and daughters because of the publication of *Oranienburg* and Gerhart's subsequent book tour in 1934–35 throughout Europe and the United States.

I went into Renatchen's room to find her wide awake after her afternoon nap and quite willing to get out of bed. I dressed her and gave her a little snack and went back into the living room to read her a little story. It was a cold, unfriendly day, the 19th of January 1934, and it had already started to get dark when the bell rang. I let one of the detectives open the door—again I had not heard the police siren—and it was Commissioner Heisig.

He quickly came into the room, greeted me with "Heil Hitler," looked around for a moment, and then said in a businesslike tone, "Mrs. Seger, you have heard what has happened. Herr Reichsstatthalter Loeper feels that you are not safe here alone in this apartment any longer, and I came to tell you that we have a little apartment for you in Rosslau."[2]

Rosslau! So that was it! For a moment, I lost control over myself and really shouted at him, "You mean the concentration camp, don't you?"

But before I could say any more, he continued, "I think, too, this is the best way. You will, of course, have your own room there. I hear there is even a piano in it. You are absolutely under my jurisdiction. If there is anything you need, the commander has orders to get in touch with me or let you phone me. In an hour, I will send a nurse who can help you pack the things you and your child might need, and then these two officers will bring you out to Rosslau."

I had caught myself by now. I knew, of course, that any protest would be useless. Again, I had the feeling that this decision was not his, but this time he had to give in to Loeper. There was no sense in making a scene. I might lose his sympathy and gain nothing. So I just asked him about Renatchen's food. She was only seventeen months old. Where could I prepare her meals? What about milk, or a bath for the child? All these things seemed so important and so impossible at the same time. I fought very hard not to lose control over myself again. His reply was to tell me not to worry about that. I could cook the kind of meals she needed in the camp kitchen. I should give the cook a list, and he could get these things when he did the shopping for the camp every day. Of course, I would have to pay for these "extras" myself. Then he got up, went to the door, turned around, and said, "You have the permission to call me any time if there is something you might need, as I told you before. Heil Hitler." Then he left.

For a while, I could not bring myself to get up. I sat there with Renatchen on my lap, thinking what to do first. I was scared. How could I get a message to the Posses? But what good would that do even if I could find a way? They could not help either. I felt terribly lost.

Finally, I got up. I had to decide what to pack. I took all the money I had out of the desk, and without much thinking as to why, I took our family book, which contained our marriage license and Renate's birth certificate, and put all this in my handbag. The two detectives, who had waited outside as long as Heisig was there, came into the room now. I had the feeling they were a bit embarrassed and did not know what to say. I ignored them and fixed Renatchen's supper. She was used to drinking a bottle of milk when she was in bed, so I filled one to take with me.

Then I went up to the attic to get a suitcase. The little stall that came with the apartment was filled with all sorts of things for which there was no room in the small apartment, especially big boxes of books. These stood in front of the suitcases, and I could not get to them without help. They were too heavy. So I went downstairs again to ask one of the detectives to help me. When I opened the apartment door, I heard a woman's voice inside—the nurse had arrived. When I came in, she turned around and greeted me with a raised right arm and a very loud "Heil Hitler." She was a big, heavyset woman, around fifty or so, in a nurse's uniform with a big swastika brooch on her blouse. I disliked her the minute I saw her. "In which way can I help you?" she demanded, not asked. I told her about the suitcase, and she sent the two men up to get it for me.

They finally came down with it, and when I opened the suitcase, the first thing that fell out were two red flags with the three white arrows, the famous anti-Nazi symbol![3] I had completely forgotten that I had put them into this suitcase with some summer dresses. I quickly grabbed them before the nurse could get a good look at them and put them away with the other stuff in there. The Posses had warned me about the flags because it was now forbidden to have them, but I just couldn't bring myself to throw them out. It did not really matter either. What more could happen to me?

I put whatever I could think of at the moment into the suitcase, mostly things for Renate, even some diapers although they were not really necessary anymore. The nurse was always in my way. I had the feeling she was looking over my shoulder into every drawer I opened. When I finally closed the suitcase, she asked, "Did you bring some handkerchiefs? I haven't seen you pack any." Instead of watching me pack, she should have taken a little care of Renatchen. The poor thing, feeling neglected by her busy mother and with all these strangers around, somehow had got ahold of the milk pitcher and, trying to catch up with me, running from one room to the other, had dripped milk all over the place. So that had to be cleaned up too. I did not say anything to the nurse, but she must have read my thoughts and now tried to busy herself a little bit with the child.

Finally, I thought I had everything and it was time to go. I put Renatchen's and my coat on and took an extra blanket for her—it was bitterly cold outside—and with one last look around, I closed the apartment door. Funny, I never really liked this apartment, but at this moment, it seemed like a lost paradise!

On the way downstairs, I suddenly remembered the baby carriage. I had to take that with me! It was always standing in the entrance hall of the house in a corner, covered with an old blanket, so I would not have to carry everything up and down all the time when we went out. Luckily it was a collapsible carriage, so it could fit into the police car. The men hesitated a moment when I made my request, but I guess they saw it was not an unreasonable one, and so the baby carriage landed in the police car too.

The nurse now turned to me and told me she would look me up in Rosslau, and then shouted her "Heil Hitler" again and disappeared in the dark. The trip to the concentration camp started!

It was not a very long ride. When we entered the main street of Rosslau at the end where the concentration camp was situated, there seemed to be hardly anybody on the street. It was just too cold to be outside unless one really had to be.

When the car finally stopped, I had quite a surprise. Through the car window, I noticed a group of about fifteen people standing quietly on the sidewalk just opposite the entrance to the concentration camp. At first, I thought they were Nazis. But they would have shouted "Heil Hitler" and made some degrading remarks as had happened to me before in Dessau. But these people stood very quietly, just watching. They had come out of sympathy! Word had gotten out through the grapevine again. With all the secrecy, coming out here so late and not using the dreaded sirens, people who cared knew what was going on. As I learned much later from one of my visitors, this group had waited there for over an hour just to show me we were not forgotten. I don't think I knew any one of them, but Rosslau had a lot of factories; most of their workers were Social Democratic voters, and Opi was well known there.

Now the big wooden two-wing gate was opened. The car moved slowly inside, and the gate was closed behind us.

In the hallway, the guards, all in SS uniforms, stood lined up, peering curiously into the car. The so-called commander of the camp, a former gendarme of one of the little villages around Dessau, stood in front of them. I had met him when he still belonged to our party and was "honored" to meet "his" *Reichstagsabgeortneten* [Reichstag representatives] at one of the election meetings before Hitler took over. Now, he still wore his old gendarme uniform but with a big swastika on his cap and his epaulets!

One of the detectives opened the car door. I took a deep breath—nobody should see how scared I really was! I took Renatchen in my arms and stepped out of the car.

A loud "Heil Hitler" greeted me, and the outstretched arms of the guards nearly touched my face. I answered with a cool "Good evening" and waited. Then the commander stepped forward, a man of about sixty, heavily built, with a cruel face and shrewd eyes. I even remember his name: Marx. Of course he recognized me, but evidently thought it better not to mention that at the moment. He told me that my room was ready, ordered two prisoners who stood in the backyard watching the reception to pick up our things, and then went ahead to the end of the entrance hall, where we walked up a narrow staircase to the second floor. We arrived at a half-finished attic. In the dim light of a small electric bulb dangling from the ceiling, I saw some odds and ends of furniture piled up, evidently things that had been stored there when the restaurant downstairs had been changed into the guards' quarters.

When I turned around, I saw that the other side of the attic was finished. The commander went over there and opened a door, and when he switched on the light, I was looking into a medium-size room with a low ceiling and two windows at the other end. It was furnished with two narrow iron beds, an old-fashioned washstand with a basin and a water pitcher on it, a big bucket next to it, a small table with two chairs in the middle of the room, and, oh yes, the piano Heisig had mentioned, an old battered instrument. Here, too, the source of light was an uncovered bulb up on the ceiling, but at least it was a brighter one. The room was comfortably warmed by an iron stove that stood in one corner, and a wooden box filled with briquettes stood beside it.

I looked at the beds. They seemed to be old army cots. The bedcloth was a faded, coarse, blue-and-white-checked material. On each bed were two folded heavy blankets of a dark grayish color. It did not look very tempting. The idea that Renatchen would sleep on something like this seemed completely out of the question for me. Besides, she was still much too little to sleep in a bed without a rail around it. She had to have her own bed! So I told the commander that night she would have to sleep in her carriage, but the next morning I would have to talk to Heisig about this. He didn't object, just told the two prisoners to bring up the carriage. I quickly undressed Renatchen, whose eyes were already half closed. She fell asleep the minute I put her down. Poor little thing! It was the first time in her life that she had to stay up that long.

Now Marx told me he would show me the kitchen and the other "facilities." I left the light on and followed him downstairs. The police car had left, and the guards had disappeared into their quarters.

We went out to a little backyard. There I had quite a shock. A full-grown Great Dane came rushing out of a doghouse next to the house and growled at me. I jumped back. The commander laughed. "She can't hurt you. She is on a chain. Besides, I trained her. She wouldn't do anything until I tell her so, but she is trained to attack a man when I say, 'Get him!'" He could have warned me, but this was his sense of humor, and he got a kick out of this.

Then I had a different kind of shock. The "facilities" he showed me were an outhouse divided into three small cubicles; each had a wooden seat and a tank underneath with a terribly strong disinfectant that one could already smell through the closed door. One of these toilets had a special lock on the door because this was reserved for the commander. I was allowed to use this one, but the key was kept in the guards' dayroom, where I would have to pick it up, which, of course, was quite embarrassing. After all, I was the only woman in this camp.

On the other side of the yard was the former dance hall, which was now the dormitory for the prisoners. We entered a small hall. On one side of it was the kitchen, on the other side a big room with long, narrow tables and benches where the prisoners had their meals and where they could spend their free time. This was also the place where they could receive their visitors on Sunday afternoons. Between these two rooms, a big door opened into the dormitory. I got a quick glimpse of rows and rows of wooden bunk beds, three on top of each other, and men sitting on them or standing around in little groups talking with each other. They turned around and looked at us. The commander quickly closed the door, and then we entered the kitchen.

It was a large room with two normal big kitchen stoves and, in one corner, an extra stove that evidently was new. It had room for only one very big kettle, which seemed to be built in. Lots of small and big pots and pans were hanging on the walls, and everything looked very neat and clean.

Three men, who were sitting at the table with coffee mugs in front of them, jumped to attention and shouted "Heil Hitler" when we came in. They were the cook and his two helpers—prisoners, of course. When Marx told them who I was, which, of course, they knew very well, I quickly went over and shook hands with them. After all, we were in the same boat. Marx cleared his throat, a little embarrassed; he certainly had not foreseen something like this. In a very strict tone, he told the cook, a man with a nice friendly face, that I was allowed to cook for my child and that he should buy whatever I needed when he did the shopping for the camp the next morning. Then he turned to me and said, "You can have your meals sent in from a restaurant if you want to. I eat there myself and it is quite good." Of course, I refused this offer. He ordered one of the prisoners to bring up my breakfast every morning at eight o'clock. After I had told the cook about the few things I needed for Renatchen, we left and went back to the front of the house.

He walked with me to my room, where he told me that I could have visitors every Thursday for two hours in the afternoon. Of course, I could write letters, but he had to read them first before they could be mailed. I had to turn off my light at ten o'clock, and at eight o'clock my door would be locked from the outside. Then, he showed me a bell next to the door that I could use in an emergency and that could be heard in the guards' room. Then, he went to the door, turned around toward me, and said, "Well, I am sure you won't be here very long. As soon as your husband finds out about this, he will come back—that is the only decent thing to do!"

Then, with a loud "Heil Hitler," he marched out of the room and closed the door behind him. I heard the key turn in the lock and his heavy footsteps on the stairs, and then everything was very quiet.

I sat down at the table and looked at Renatchen, who slept peacefully in her carriage. All of a sudden, it dawned on me what Marx had just said! The last few hours I had been so occupied with all that had happened to us that I had not thought of anything else. This, of course, was what they wanted. They were not interested in me; they wanted to force Opi to come back by keeping us as hostages. That would do the trick! And there was nothing I could do but pray that he would not lose his head and do just that. They would kill him on the spot—an escaped prisoner! But he would know that too. He would know that would not help us at all!

A feeling of absolute helplessness overcame me. My self-control, which I had tried so hard to maintain the whole time, suddenly disappeared. I put my head on the table and cried bitterly.

A harsh voice shouted from the foot of the staircase, "Lights out!"

That brought me back to my senses. I stopped crying and went over to the wall and turned off the light. After a moment, my eyes got used to the darkness, which was not as complete as it seemed at first. A searchlight from the roof of the dormitory lit up the former restaurant garden that bordered the side of the house on which my room was situated. I could even see a small part of the dimly lit street behind the wall. I stood for a little while at the window and looked at the high wall that separated me from the outside world. For how long?

Finally, I undressed and went to bed. The mattress was a sack filled with straw. It was hard and uneven. The pillow was certainly anything but soft. The blankets were very heavy, but at least they kept me warm. The fire in the oven had gone out by now, and it was quite chilly in the room.

It took me a long time until I finally got to sleep. It was still pitch dark outside when I was awakened by loud singing. At first, I didn't even know where I was and what was going on. Then I remembered, and I also remembered that Opi had told me that every time a troop of prisoners was sent for outside work, they were ordered to sing as they marched through the streets. I am sure none of them felt like singing, but this was one of the ridiculous rules, at least a harmless one. It happened every morning except on Sundays. Later, I heard that some people in Rosslau had complained about this to the commander, but to no avail.

The singing had awakened Renatchen too, and she started to get up in her carriage. I picked her up and brought her into my bed for a little while and then got up, and I dressed her and myself. I didn't bother her too much with washing because the water was very cold. Something had to be done about this too.

At eight o'clock, I heard someone coming up the stairs, the key turned in the door, and then there was a short knock. When I opened the door, one of the men I had met in the kitchen the night before stood there with a tray in his hands. This time he skipped the "Heil Hitler," and we both said, "Good morning." He put the tray down on the table a little awkwardly. On it was a coffee pot, a pitcher with milk, some slices of bread with a piece of margarine next to them, and two cups. He told me he would be right back with some wood to start a fire in the oven. He was back in a few minutes, and while he worked on the fire, he gave me some advice on how to handle the oven, especially not to forget to close the shutter in the back before I went to bed so that the fire would not go out completely during the night.

When he started to leave, he hesitated a moment before the door, and turning around again, he said, "We prisoners, at least most of us, want you to know that we are on your side, and the cook and I want to help you whenever we can. I know it won't be much, but we will try our best. I and some others were together in the same ward with your husband in Oranienburg. He was a real comrade. He shared everything with us. It did not make any difference to him that we were Communists." After this little speech, he quickly left the room. I knew he could not do much, but every friendly word was a little helpful already.

When we had finished our breakfast, I started to unpack the few things I had brought. A small chest of drawers, which I had not noticed the night before, stood between the two windows, and there were a few hooks next to the door so that I could hang up our clothes. The few toys that I had brought found their place on the chest, or rather would eventually because Renatchen greeted every piece with joy and wanted to play with them all at once. I was glad that at least she felt a bit at home in these strange surroundings.

I had brought some stationery and some stamps with me so I could write to my parents. But first I wrote a short note to the Posses telling them where I was and that I was allowed to have visitors for two hours every Thursday, hoping fervently that they would come, but I did not ask them to. That had to be their own decision. But deep down in my heart I was quite sure that they would come!

Then I put a coat on Renatchen, and we went downstairs. When we entered the little backyard, the Great Dane came out of her doghouse and looked at us. Before I could catch her, Renate had run over to the dog and started petting her. And strangely enough, the dog stood quite still, then turned her head and sniffed at the little girl, and from that moment on, the two were great friends. As fiercely as the dog would growl if some of the prisoners—besides the cook, who fed her—went near her, Renate could do anything with her. She just stood still and wagged her tail.

When we entered the kitchen, the cook was just finishing his shopping list. I gave him some money and told him what I wanted: some vegetables, some fruit, milk, a little butter (we got only margarine, but this was not the kind one gets today, and it did not taste very good), and eggs. Renate's daily supper was half a soft-boiled egg and a piece of buttered bread.

Then, the cook and I tried to figure out how I would give Renate her morning bath. It simply did not occur to me that I could have just washed her; she was used to her bath, and that was that! The only solution we could find was the big tin dishpan that the prisoners cleaned their plates in after their meals. It would not be needed in the mornings because they had to rinse their coffee mugs in cold water under the faucet in the back of the dormitory. The cook promised to send up the pan with some hot water every morning after breakfast, and I was grateful for that.

But I will never forget the next morning when I took Renatchen out of this improvised bathtub, which she enjoyed very much. The cook had cleaned the dishpan very carefully with some cleansing powder, and the powder, along with some residue of fat and tin, had made a sort of silvery paste that covered her whole little behind! I had a hard time getting it off, using a lot of soap and some pressure, which she did not like at all! From that day on, I put a diaper on the bottom of the dish pan, and that took care of this obstacle.

When the commander came in, I gave him my open letter to the Posses, and he promised to have it mailed later after he had read it. Then, I reminded him of my telephone call to Commissioner Heisig about the baby bed. He went with me into the front room of the main house, which was nearly empty because most of the guards were out with the working prisoners, and a few were in the dormitory watching the cleanup there, woodcutting in the yard behind the dormitory, or doing whatever else had to be done to keep the camp going. Last but not least, there was always a big pile of potatoes to be peeled, one of the most substantial parts of our meals, which, as a matter of fact, were quite simple, of course, but not half as bad as they had been in Oranienburg.

Heisig was quite polite, asked if everything was all right so far, and agreed to let me have Renatchen's bed after I explained to him that she was too little to sleep in an adult bed yet. He would send two policemen over to the landlord of my apartment house to get the key, and they would pick up the bed with all of its contents and bring it to Rosslau. Marx, who stood right next to me as if he were afraid that I might say something he did not like, had a silly smile on his face when I started talking to Heisig. I saw it change to an astonished grin. I am sure that he was convinced that I would never get anywhere with my request.

In the evening, a police car arrived with two plainclothes men and Renatchen's bed! This is the same bed all three of you slept in here in this country [America], and I hope very much your children will sleep in it too many years from now![4] I think this was the first time a police car had done something as nice as transport a baby bed!

Again, all the guards came out to watch, just like the night before when we arrived. There were quite a few astonished faces when, instead of a new prisoner, a baby bed arrived. Marx ordered two of the guards to bring the bed upstairs and to set it up. A third guard had to bring up the blankets and the bedclothes, which were very nicely folded. I guess one or both of the policemen might have been fathers themselves and somehow sympathized with us. This was at the very beginning of the Nazi regime, and quite a few men in the police force were not Nazis yet. People were not as cruel then as many of them became later on, maybe out of fear or maybe because the Nazi psychology brought out all the worst instincts in people, such as the hatred for anyone who had a different political opinion or who was not as Nordic as they imagined themselves to be—something that they thought made them superior.

The two guards had taken the iron bed out of the room and set up the baby bed. Renate had watched the whole procedure very quietly, holding my hand. All of a sudden, she let my hand go, ran over to her bed, and touched it all over, laughing happily. She had finally recognized it. This was another familiar thing in all these strange surroundings. I very much hoped it would help her adjust more quickly.

I can hardly describe my feelings when a little later, I could put her into her own bed. She lay there so content, drinking her night bottle, stopping from time to time for a second, giving me a quick smile, and then continuing to drink it to the last drop. For a moment, it was as if we were on a little island, far away from everything that had happened in the last twenty-four hours. Looking down at my child in her nice clean bed made me feel a little more at ease. That night I slept better too.

After breakfast the next morning, when the room was a little warmer, the cook sent up a big dishpan with warm water, and Renatchen had her first bath. I already mentioned the tragicomic success of it.

I made our beds and tidied up the room a little, and then there was very little else to do. When I tried to open a window for a bit, I found out that the window catches were secured with strong wiring twisted around them many times. It would be impossible to get it off without a wire-cutting tool. So we had to be content with the draft that came through these not-very-tight-fitting old windows, especially when the wind was blowing in this direction at the house.

Renatchen was occupied with her toys, and I decided to write to my parents. I dreaded writing this letter, but of course, it had to be done. I tried to describe the situation in an as matter-of-fact way as possible, without mentioning my greatest worry—that Opi might do what the Nazis wanted him to do and what they hoped to achieve by taking us as hostages: that he might come back. As Opi told me much later when we were together again, this thought had entered his mind the first moment when the news of our imprisonment finally reached him in Prague. But luckily, by thinking it through less emotionally and talking it over with his friends, who convinced him that going back to Germany would mean his certain death without any guarantee of our freedom, he gave up this idea. There was very little that I could write to my parents. It is an awful feeling to know that someone is reading your letters with the sole purpose of finding something that might incriminate you. And I was quite certain that nothing would have made Marx happier! So I just told them that we were all right, that Renatchen had the right kind of food, that she even had her own bed, and that they should not worry too much about us.

Then I went downstairs into the kitchen with Renate to prepare her lunch and to pick up my own. This was the main meal. The prisoners came home and had an hour before they had to march out again to work until five o'clock. As I mentioned before, the food was not too bad, usually potatoes and vegetables and a little bit of boiled meat, all cooked together in that big built-in kettle, or dried split-pea soup or beans cooked in a thick mash, or noodles cooked together with dried fruit—something the men liked very much. I thought it was terrible, but Renatchen liked it too. What made it a bit difficult was that the cook knew only five or six recipes that were repeated each week in the same order without any change. As he told me later on when we were better acquainted, he had never cooked in his whole life but had volunteered for the job so that he did not have to work outside. His wife had given him some [cooking] advice during her first visit which had helped. As his friend told me, the food was hardly edible the first few meals before that.

After lunch, Renatchen had her afternoon nap. I had brought a couple of books with me that I had grabbed at the last moment. One of them was written by a Norwegian author—I have forgotten his name—that I had started reading at home. Its German translation had come out shortly before Hitler came to power, and this book was widely read in our circles.[5]

I had just opened the book and started reading when I heard someone coming up the stairs and then a knock at my door. When I opened it, a guard stood there. He told me to come downstairs because someone wanted to see me. I looked at Renatchen. She was fast asleep and would not wake up for at least another hour. So I went down with him and into the guards' room. There was my visitor: the same nurse Heisig had sent with the police when we were brought here. When she saw me, she got up from her chair and greeted me with an outstretched arm and a loud "Heil Hitler." Then she told me that Commissioner Heisig had sent her to see if everything was in order and to look over my quarters. Then she took a book out of her big handbag and said, "I brought this for you to read. It is a very interesting book, and you will learn a lot from it. Every German should have it." After this little speech, she handed me Adolf Hitler's *Mein Kampf*. I gave it right back to her and told her that we had it in our library, and I had read it. I wanted to say also that I wished that more people had read and understood it. Maybe Hitler would not have been where he was now! But I thought better of it. Nothing would be gained by that, and it would only make things worse. We only looked at each other with not-too-friendly eyes. Then she put the book back into her bag, turned to the guard, and told him that she wanted to see my quarters now. We went upstairs without the guard. I guess he thought this was the kind of visitor he could leave me alone with.

She looked the room over, which didn't look as bare and disconsolate as it did when we arrived two days ago, with a little sunshine coming in, Renatchen's white bed, some toys lying around, and a big, framed picture standing on that old piano. She looked at the little bed but didn't say anything. Then she walked over to the table and looked at the books. When she saw the title of the book I was reading, she picked it up and said, "I have to confiscate this book, it is on the forbidden list" and put it into her tremendous handbag.[6] She must have been quite active in her party besides just being a nurse. I forgot to mention that this book had quite a socialistic tendency, just the opposite of Hitler's ideas. I told her that I had only two or three more chapters to read, so I knew its content anyhow, but of course, I did not get it back. With the words "Everything seems to be all right. Heil Hitler!" she turned around and left. Not one question about the child or if I might need anything; after all, I was the only woman in that concentration camp. For her, I was just an enemy, and that was that. I never saw her again.

Now Renatchen woke up. As I made Renate's lunch, Marx came into the kitchen and told me that I could take the child into the former restaurant garden every afternoon for an hour or so if the weather

A Hostage in Rosslau 119

was nice; he would leave orders with the guards to open it up for me. It was cold, but the sun was shining, and we both needed fresh air. I put Renatchen into her carriage that was now standing downstairs in the corner of the big hallway and knocked on the door of the guards' room. A rather nondescript-looking SS man, about thirty years old, whom I had not seen before, opened the door. When I told him what I wanted, he put on his coat and cap, took a large key from a board on the wall, and asked me to follow him. No "Heil Hitler," which I thought was a bit unusual. When he opened the garden door and let us in, I thought he would go back into the house. But he didn't. He just walked next to me around the garden without saying a word. After the second round, I stopped and asked him why he did not go inside again. "My orders are to stay with you as long as you are out here," he answered. I thought that was kind of silly because I could not climb the high wall, and nobody could come in to whisk me away. We walked another round in complete silence.

Then I decided to try to find out a little about him as a person. I have forgotten how I started our conversation. He was quite easy to talk to and willingly answered all my questions. Pretty soon I knew his name, Meinicke; the name of the little neighborhood village he came from; that his parents were farmers; that he was the younger son; and that his brother would inherit the little farm one day, so he had to look for a job, and so on.[7] Somehow, he did not at all seem like the type of person to become an SS man. So I asked him quite frankly how he happened to join this outfit. I got the most unexpected answer! He said he knew very little about politics. He knew about Hitler and Göring, of course, and thought they were great men.[8] All the others didn't mean anything to him. He had joined because there was not enough work on the farm. Besides, he did not get along with his older brother very well and would have to leave the farm anyhow as soon as his father died. He needed a job. This one did not pay too much, but he had his nice uniform and room and board, and the work was easy. He had gone through some training first, of course, but he had already advanced to the rank of sergeant, as he told me proudly, showing me the stripes on his sleeves. All in all, he seemed not too intelligent to me but otherwise quite a nice person, an impression that some of the prisoners, who all liked him, confirmed later on. "Meinicke is all right," I was told. "When he is in command, everything is easier." Finally, I thought we'd had enough fresh air, and we went back into the house. At least part of the long afternoon was over.

The next day would be Thursday, my first day for visitors. Would the Posses come? After all, he was a teacher, a public official, paid by the state. People were now judged not only by what they did and which party they belonged to but also by whom they kept in contact with. I should not have worried—of course they came! Long before the visiting time, Renate and I were sitting at the window looking out for them. It didn't help very much because I could see only a small part of the sidewalk opposite the house, but I was much too excited to do anything else.

A few minutes after two o'clock, we were called down—they had come! It was quite an emotional moment for all of us! Leni and I had to fight hard not to cry when we embraced each other, and even Otto had some difficulties keeping his composure. But Renatchen saved the situation. As soon as she recognized her old friends, she rushed over to hug them, happily babbling something in her own language.

Before we could sit down, Marx, who had been sitting at his desk near the window watching us, came over and asked to see the package Leni had brought with her and wanted to give to me. There were some cookies and chocolate for Renate, some fruit, a piece of salami—in short, some foodstuff, so that was all right. After the inspection, he ordered two guards to stand next to the door, and he went back to his desk, listening intently to everything we said to each other. I was used to that because of my long experience visiting Oranienburg, but the Posses were quite uneasy at first. After a little while, they got used to it too. Everyone could hear what we talked about. I was much too happy to see them to say something that might cause him [Marx] to shorten their visit. They told me about mutual friends, naturally mentioning only their first names, and how many people had asked about us since the news of us being here had spread fast, at least in our circle of party members and sympathizers. Some of them would come and visit me too. All this was thrown in between some harmless chitchat, just a few words and hints here and there.

My practical friend Leni offered to take home some of my dirty laundry to wash it for me and to bring it back on their next visit. I was very grateful because that was something that had worried me too. The prisoners gave their laundry to their wives or relatives when they came to visit. The cook had told me that there was some old washtub in the back of the dormitory where the showers for the men were. The prisoners used it sometimes for their work pants, and it was said to be in very bad condition. So I had been quite careful with our underwear;

changing them every day was out. Thank goodness Renatchen was completely toilet trained!

Leni also promised to go over to my apartment and get whatever I might need. I had given her a spare key a long time ago, so that could be done without any trouble. I was very grateful for that offer because in my excitement on that terrible evening when I had to pack for our stay here, there were, of course, a few things I had not thought about since I really did not know what to expect.

The two hours the Posses were allowed to stay passed very quickly, and only their promise to come again the next Thursday made the parting a little easier. But when Leni told me that they'd had to sign their names and address when they arrived, I became a little scared for them and told them it was better not to come again so soon. But they just smiled, kissed Renatchen and me, and left. I knew they would be back again the next week.

When the heavy door had closed behind them, I rushed upstairs with Renatchen to have a last look at them from our window. I had described to them where our room was situated. They had gone over to the other side of the street, and as soon as they saw us at the window, we waved at each other until the guard came out and ordered them away. I felt very lonely when they were out of sight. Now I understood only too well Opi's remark one day when I had to leave him after one of the many visits in the Dessau prison. Now I experienced it too, this terrible feeling of being deprived of one's freedom. I had not felt it so strongly as in that moment when I saw the Posses disappear from my view. I am quite sure that no one can conceive that feeling unless he has lived through a situation like this himself. I looked at my little girl, who played happily with some blocks that the Posses had brought for her. And as so often was the case in these unhappy days, her being there with me slowly helped me to overcome my despondent mood.

By and by, I got to know some of the other prisoners a little better. The cook, whom they seemed to regard as sort of a leader to whom they came for all kinds of advice, gave some prisoners, men who came from the same village as him, special privileges. They were allowed to come into the kitchen in the evening and get a mug of his terrible coffee, which he always had a big pot full of on the stove. I myself had gotten into the habit of having a cup of tea when Renatchen was asleep. Just going down and fixing it was already a pleasant interruption on those long, lonely evenings. Sometimes, when everybody knew that Marx had gone out and Meinicke was in charge, we had quite a political session. Most of the men were laborers and members of the Communist Party. One of them was a former district leader, quite intelligent and evidently on a higher educational level than most of the others. Since they all came from the same district as we did, they all, of course, knew Opi, and some of them had even been in Oranienburg with him. They had fought against him and our party as long as that was possible, but now we were all in the same boat. That made our debates much more conciliatory than they would have been under other circumstances. As a matter of fact, we all agreed that the only way out of the Hitler spook would be a *"Vereinte Front"* (united front) between our two parties. My argument that all this might have been avoided if their party had not blocked us all the way and sometimes even voted with the Nazis was refuted with the district leader's argument that all this had been done for "tactical" reasons, one of his favorite expressions. Oh yes, we solved all the problems in that kitchen. I nearly became a Communist too!

When the weather started to turn more springlike, I was allowed to go out to do some of the necessary shopping myself—for instance, to get things I needed from the drugstore. There was a little library on the main street where I could borrow a book for ten pfennig each. On our own bookshelves, we had the few good books it contained (the whole library was just a little store, called a lending library, which sold some stationery and things like that too), and I had already read them all. So I borrowed all the mystery stories they had there, just to have something to read in the evening. These little excursions were kind of funny. Meinicke was usually our guardian. Before the door to the street was opened, he uncocked his pistol and put it into his belt. Then another guard brought the Great Dane on a leash, and we marched into the street. Meinicke walked next to me and the baby carriage and the SS man with the big dog about twenty feet behind us! It really was something! I never did find out whose idea this funny business was. Meinicke only said, "Orders," when I finally asked him about it after a few of these excursions.

I certainly became well known to the good people of Rosslau during that time! I did not mind when people stared, some sympathetic and some hostile; it was so easy to read their thoughts! It just felt good to be outside in the world for a little while, no matter what kind of world it was! I also found out that we had a lot of anonymous friends in that little town. Every so often, when I came out of the library or a store, I found something in Renatchen's carriage—some fruit, some chocolate, or even a little toy. Since Meinicke always went inside with me, the people must have waited for the moment when the SS man with the dog had walked a little farther up the street because that big animal never liked to stand still. I never saw anyone doing it, had no idea who these people were, and could never thank them. I also think part of their doing this was some sort of protest, just like my action on the day of the Jewish boycott some months earlier.

Weeks and weeks passed by, and the Thursdays when the Posses came always mattered most. Sometimes they brought other people with them—some I knew, some I had never seen before, just as they had come to visit when I was still in the apartment out of loyalty to Opi since there was not much else they could do. I appreciated that very much, and I knew they took some risk since they all had to sign their names. I heard later from the Posses when I was in Switzerland that some of them had been taken into "protective custody" since all of them had worked for the Social Democratic Party in one way or another. Their visiting me might not have been the reason for it, but their name on that list certainly did not help either.

I was not quite so nervous about Opi coming back. If he had thought that would help, he would have done it right away. I did not know then that it had taken awhile until the news of us being in Rosslau had reached him. For one reason or another, the grapevine had not functioned so well this time; the Nazis had imprisoned many more people and had closed many loopholes. I asked the Posses if they had heard anything about him, but they had not. They hoped just as much as I did that he would not do what the Nazis evidently had expected him to do—to come rushing home.

But then something happened. I was awakened by a terrific commotion on the street—something was going on in front of the house. There was loud shouting and the sound of car motors and motorcycles, mixed with the deep barks of the Dane. When I looked through the closed window, I could see only that the street was lighter than usual. Everything seemed to be happening in front of the house. A terrifying thought came to my mind—fire! I ran to the locked door and hammered against it with my fists, but with that noise down there, nobody could hear it. Then I remembered the bell and frantically pressed the button—no reaction either! I just went to grab Renatchen when I stopped myself because I did not smell any smoke. If there was a fire downstairs, there would be smoke up here on the second floor by now, but there was not even the slightest smell of it. But what was going on? I ran back to the window. I still could not see anything, just that there was more light than usual. All of a sudden, the noise of the cars and motorcycles grew to a terrific roar, and then it became less and less noisy, and after a short while I couldn't hear anything anymore. The street had become dark again too. I walked over to Renatchen's bed. She had slept peacefully through all that noise. But I was wide awake now.

I had to know what had been going on downstairs. I pressed the bell button again a few times. Finally, I heard footsteps on the stairs. Someone outside asked what I wanted but did not open the locked door. It was Meinicke. His voice sounded a little strange, quite unfriendly and as if he were in a hurry. All he would tell me was that there had been a brawl. I should go back to bed and by no means turn on the light. This was an order. He had never spoken to me that way before. But before I could ask more, I heard him go downstairs, and everything was quiet. His last remark made me realize that in my excitement, I had not even thought of turning on the light. With the help of a match, I looked at my watch; it was way past midnight. I crawled into my bed. But it took quite some time until I finally fell asleep again.

The next morning, I asked the cook's helper when he brought our breakfast if he had heard something unusual the night before. He said yes but that he did not know what it was all about, and then he left quickly. I definitely had the feeling that he was not telling the truth. Later on, when I went downstairs to make Renatchen's lunch, I also asked the cook. I got the same short answer, and then he left the kitchen. It was quite obvious that he did not want to talk about it either.

When it was time for our daily outing, Meinicke was nowhere in sight. Another SS man, who was usually in charge when Meinicke had his time off, took over. I had seen him a few times in the kitchen before. The cook had warned me about him and had told me that he was one of the most brutal guards in the camp. He had beaten many prisoners until their heads were bloody if they did not follow his orders quickly enough, especially when he was drunk, which happened quite frequently on payday. Marx was afraid of him too. His switch to the Nazi Party shortly before Hitler came to power did not make him too attractive to the dyed-in-the-wool Nazis. He knew that quite well and tried in every possible way to make them forget his past. He had sometimes assisted the guard by letting the big dog scare the prisoners half to death before he called the Dane back. The cook told me that all this had changed since I was there, and everybody thought that the reason for this was that I might talk to Heisig about it. I don't know if this would have helped very much, but whatever the reason might have been, truthfully, I must say that only once I saw two men with blood on their faces. Some new prisoners had arrived one day, and the detectives who had brought them in interrogated them in the dining room next to the kitchen. In the afternoon, the prisoners were led out into the biergarten that I could see from our windows. They were ordered to walk around in a circle for half an hour, and I happened to see this. Later, I was told that this special SS sergeant had participated in the interrogation.

There was quite a fluctuation in this little concentration camp. Some of the new prisoners were there for only a few days, some were sent to larger camps, and some were discharged after a short stay. During the time that I was there, there was never any really important opponent of the regime among them.

The next day was a Sunday, and Meinicke was back. We went to a nice little park near the concentration camp for our outing. Then, I tried to find out from Meinicke what had been going on two nights before. At first, he did not want to talk about it. But after some persuasion, he came out with it. A group of about twenty SA troopers had come from Oranienburg. Their intention had been to pick Renate and me up, take us to Oranienburg, and let this be known everywhere. They thought this would certainly bring Opi back right away, and their honor would be restored. They could not get over that it was *their* concentration camp from which a prisoner, and an important one, had managed to escape.[9] There had been a fistfight after he refused to let the SA into the house, but he and his men had stood up to them. He had told them that only Commissioner Heisig of the Gestapo in Dessau could give them permission and that they could call him if they wanted to, which they did not. And after some punches between both parties, they finally left. Meinicke had gone to Dessau the next day and told Heisig the story and was very much praised for the way he had handled the affair. Then, he made me promise not to talk about this to anybody because he was not supposed to tell me all this.

I had listened to him with some skepticism. The whole story sounded so incredible! But then, I had heard the cars and the shouting. If all this was true, I really had to be very grateful to Meinicke. I don't know what would have happened if the other sergeant had had the night watch and if the whole story was really true!

It was true! I found that out a few days later when a new prisoner transport came in. One of the detectives who came with them had been on duty during my house arrest, and I had talked a lot with him. I saw him on my way to the kitchen when he came through the hallway at the same time. He stopped to talk to me for a few moments and then mentioned that I had escaped some danger the other night. That was all he told me. But it did fit with Meinicke's story. So I really had to be grateful to him. A few years later, when we were already in America, I could do something for him. Shortly after the war was over, the Posses wrote to me that he needed help to get through the denazification procedure. As a former SS man, he was certainly in trouble. I wrote some sort of an affidavit for him, and that, together with some letters from other former prisoners, helped him, as I learned later from the Posses.[10]

A few days after this happened, our lawyer visited. He had received a letter from Opi, who asked him to help me start divorce proceedings! This was exactly what Opi had asked me to do when we were together the last time in Oranienburg. I was just as reluctant to do this now as I was when Opi talked about it then. The lawyer tried very hard to convince me that this would be the best way out of our troubles—maybe the only one! If I divorced Opi, there was certainly no longer a reason for keeping us here in Rosslau. So I finally filled out the necessary forms and signed them. It was terribly difficult for me to do this, and it took all my willpower to go through with it. In my heart, I had the feeling that this was all wrong. The lawyer, a very nice person whom we had socialized with quite often in better times, was very helpful and understanding. He really seemed to be convinced that this step would be the best thing to do. But just the same, I hated it. Luckily, it never worked out. Marx, who asked me that same evening whether I really intended never to get together with my husband again, had promptly forwarded my answer that I was not serious about it [the divorce]. I could not help myself; I simply could not say no, which would have been the right thing to do. Instead, I said that someday we would have to get together to decide about the future of our child. Our lawyer later told me that this answer had been the main reason that the request for a divorce had been denied. For once, Marx had done me some good, even if it wasn't at all his intention!

I had been in Rosslau about eight weeks when the Posses brought the exciting news that Opi had written a little book about his experiences and life in Oranienburg and that it was secretly circulating in

Germany already! They had just heard about it from a comrade who had heard it from someone else. They themselves had not seen it yet, and, of course, it would be very dangerous to possess it. I don't remember if they ever got it while I was still in Rosslau. I should mention that Marx had long ago lost all interest in our conversations. Now it was usually one of the younger SS men sitting in a corner with a newspaper or playing a game of cards with another one, and even if they wanted to, they were too far away to understand every word we said. So we speculated about this exciting news. I argued quite naively that if the book was out, and that was what the Nazis had wanted to avoid, what reason would they have to keep us any longer? I tried very hard not to get my hopes up too high, but I could not help thinking about this possibility during the next few days.

But instead, something else happened. One morning, a week later, I was called down to the guardroom, and there was a detective from Dessau. He explained to me that it was necessary to evacuate my little apartment because there was a great shortage of housing in Dessau, and it was needed. My furniture would be taken to a warehouse. When I asked where I would go when I was discharged from Rosslau someday, he just answered with a shrug of his shoulders: "You can stay with friends and find another apartment." I would be allowed to be there when the moving date was set. What could I do? I had to sign a piece of paper that he had brought with him that said I agreed to the moving. He informed me that I would be picked up on the moving day, and I would have the necessary help so that everything would be done in a few hours. Then he left. I walked upstairs in a sort of a daze. It certainly did not look as if we would be released in the near future. Why would they go through all that trouble if there was even the slightest chance? It looked very hopeless and bleak again.

And then something also came to my mind that I had completely forgotten. The little suitcase that I had packed that day when I was supposed to meet that Czech woman was still in the cellar—how could I explain that? My claim that I did not know anything about this plot could hardly be upheld if they opened that little suitcase and looked at its contents! Suddenly I was very scared. I could think of nothing that would sound like a plausible explanation for it. Maybe something would come to me when I was there, but at the moment I could not think of anything. Needless to say, I did not sleep very well the next few nights.

A couple of days later, Marx told me that the moving date was set for the following day and that I would be picked up early in the morning so that I could be there at the same time as the movers. When the police car arrived, I was a little relieved to see that one of the detectives was the one I mentioned before, who was a sympathizer of our party. I asked him if I could call the Posses and ask Leni to take Renatchen as long as I was in the apartment. He thought it over for a moment and then agreed. I quickly explained to Leni what this was all about. Of course, she agreed right away to take care of her, which took a load off my mind, and I knew that Renatchen would be very happy to be with her.

It was a strange feeling being in a car and driving through all the well-known streets. Coming back to the apartment was somehow strange and unreal too. After being in that drab room in Rosslau for nearly eight weeks now, the apartment looked more comfortable and elegant to me than when I lived in it!

The movers arrived a few minutes after us. They had brought boxes and barrels with them and started to pack the books and the dishes right away. With the help of the two detectives, I brought all the suitcases down from the attic. They really helped me a lot and were not just standing around watching. I thought that this was quite decent of them. I don't know if they were ordered to do so, but they looked all the books over before they were packed, and when I tried to empty Opi's desk, they told me to leave most of the stuff in there and just lock the drawers and give them the key. The movers worked very quickly and efficiently. I think it was new to them to work under police supervision, so they did their best. Maybe they were a little scared too.

Everything was now in the van. Only a few things in the cellar were still left, including the little suitcase. The detectives locked the apartment door, and we went downstairs. One of them went outside, and the other followed me with one of the movers into the cellar. There were only a few things I wanted. But there on an old table was the little suitcase! It was an elegant, rather new leather suitcase that Opi had given me as a wedding present for our honeymoon, a piece one does not usually keep in a damp cellar. He went over and opened it. He looked at the baby clothes that were lying on top, and then he looked at me. But before he could say anything, I went over, closed the suitcase, and said, "Oh, yes, I forgot all about it when I had to leave so suddenly. We had spent the night at a friend's house a day or two before, and I left it here when I brought Renatchen upstairs. I will take it with me now. There are things in it that I can use now for the baby." I don't know if he believed me. I don't know what would have happened if he had looked through everything and found the money and the few family papers that I had at the bottom of the suitcase. But I guess this explanation that came to me at the spur of the moment seemed plausible to him. He took the suitcase upstairs for me and put it into the police car. I know now how lucky we were in all our troubles. Everything really worked out quite miraculously, as I gratefully can say now. But as one was going through it, it certainly was not as easy as it sounds now forty years later. It did cost a lot of nerves.

The moving van had left already. I saw it drive around the corner. For a fleeting second, a thought went through my mind: would I ever see any of our belongings again? But it didn't seem very important anymore. Too much had happened; too much had changed our lives. We drove over to the Posses' and picked up Renatchen and then went back to Rosslau. For how long would it still be my "home"?

I remember two more events very distinctly about the rest of the time I had to stay there. One day, when I had just started to dress Renatchen for our afternoon outing, two of the guards came upstairs carrying the baby carriage with them. One of them told me that there would be no outing today and that I was not allowed to go down to the kitchen for the next few hours. Before I could ask why, he turned around, closed the door, and locked it from the outside. What on earth was the reason for this? I went to the door and listened, but everything was completely quiet; there seemed to be nothing unusual going on downstairs. I finally settled down near the window and tried to read. Renatchen was very busy with my handbag, unpacking it and then putting the things back again, never getting tired of playing this fascinating game over and over again. I let her do it this time, as it kept her beautifully occupied. My book did not interest me very much. A little bored, I looked out of the window, and I saw Marx entering the garden. A tall man in civilian clothes was with him. Both men talked to each other for a moment. The stranger looked around but not up to my window, and then both men went inside again.

An hour or so later, somebody came up the stairs, and my door was unlocked. I rushed over to open it. This time it was Meinicke. He grinned at me and said, "Your husband is fine. He is still in Prague." He told me that they'd had a visit from a Czech newspaperman who knew Opi, and Marx had shown him the layout of the camp. So that was the stranger! If only I had known about that, I would have knocked on the window or done something to attract his attention so that he could tell Opi he had seen us! But just the same. This was the first time that I had heard anything directly about Opi since the day my mother-in-law had brought me the news that he was in Prague. If only I could have talked to that man!

Later, when we went down to the kitchen to make supper for Renatchen, I asked the cook if he had seen the visitor. He had. Marx had brought him into the kitchen to show him what the prisoners would eat for dinner. Of course, it was the day where we had a beef noodle soup, one of the best dinners on the weekly menu. The journalist had asked the prisoners how they liked the food, and of course, the answer was "fine." But then the man had turned to Marx and told him that he had heard from Opi that I was in this concentration camp and that he would like to talk to me. Marx had answered, "Did you see any woman around here?" And with that, he had led the visitor out of the kitchen. It was understandable that none of the prisoners had dared to say anything. So the Czech left under the impression that what Opi had told him must have been just a rumor or something. I don't remember if Opi had ever spoken to the man again later. He may have left Prague already when the journalist returned. I never found out if it was only Marx's idea to keep my presence in the camp a secret. It was just in contrast to the Nazis' idea that holding us hostage would bring Opi back.

Later in the evening, as I made my tea, Marx appeared in the kitchen. Naturally, I asked him why I could not have seen the Czech and quite innocently added, "He might have known my husband." Marx was annoyed at first and said angrily, "Somebody has talked too much. How did you find out who the visitor was? And how did you know that I had a visitor at all?" I answered that I had seen the man from my window standing with him in the garden and had simply asked who he was. I did not tell him that Meinicke had told me first about him [the Czech journalist], and I did not tell him that I knew he had lied about us being here either. Now he turned to me, and with an unpleasant grin, he said, "Your husband seems to be having a very good time in Prague. I have heard he has a very beautiful secretary and doesn't seem to miss you at all; otherwise, he would have come back long ago." With this friendly remark, he left the kitchen.

"That filthy dog," the cook said furiously. Then he turned to me. "I hope you know your husband better than that. Don't get any silly ideas."

I went upstairs. And then I started to think about what Marx had said. Of course, it was silly, and the cook was right. But sitting here in that dreary room, all of sudden it didn't seem so silly anymore! We were young, and we had been separated for such a long time. After all he had been through, and now all of a sudden he was free to go where he wanted to, to do what he wanted to. . . . Was it really so hard to understand that there might be a wish for companionship (other than just political friends)? When would we be together again? But when I got that far with my noble thoughts, a terrible anxiety started to get the better of me—would we ever be together again? I tried very hard to push all these thoughts from my mind and to instead remember the last time we had seen each other, the day before Opi's escape, and all the love I had seen in his eyes. Why should a malicious remark make me so unhappy? That was just why Marx had said it; that was his way of torturing me. I didn't even know if the Czech had said anything to him besides asking about us being there!

The next day we had our walk to the bank of the Elbe River. It was a nice warm spring day. Being outside the camp in the warm sunshine made me feel better again—not quite as hopeless as the night before. We watched the big barges passing by, going up and down the river. Often children were playing around the cabins at the end of the ships, and laundry was blowing in the wind. It all looked so peaceful. I read the names of the ships. Most of them were German or Dutch. But then came one with a very strange flag, going slowly upstream. On its bow, it said *Praha* (Prague). All of my longing, loving thoughts went with that boat, and I looked at it until it went around a curve of the river and out of my sight. If Renatchen and I could only have been on that barge, going there too!

I turned to Meinicke and told him what I was thinking. He laughed and said half seriously, "If I could help you get there, I would do it. But you would have to take me with you. Maybe your husband could find me a job there." We both laughed and talked about something else. But I can still see the children playing on that barge and remember only too well that longing feeling I had when I saw that name on the barge.

I would like to mention here that on our outings, I had lots of talks with Meinicke about the situation in Germany and did my best to enlighten him. He was really politically innocent and had never bothered to think very much about the goals of the National Socialist Party before he joined it. He was against violence, and the only fights he had were with his comrades when he discovered that they maltreated prisoners. Our talks gave him something to think about. One day, after he had an argument with the other sergeant about something to do with camp rules, he came into the kitchen and said to me and the cook quite bemused, "I wonder what will become of me if things should change someday. I don't quite feel like a Nazi, and you people will not accept me either!"

One Sunday at the beginning of May, I had a wonderful surprise! When I brought our breakfast dishes down to the kitchen, a guard came in and told me to go into the guardroom because Marx wanted to see me. Wondering what this was all about, we went with him. And there, standing next to Marx, was my father! This was certainly completely unexpected. My parents hadn't mentioned anything about this in their letters so as not to disappoint me, in case it did not work out. But it did, and here he was! After the first excited embrace and a careful introduction to Renate, who did not recognize her grandfather at first and shied away from him a bit in the beginning, we sat down and talked under the watchful eyes of Marx.

Father had written to Commissioner Heisig and received permission to see me even if it was not my regular visiting day. And since he had come from as far as Freiburg to Dessau (about a sixteen-hour train ride), he was allowed to stay with us all day! Marx invited him to eat with us in the dining hall after the prisoners were through with their meal and even to go along with us on our afternoon walk, of course under guard. Just as it had been with the Posses the first time they visited me, it made my father a bit uneasy in the beginning, but soon he forgot about it. Besides, we had no secrets to discuss. He had heard nothing from or about Opi, which, of course, was my first question. He mostly wanted to know how Renate and I were doing. It was touching to see how he tried to get acquainted with his grandchild. She had forgotten the very short time he had been with us in December. But it didn't take very long for the two to become good friends.

Mother had sent a sweet little dress, which fit Renatchen perfectly and in which she walked around like a fashion model, very proudly showing it to everybody who cared to look. It was so good to see her in something different, something that really fit. The few things that I had with me were already outgrown and faded from washing them so often. She was so happy with the new dress that I had quite a difficult time when I wanted to undress her at night; she wanted to sleep in it. She finally gave in when I promised her that she could wear it the next day and that her grandmother might even send her another one if she was a good girl.

But, as all good things pass quickly, Renatchen didn't want to let go of Father's hand and started to cry bitterly. I did not feel much better, but there was nothing we could do about it; he could not take us with him. He was just as upset as we were. I was only glad that he would have time to visit the Posses and talk with them before he had to catch the night train back to Freiburg, where he had to be for a performance the next night. I went up the staircase to our room with a very heavy heart and a tired little girl in my arms, but just the same grateful for this exceptional day.

Father had told me that he had written many letters to people he thought had some influence in the Nazi Party who could do something to get us out of the concentration camp, but so far to no avail. The Nazi leader of Dessau, the Reichsstatthalter Loeper, had to order our discharge, and this man would never forget that his archenemy, who had fought so hard against him, had escaped and was completely out of his reach. This was his revenge.

All the excitement over Father's visit finally died down, and the days went on as usual. I got quite depressed. It all seemed so hopeless! If one has done something against the law and has to go to jail, one knows at least how long one has to stay, and every day gone by brings one closer to freedom again. But for us, there was no such set date. I even started thinking about finding a way to escape—but how? What could I do with a little child without endangering her life? And with Meinicke's help? His uniform could help make matters easier, at least the getaway part. After nearly three and a half months, the second guard with the dog was not with us anymore when we went for our walk. They needed every man for guard duty outside of the camp since most of the prisoners had to work in the fields now. So we could disappear on one of our walks. But was Meinicke really serious when he said he would help? I knew he was infatuated with me, even if he never said a word about this, but would that give him enough courage to run away with us? But if we really got out of Rosslau, what then? I had very little money, no passport, no way of getting across the border, and so on and so on. No, the idea of escaping was impossible. Besides, I had to make a decision not only for myself; there was my child. There was not the slightest chance of success without outside help, which I did not have and could not get.

I tried very hard not to occupy myself with such impossible thoughts, but of course, that was easier said than done. I told myself in better moments that someday everything would be all right again—it just had to. Opi would find a way to get us out of all this, and we would be together again. I had no idea whether he was still in Prague, but wherever he was, he would not sit still. He would do something to help us; I was very sure of that.

And then it happened! I was in the kitchen to iron a few things I had washed. Renatchen was sitting at the kitchen table, playing with a little doll that Leni had brought her on one of her last visits, when I looked out of the kitchen window and saw Marx crossing the yard. I warned the cook, who was reading a book, which he quickly put away and started cleaning some vegetables. If Marx saw someone not working, unless it was official rest time, he quickly invented some job, no matter if it made sense or not, like sweeping the kitchen floor again even if it had been done just a minute before.

With a loud "Heil Hitler," Marx marched into the kitchen and turned to me: "You can go and pack your things. You are discharged!" For a moment, I thought I had not heard him right—was this one of Marx's jokes? I looked at him unbelievingly. He grinned a little. "Commissar Heisig just called.[11] You can leave whenever you are ready."

So it was true! I grabbed my laundry, picked up Renatchen, and ran out of the kitchen without a word. Upstairs in our room, I sat down and cried. I could not help myself. But it was a good cry. It took a lot of the tension away that had built up in me during these dreadful weeks and months. Free—that was all I could think about at the moment. Renatchen stood in front of me quite still, and all of a sudden, the corners of her sweet little mouth went down. She had never seen me like that—she was scared. In a moment, she would cry too. This brought me back to myself. I kissed and hugged her until she smiled again; her mummy was back to normal. I packed as quickly as possible. Then, it occurred to me that I had to call Leni and find out if she would be home. There was really nowhere else I could go. For a moment, my excitement dwindled a little, but only for a moment. If she was not home, we would sit on the staircase and wait, but I would be sitting there of my own free will.

I went down and got the permission to call. Luckily, she was home and became nearly as excited as I was. Before I could say anything further, she told me she would leave right away and come pick us up. I knew it would take her at least an hour until she could get here. I would have liked to rush out of this place as fast as possible. But with Renatchen and the luggage, it would have been very difficult to get to the streetcar without help. The stop was a few long blocks from the concentration camp, so I just had to wait.

I used the time to say goodbye to the cook and his helper. A few prisoners who worked in the camp came into the kitchen and wished me luck. I really had the feeling that as much as everyone was longing for his discharge, none of these men begrudged us. I was sorry that Meinicke was not there, as he was on an errand in Dessau. So I asked the cook to say goodbye to him for me. I left the Posses' telephone number so he could call me, but I don't remember if he ever did.

Finally, I was told that Leni had arrived. I left Renatchen in the kitchen and rushed upstairs to get our suitcase and Renatchen's blanket and pillow. The cook's helper had come upstairs with me and helped me carry my things down. I took a last look at the room, which looked as unfriendly and strange to me as on the evening we had arrived there. With a deep sigh of relief, I closed the door behind me. I had to leave Renatchen's bed there, but that was quite unimportant at the moment. All I could think about was getting out of there as quickly as possible. I rushed into the kitchen to pick up Renatchen, said goodbye once more to the men there, and ran into the guards' room, where Leni was waiting for us with a happy smile and a big hug. And then the large front door was opened, and we walked out into the sunny street. As far as I was concerned, it could have rained cats and dogs, as the saying goes. I think nothing could have spoiled this indescribable feeling—to be free!

When Ilse started to pack for Rosslau, she realized she had the Three Arrows anti-Nazi flags in her suitcase. The storing of such material after it was banned certainly could have resulted in punishment from the Nazis. Even after realizing this, she still refused to throw them out, claiming she could not bear it. Everyday acts like this in normal times would hardly receive notice; they were once "part and parcel of daily life," as Nathan Stoltzfus, Mordecai Paldiel, and Judy Baumel-Schwartz argue. But "the difference is rooted in timing, location, and perspective."[12] Such a simple incident now became an act of defiance under Nazi occupation.

Ilse's detailed description of the layout of Rosslau, as well as of the guards and prisoners, may be one of the most intimate portrayals historians have of this camp. When Ilse arrived at the camp, she noted a number of SS guards. Although the SA had started setting up this transitional concentration camp in August 1933, the SS and Gestapo took control of the camp the month Ilse arrived, in January 1934.[13] She had extensive interaction with Sergeant Otto Marx, the commandant of Rosslau, after she first arrived, as he took her through the facilities and laid down some ground rules. As Marx was showing her around, Ilse met the Great Dane they kept on the premises. She was surprised by the dog but especially by Marx's comments that he had trained her to attack when directed. We know that Rosslau was a site of murder and torture; we know of at least one murder and two public hangings there.[14] Even Ilse recounted in the previous chapter that people who passed by the camp reported hearing the screams of prisoners.

Ilse mentioned the fluctuation of prisoners; some stayed only a few days or were discharged after a short stay, whereas others were sent to larger camps. This was typical of camps created to house detainees in "protective custody." We know that at least forty of the prisoners had been transferred from Oranienburg, and Ilse noted that they knew Gerhart while imprisoned there.[15] She never encountered any Jews in the camp. All the prisoners were either Social Democrats or Communists, and she remarked that they were all allied in the camp despite their past differences. She even made light of the fact that they still could not agree as to who was at fault for their political divisions, but she certainly found solace and camaraderie in the presence of the other political prisoners in the camp.

The division between Social Democrats and Communists in Germany originated in the German revolution in 1918–19, when the Social Democratic government in charge used the military and right-wing paramilitary groups to fight and murder the leaders of the recently formed KPD (Kommunistische Partei Deutschlands; Communist Party of Germany), Karl Liebknecht and Rosa Luxemburg. After this, the once organized working class became deeply divided, and resentment grew. Thereafter, Communists blamed Social Democrats for the murder of Luxemburg and Liebknecht and "perceived the SPD [Sozialdemokratische Partei Deutschlands; Social Democratic Party of Germany] as an ally of the bourgeois parties and the capitalist system." Meanwhile, the SPD "accused the Communists of undermining the parliamentary republic and seeking to establish a dictatorship along the lines of the Leninist Soviet Union."[16] As the National Socialists emerged in the late 1920s as a political threat, the KPD continued to view the SPD, not the Nazis, as its worst enemy, and the Social Democrats viewed Communism and Nazism as "two sides of the same coin"; they perceived both as "totalitarian" movements that wanted to destroy democracy and establish a dictatorship.[17] Noncommunist historians and critics, naturally, have blamed the KPD for being one-sided, deceptive, and manipulative in its attempts to bring Social

Democratic workers into a Communist-led united front of the left against the Nazis. And Communist historians, naturally, have blamed the SPD for rejecting any form of cooperation with the KPD that might have brought about the demise of the NSDAP (Nazi Party).[18]

One can see how this history led to political debates between Ilse and some Communists about which party was at fault, but they all agreed now that forming a united front was the only way to root out Nazism. If before 1933, Social Democrats and Communists generally felt a mutual hatred and distrust toward one another, then after 1933, Gestapo reports confirm that Socialist-Communist united fronts were established in several states throughout Nazi Germany and that close cooperation between the KPD and SPD was common.[19] A united front strategy became popular among many rank-and-file SPD and KPD members, even if the German Social Democratic Party in Exile (Sopade or SoPaDe; short for SPD) remained skeptical of this tactic. The leadership of the KPD officially adopted a united front policy in 1935.[20]

Ilse's emotions varied and were directly tied to her new condition of being held hostage at Rosslau. Upon first learning that she had to go to Rosslau, she felt very defeated and lost, even struggling to figure out what to take with her. When she finally arrived at the camp, though, she did not want anyone to see that she was scared. Moments of resiliency like this were mixed once again with feelings of helplessness—for example, when Ilse learned there was nothing she could do to get herself out of her situation because they only wanted Gerhart. She had very dark moments, feeling hopeless because she did not know whether she would ever get to leave Rosslau. At times, she also questioned her husband's love for her since they had been apart for so long. This uncertainty also resulted from the "mental torment" tactics the Nazis employed, at one point even telling her Gerhart had a new girlfriend in Prague.[21] Other times, she found humor in her tragic situation, as she described in the story of Renate's first bath in the camp. Turning to humor was certainly a way for her to cope—gallows humor, if you will—but it also demonstrated Ilse's defiance in making light of the situation the Nazis put her in. She certainly felt deprived of her freedom to just leave the camp (or her room, for that matter) whenever she wanted to, and yet there was solace in being allowed to go into town, even if there were always guards accompanying her.

At several points throughout her time in Rosslau, she felt hope, especially when she witnessed the acts of kindness or sympathy or even what she considered to be resistance from other people. When she first arrived at Rosslau, people were awaiting her arrival even though the Nazis had tried to keep it a secret. Ilse perceived this as people showing sympathy for her, similar to when people in the town of Rosslau left gifts for her in her daughter's carriage when she was out walking. Even more than showing sympathy and solidarity, she recognized this as a small act of resistance and even related it back to her own resistance against the boycott on Jewish stores. Such an act could have resulted in punishment from the officers who were accompanying Ilse on her outings. She recognized that an even greater risk was the one people took by coming to visit her, especially because they had to leave their names and addresses. Some of these folks did not even know her, and many of them were later taken into "protective custody" (probably more so because of their work with the SPD). This was their way of exhibiting agency in the face of a repressive government. Regardless of who came to visit each week, Ilse's optimism was ostensible even some thirty-five years after the fact.

Ilse enjoyed certain privileges at Rosslau that other prisoners did not. She may have been permitted some liberties because of her status as a hostage rather than a prisoner and still others because she was the only woman and mother in the camp. It was likely this latter fact (and a bit of luck) that resulted in the Nazis treating her graciously when she demanded certain things for her daughter, or not prying more than they normally would have, for example, when they were repossessing her apartment and found a packed suitcase she had for her planned escape. She was able to use the commandant's private toilet—the only one with a lock—so that she would not have to share with the men. She was allowed to ask for whatever she needed for Renate in terms of food items, although she paid for it all herself. Commissioner Heisig accommodated her request to bring Renate's crib to Rosslau, which was no small task for the police and likely appeared out of place altogether at a concentration camp. These were some of the practical concerns of housing a toddler in otherwise dismal quarters that the SS obliged. Of course, Ilse was not Jewish, but this was a far cry from later Nazi policies of separating Jewish women from their children or consistently labeling pregnant women and mothers with small children "incapable of work" and sending them directly to be killed in gas chambers in the various death camps.[22]

One privilege she enjoyed almost daily was the ability to go out in the garden or to go on outings outside the camp to the park, the library, or stores, or just on a walk in Rosslau. She was not performing forced labor like the other prisoners. This was likely due to her status as a hostage who did not do anything wrong but who was just being used as a pawn to goad Gerhart back to Germany. One of the people she befriended on these excursions was the SS officer Meinicke, who, she learned, joined the SS only because he needed work. Such reasoning was likely many men's motivation for supporting the Nazis early on. The ongoing effects of the Great Depression in 1934 in

Germany made jobs scarce. Ilse certainly influenced Meinicke's thinking, as he came to question his loyalty to the Nazi Party. Meinicke protected her when SA officers from Oranienburg came to take her one night, demonstrating how instead of being a true believer of Nazi ideology, he participated in small acts of resistance against the regime he was working for. Even Ilse commented on how initially the officers were not that Nazified and therefore not that brutal and sympathized with her, perhaps because they were fathers themselves.

However, not everyone at Rosslau looked out for Ilse or sympathized with her as a mother. Her encounters with the nurse showed that there were clearly others at Rosslau who were true believers or at least wished others to perceive them as true believers. Interestingly, Ilse expected the female nurse to sympathize with her because she was a woman and mother. We learned very quickly that this was not the case. Wendy Lower has demonstrated that women were just as indoctrinated as men during the Third Reich and that female perpetrators were not exceptional but part of the everyday machine.[23]

Notes

1. White, "Introduction to the Early Camps," 9.

2. *Reichsstatthalter* referred to the Nazi-created office of Reich governor. Loeper was Reichsstatthalter of the state of Anhalt.

3. The Three Arrows was the political symbol originally conceived for the Iron Front, a German paramilitary organization made up of Social Democrats, trade unionists, and liberals that then became associated with the SPD. The party officially adopted this symbol in 1932. It represented resistance to Nazism, Communism, monarchists, and other reactionary conservative movements. See Harsch, "The Iron Front," and Potthoff and Faulenbach, *Sozialdemokraten und Kommunisten nach Nationalsozialismus und Krieg*, 27.

4. Here, Ilse was addressing her three grandchildren, Mark, Andrew, and Jennifer Brandt. According to Mark, all three of them did, in fact, sleep in that crib at some point. Personal correspondence with Mark Brandt, grandson of Ilse Seger, January 15, 2021.

5. I do not know which author or book Ilse is referring to here.

6. Wolfgang Hermann, a member of the Nazi party and a librarian, drew up a "black list" of banned books, starting in spring 1933. These books were then looted from libraries, bookshops, and scientific institutions. This list was also distributed to the German Student Association that organized the book burning on May 10, 1933. See Wolfgang Hermann's list, titled *Prinzipielles zur Säuberung der deutschen Büchereien*, through the *Deutsche Digitale Bliothek*: https://ausstellungen.deutsche-digitale-bibliothek.de/verbrannte-buecher/items/show/82.

7. I could not find the name of whom Ilse was referring to here. His name could have been spelled Meinicke, Meinecke, Meineke, or Meinike. Ilse spelled it a couple different ways throughout the memoir. I have used the spelling Meinicke, which is one of the ways she spelled his name, just for consistency.

8. Hermann Göring was an early member of the Nazi Party who eventually became commander of the air force.

9. Emphasis mine.

10. During the denazification proceedings, documents that attested to the good character of one's political past were dubbed *Persilscheine*, named after Persil laundry detergent, which

removed brown stains. These documents helped whitewash former Nazis of their crimes, but there was a lot of corruption with people buying and selling these on the black market. See Biddiscombe, *The Denazification of Germany*, 72, 113.

11. Here, Ilse mistakenly used *commissar*, used to refer to a government official in the Soviet Union, instead of *commissioner*.

12. Stoltzfus, Paldiel, and Baumel-Schwartz, "Women Defying Hitler," 10.

13. White, "Rosslau," 157–58.

14. Ibid., 158.

15. Ibid., 157–58.

16. Berger, *Social Democracy and the Working Class*, 98, 103.

17. Ibid., 105.

18. Peterson, *German Communism, Workers' Protest, and Labor Unions*, 400–401.

19. Horn, "The Social Origins of Unity Sentiments in the German Socialist Underground," 343–45.

20. Berger, *Social Democracy and the Working Class*, 152. The Sopade operated in Prague from 1933 to 1938, in Paris from 1938 to 1940, and in London until 1945.

21. Seger, *A Nation Terrorized*, 200.

22. "Women during the Holocaust," *Holocaust Encyclopedia*, United States Holocaust Memorial Museum, https://encyclopedia.ushmm.org/content/en/article/women-during-the-holocaust.

23. Lower, *Hitler's Furies*.

6

Meeting Marvis Tate and Leaving Germany

Ilse was unexpectedly released from Rosslau some four months after being taken hostage. This chapter begins with her happily leaving Rosslau with Leni Posse, who came to pick her up, but she was still dumbfounded as to how this happened. She spent a couple days at the Posses', learning that several members of the SPD (Sozialdemokratische Partei Deutschlands; Social Democratic Party of Germany) had betrayed their party, before getting a surprising visit from Marvis Tate, whom she did not know. Marvis Tate was a member of Parliament (MP) from the Conservative Party from 1931 to 1945 who was largely responsible for getting Ilse and Renate released from Rosslau, out of Germany, and reunited with Gerhart.

This all came about due to Gerhart's transnational connections, which he had fostered during the Weimar Republic primarily through his interconnected work in the SPD and German Peace Society. These connections and his reputation had already hastened a foreign exile after his escape from Oranienburg and helped him get Ilse and Renate out of Germany.[1] When Gerhart arrived in England on a lecture tour, he gave two lectures in the House of Commons, one for the labor members of both Houses of Parliament and one for the conservative and liberal members, which was arranged by Nancy Astor, also known as Lady Astor or Viscountess Astor, the second elected female MP; she served from 1919 to 1945. Both Tate and Astor had power, influence, and considerable resources to orchestrate Ilse and Renate's release. Once Gerhart told the MPs about his wife and daughter being held hostage, Lady Astor suggested that all the female members of the British Parliament go to Leopold von Hoesch, the German ambassador to the United Kingdom (1932–36), and demand the release of Ilse and Renate. As Ilse recalled previously, and Gerhart confirmed in the English version of his memoir, the MPs did this and gave von Hoesch two weeks to release them; otherwise they would start asking questions about the hostage situation in front of the House of Commons.² After 1933, the Nazis were angling to create an Anglo-German partnership and were quite concerned about English public opinion. The MPs recognized that the Nazis wanted to avoid the negative public attention that would result from their questions in front of the House of Commons and thus used Gerhart's story in order to facilitate the release of his wife and daughter. The MP's efforts were coupled with pressure from a bishop of the Church of England and several media outlets in Great Britain that published the story.³

International politics, transnational pressure, and Gerhart's transnational connections remarkably influenced Ilse's individual circumstances. As Shelley Rose has argued, "The absence of this transnational intervention would have been disastrous for the Seger family."⁴ Even Gerhart, reflecting on this moment after the fact in *Reisetagebuch*, recognized the importance of his reputation and connections: "Unfortunately, my wife's case was and is by no means the only case of hostage-taking; there were and are not only many more, but far worse cases."⁵ One week later, on May 19, 1934, Ilse and Renate were released from Rosslau.

When we were finally settled into the streetcar, the conductor gave us our tickets, then he looked around to the few passengers who were sitting at the other end of the car, bent down to me, and whispered, "Seems you are going home, comrade Seger. Good luck to you!" This was certainly a nice beginning in the outside world!

We traveled to the last stop, which was at the Dessau railroad station, and from there we took a taxi to the Posses'. Renatchen recognized the apartment right away and ran happily around, feeling at home again. Leni made something to eat, and then we sat and talked and talked, and nobody tried to listen in! Leni told me many things that the Posses couldn't have told me in Rosslau. And it was not all pleasant. People had changed. Even some of our own party members whom I knew quite well and whom we never expected to went to the other camp. But everybody was under enormous pressure, and some of them just wanted to be on the right side of the fence. That, of course, was sad news and something I had not expected from the people Leni mentioned.

Finally, Otto came home from school and, quite surprised, greeted me warmly. After we had talked for a little while, he disappeared and came back with a bottle of a good Rhine wine, saying that this was a day we really had something to celebrate.

Before our celebration, I tried to call my parents in Freiburg. This was not as easy as it sounds. They had no telephone. First, I had to get the number of the physician who lived in the same house, and somebody had to be sent downstairs to fetch them. Luckily, they were home, and naturally we talked for quite a while. I promised to come to Freiburg as soon as possible. One thing I was not quite sure about yet was whether I could travel now or if was I still bound to the promise I'd had to give not to leave Dessau without permission when my house arrest was lifted. I had not thought about this until that moment when I talked to my parents. I had not really thought about any future plans since I had passed through the doors of the concentration camp. I just didn't want to let anything spoil that beautiful feeling of being free! I somehow had to get in touch with Opi, but how? I didn't even know if he was still in Prague. There was so much to think about and to decide. Nothing seemed to be real—I had to adjust myself to this new situation—but not right now. It is funny, writing this after nearly thirty-nine years; I still remember this dreamlike feeling of tremendous relief![6]

In the evening, we had a lot of visitors. The news of my release was all over Dessau. I was grateful that people came, but I just as much would have liked to be alone with the Posses, enjoying their company and their nice comfortable home. Finally, everyone left, and I felt dead tired. Renatchen was long asleep on a couch upstairs that we had surrounded with heavy chairs, and I was in bed down on the sofa in the living room. But tired as I was, when the house was quiet and dark, I thought of Opi and when we would be together again and how I could reach him. It took a while until I fell asleep too.

I hardly remember anything about the next few days. I guess we had some more visitors, and we might have taken some walks with Renatchen. I had to make up my mind when to go to Freiburg, and I had to call Heisig to find out if I could go.

But then all these decisions were taken out of my hands. It was shortly before noon, and we had just finished tidying up the apartment and talking about this when the doorbell rang. Leni went to open the door, and I heard a woman's voice asking for me. Leni hesitated a little, but then she called me. In the doorway stood a very elegantly dressed, good-looking woman with a photograph in her hand. She looked at me and then at the picture, smiled at me, and said in heavily accented German, "Yes, you are Mrs. Seger. I recognize you from this picture, which your husband gave me a week ago in

London." She gave me the snapshot. It was one of the last ones Opi had taken in Dessau before he was put in jail and showed me carrying Renatchen in my arm, standing on the balcony of our old apartment. She introduced herself as Mrs. Tate from London and said she had good news for me. Leni asked her to come in. We were both a little hesitant, yes, even a little suspicious. We all sat down and waited to hear what this mysterious visitor had to say.

She looked us over for a moment, and then she gave us a winning, warm smile. "I can understand that you are a bit surprised about my visit. I am here to help you, Mrs. Seger. I am a member of the British Parliament, and I am here to take you and your child with me back to London, where Mr. Seger is anxiously waiting for you." And then she told us that a lot of politically well-known British people had gotten together after they heard about our plight through Opi and had decided to do something about it. She also told us that she had come from Berlin, where she'd had a long conference with Ernst Hanfstaengl, who was the chief of the Nazi Foreign Press Bureau. She had told him how indignant the English were about our imprisonment as hostages, which undoubtedly the German ambassador had reported to the German government. The famous American-born Lady Astor, a conservative member of Parliament, as well as the Duchess of Atholl and some others, including Tate, had gone to the German ambassador, Herr von Hoesch, and asked him to do his best to get us free.[7] Otherwise they would start publicly asking some questions about this hostage business in the House of Commons.

I would like to mention that at that time, in 1934, the Nazis were trying very hard to gain the friendship of Great Britain for various reasons, and it was very important to them to let nothing interfere with that aim. This, of course, was a great advantage for us. Hanfstaengl had called Heisig from Berlin and given the order to release us and let me have a passport. I was even allowed to leave the country with Mrs. Tate if I wanted to!

All of this was hard to believe after all that had happened to us. I was completely in a daze, not capable of making any decisions at the moment. Mrs. Tate realized that. She was not only a very warm-hearted, understanding woman but a very energetic one also. She had already visited Commissioner Heisig before she came to see us. The police had my old passport, which they had confiscated before they had taken me to Rosslau. He [Heisig] had promised her to have a new one made out and sent to me. Now, she wanted me to pack up our few possessions and be ready when she would come back to pick us up to take the evening train to Berlin. She had rented a hotel room for the day where she wanted to go in the meantime to do some work and rest a little.

When I told her that I had promised my parents to visit them first before I made any decisions about our future, she convinced me how important it was that we go to Berlin right away and see Hanfstaengl. Everything would be decided there. I wanted to be with my husband, didn't I? One never knows in these times what could happen! She advised me not to telephone my parents now. I could write them a long letter and explain everything; they certainly would understand. I knew she was right, but I knew also how terribly disappointed they would be—and I was too. If I really left the country, when would I ever see them again?

Mrs. Tate looked at me, as she understood my hesitation. "It will be all right. Believe me, Mrs. Seger," she said. She came over to me, stroked my cheek, bent down and gave Renate a quick kiss, waved to Leni, and went to the door. There she turned back to us. "Be ready at six o'clock. I will pick you up." Then she left, and pretty soon we heard the taxi that had waited for her drive away.

Leni and I sat down and looked at each other. Was this real? Was all that she had told us true—the meeting with Hanfstaengl, that I should get a passport and leave the country? But I was out of the concentration camp, so what Mrs. Tate was telling us must be true; I was not dreaming!

Leni was the first to come down to earth. "Start packing, I have to go and make lunch—Otto will be home very soon," she said and went into the kitchen. I picked up Renatchen and put her on my lap. She had behaved so well during Mrs. Tate's visit, not interrupting anything, as if she had sensed that something important was going on.

I thought the whole conversation over again. It slowly entered my mind that if all went well, we would be reunited with Opi in a few days! And tonight, I would be in Berlin! Suddenly, I had an idea: Leni had to come with me! I rushed into the kitchen and asked her if she would do that. At first, she gave me all sorts of reasons why she couldn't, but then she warmed up to the idea. "Let's see what Otto says." Well, if she wanted to come, Otto certainly would not say "no," I was sure of that. If everything worked out the way Mrs. Tate thought it would, it would be for only two days. Otto came home just then, and after he had heard the whole fantastic story, he didn't say "no"! It made me feel much better to know that Leni would be with me through these decisive hours.

We had started packing when we heard police sirens, and then a car stopped in front of the house. My first thought was it was all over—they were picking me up again! I looked at Otto and Leni. I could see in their faces that the same thought went through their minds. Maybe Reichsstatthalter Loeper had interfered! The bell rang, and Leni went slowly to open the door. Commissioner Heisig and another police officer whom I didn't know stood in the hall.

"Mrs. Seger, I came to bring you your passport. Please sign it." He came in and put the passport on the table in front of me. So, everything Mrs. Tate had told us was true! I looked at the passport. They had taken the picture out of my old one and put it into the new one. The only unusual thing was that instead of being valid for three years, it was made out for four months. I signed it and looked at Heisig, still a little unbelievingly. "Does this mean I can travel, can even leave the country if I want to?"

He smiled at me and said, "You don't seem to understand. You are perfectly free now. You can go wherever you want to. I wish you all the best, Mrs. Seger. Goodbye." He turned and left. The other officer looked a bit astonished, gave a very loud Hitler salute, as if he wanted to make up for the omission of his superior, and left too.

We looked at each other. The whole thing was so strange: the chief of the Gestapo coming in person, as if he wanted to make quite sure that the passport reached me. Well, we did not have much time to ponder this. It was not important. We finished packing; there wasn't very much anyhow. Renatchen got her supper, and then Mrs. Tate came. I explained to her that Leni was coming with me and that I hoped she did not mind. She didn't at all. She was glad that I would have company since she would be quite occupied the following day in Berlin. Soon we left for the train. Otto came with us. I still can remember his face and how he waved at us when the train left.

The next day, we saw Mrs. Tate only at breakfast. She told us that she would be busy all day and that she had a dinner engagement, so we would be on our own all day long. But she would call me early the next morning and tell me what to do next.

We had this beautiful May day for ourselves. And I was in my beloved Berlin! I was so happy that Leni was with us. Being interned for so long, I'd had to relearn how to make some decisions, to see so many people around me, just to be on my own again. That might sound a bit unbelievable, but it really felt that way, and I was glad that Leni took over. We went to the zoo, which was not very far from our little hotel, and Renatchen had a lot of fun. This was something she had, of course, never seen before, and it was very difficult for us to explain to her that she could not touch all the animals. I don't remember very much about those two days in Berlin. I recall only that nothing seemed quite real to me. I still could not believe that a new life lay ahead of me—no more concentration camp, no more anxiety, and we would be united with Opi soon!

Rather early the next morning, Mrs. Tate called. I was supposed to go to her room in an hour. She had good news for me, and we would go out together. Leni would take care of Renatchen during that time. "Make yourself pretty," she said and hung up. I was dressed already, and I did not have much else to wear anyhow, only what I'd had with me in the concentration camp. The rest of my clothes were, of course, still in the warehouse. So I just put on a little lipstick, which I hadn't used since I'd seen Opi the last time in Oranienburg, the day before his escape. I powdered my nose and had a quick breakfast with Leni and Renatchen and then walked over to Mrs. Tate's room, getting more and more excited as I walked along the long corridor. What would happen now? Where would we go?

When I knocked, a maid opened the door. Mrs. Tate was very elegantly dressed and just putting on a hat, exactly in the same color as her outfit. She turned around toward me, looking very beautiful, and gave me her warm smile. "I will be with you in a minute." She told the maid to order a cab and then pointed to a big bouquet of wonderful long-stemmed red roses. "Mr. Hanfstaengl sent them over to me this morning. Aren't they beautiful?" Of course, they were, but I was much too anxious to hear what she had to tell me. But she had evidently realized the atmosphere in Germany very quickly and that it was better not to trust people one did not really know, that there were informers all around, especially in a hotel that seemed to have a lot of foreign guests. She did not say anything before we were out of the hotel and settled in the taxi. Then she told me she had spent the entire evening Mr. Hanfstaengl's villa. She'd had dinner with him and had listened to his piano playing—he was known to be a very good player—and in this comfortable and pleasant atmosphere, she had settled with him my release from Germany and the permission to go with her to England!

This was all I could take in at the moment. She said something else; she spoke of the British embassy and said we would have to go to Hanfstaengl and get his personal permit or something like that. To tell the truth, I listened with only one ear. My thoughts were far away—in one or two days, I would be together with Opi!

The taxi stopped in front of a big building. Without looking around, I followed Mrs. Tate inside. I don't know what made me think that we were in the British embassy. No wonder I was quite shocked when I saw two SS men around the reception desk. Had it gone so far already that even foreign countries had SS guards in their offices? I must admit this sounds quite naive now. But my state of mind was not very rational at the moment, as one can imagine. And then I saw a big swastika flag next to the staircase, and all of a sudden it dawned on me that we were not at the embassy; we were in Mr. Hanfstaengl's headquarters! My hands got cold, and I felt very scared. Mrs. Tate must have felt my reaction. She put an arm around my shoulder reassuringly when one of the SS men, whom she had told that Mr. Hanfstaengl was expecting us, led us upstairs and knocked at a big door, which another uniformed person opened right away.

We entered a big room furnished with bookshelves and lots of easy chairs and beautiful rugs on the floor. Next to the tall windows stood a tremendously big desk. A tall, very English-looking man, his hair parted in the middle, sat behind it—Ernst Hanfstaengl. He jumped up and rushed over to Mrs. Tate, took both her hands into his, and greeted her like a long-lost friend. When she introduced me to him, he nodded shortly to me and offered me a seat on one of the easy chairs. Then, he went over to his desk with her, moved a chair right next to it, and started talking in English with her. And there I was, sitting on the edge of my chair, not understanding one word of the whole conversation. Once or twice, I heard her mention my name. So at least I knew that they were talking about my situation.

Then, Hanfstaengl turned to the SS man who was standing at attention next to the door and ordered him to make a telephone connection with a Paris hotel and ask for Gerhart Seger. My heart was beating fast. Would he be there? Would they reach him? Pretty soon the phone rang, and the SS man lifted the receiver. *"Hier Deutsches Auslands Presse Amt, ist dort Herr Seger?"*[8] When the answer came, he gave the receiver to Hanfstaengl, who, without speaking, passed it on to Mrs. Tate. She talked for a short time in English and then said in German, "Now you can speak with your wife. She is here too." When she started to pass the receiver to me, Hanfstaengl took it from her and ordered the SS man to show me into the room next door and to connect the phone for me there. Looking at me for the first time since that short introduction, he said, "I think you would like to speak with your husband in private," and turned back to Mrs. Tate.

I ran into the other room where the SS man handed me the receiver and left. My hands were so shaky, I nearly dropped it before I could lift it to my ear. And then I heard Opi's voice so loud and clear: "Ilselein, is that you?" I could hardly speak. It had been nearly six months since I had heard that beloved voice, since we had seen each other. I don't remember anything we said to each other in that short moment. We were both too excited to make much sense. And then there was a short click, and the phone went dead. I sat down for a moment and tried to get ahold of myself. I heard Mrs. Tate calling me. When I entered the other room, Mr. Hanfstaengl turned to me and said, "Mrs. Tate and you will leave Berlin early tomorrow morning by plane for London." Then, turning to Mrs. Tate, he continued, "The sooner you leave, the better. At the moment, everything has been cleared, but you never know what the 150 percenters will do."[9] In a few moments after that, our meeting ended, and we could leave.

When we were finally back in a taxi again, Mrs. Tate leaned back and laughed. "Oh, I am so glad it's over and we can fly tomorrow. He gave an order for our tickets to his secretary when you were talking to your husband, so that is taken care of. He wanted to have dinner with me tonight again, but I told him I could not make it. I will now bring you back to our hotel, and then you and your friend are on your own for the day, and I will come to your room sometime tonight and tell you when we have to leave for the airport tomorrow morning." When we reached the hotel, she let me out of the cab and went on. She did not mention the British embassy, and I was glad I did not have to go there. I rushed upstairs to our room, where Leni and Renatchen were waiting for me. I was certainly glad that Leni had come with us. I don't know how I could have survived the rest of the day without her, her understanding, and her practical help.

The weather was beautiful, and we decided to go to the zoo, which Renatchen enjoyed tremendously. It was the first time in her young life that she had seen big and small animals other than a cat or dog, and she was only disappointed that she could not touch them.[10] Then we went to a big department store, Wertheim (which was completely bombed out in the Second World War) and bought a little suit for me since I had only winter clothes. It was not very elegant, and it didn't fit too well either, but it was new, and I felt very good in it just the same. I bought a new dress for Renatchen too so that we wouldn't look too shabby when we met Opi in London. Finally, after we had something to eat in a little restaurant, we went back to the hotel. It was bedtime for Renatchen, and after all that excitement in the zoo and the walk in the big city, she nearly fell asleep before I had put her pajamas on.

We sat down on our beds and talked. Leni promised to write a long letter to my parents as soon as she was back home in Dessau and explain everything to them. I would write as soon as I could, when I was together with Opi in London. The whole situation was not quite believable to me yet. I was still afraid something might go wrong at the last moment. Hanfstaengl's remark about the 150 percenters was still on my mind. We finally stopped talking. We were both occupied with our own thoughts. Would we ever see each other again? What would the future bring for all of us?

We were both relieved when we heard a knock at the door. It was Mrs. Tate, and we talked about the next day, when to meet for breakfast down in the hotel, and when we would have to leave for the airport. When she wished us good night, she turned to me, stroked my cheeks lightly, and said, "Tomorrow will be a big day for you, young woman. Sleep well." Then she left. We went to bed soon after she was gone. We did not talk very much anymore, and soon Leni no longer answered; she had fallen asleep. It took a little longer for me because so many things ran through my mind, but finally I fell asleep too.

The next morning, I was up and dressed long before the hotel phone rang, and while Leni put her clothes on, I dressed Renatchen and packed the few things we had used, and then we went downstairs to wait for Mrs. Tate. I was very nervous and could hardly eat anything. I helped Renatchen with her breakfast and didn't participate in the conversation between Leni and Mrs. Tate at all.

Finally, it was time to go to the airport. And now, I'm drawing a blank because I don't remember how we got our tickets, whom I had to show my passport to, whether there was an SS man around— nothing. I remember only Leni's tear-streaked face when we embraced each other for the last time. And then I was sitting in the plane, Renatchen on my lap and Mrs. Tate on the other side of the aisle. I tried to get a last look at Leni, but I could not see her any longer. All the people who had been standing there before seemed to have been ordered away. The plane now started its two motors with a tremendous noise. Renatchen turned to me and looked quite scared, ready to cry. I quickly put some little pieces of cotton into her ears, which Mrs. Tate had advised me to do, and took her strongly into my arms, which reassured her. Soon we were up in the air and looking out the window. I had my last view of the Reichstag, the famous Tiergarten—Berlin!

But now I had to turn my attention to Renatchen. She had taken the little pieces of cotton out of her ears and tried unsuccessfully to put one of them into the ears of a gentleman who sat in front of us and didn't care at all for her attempts. I apologized to him, but he didn't look very friendly. Besides, with the noise the airplane made, he could not understand a word of what I said anyhow. I looked at Mrs. Tate. She just laughed and waved to me. It was impossible to talk with each other. At that time, the cabins of the planes were not soundproofed the way they are today. In the meantime, Renatchen had found something else to occupy herself with—the famous bags that even today are still in the pocket of the seat in front of you.

All of a sudden, the plane started to rock quite violently, and I had the awful sensation that we were falling down. It took only a few seconds until the pilot had straightened out the plane again. But Renatchen had had enough—no more exploring. She looked around at me a little scared, but when I smiled at her, she nestled herself comfortably into my arms, closed her eyes, and fell asleep. I did not feel too courageous either, especially when I looked out the window and saw thick, dark clouds on one side of the plane and saw crisscross lightning all over them. So I closed my eyes too and started concentrating on the thought that I really was on my way to Opi now, and in a little while, we would be together again, no more fear and worry. We would be happy again!

But then another thought entered my mind—my parents, who were expecting us in Freiburg, and instead they would get a letter telling them that we were in England without even having said goodbye to them. How disappointed they would be. I felt a terrible longing for them. When would I see them and my brothers again? I am not a writer. It is impossible for me to describe that mixture of feelings that went on in me on that flight to England. Can one be happy and sad at the same time?

There was a very famous German author, Friedrich von Schiller, who wrote a verse in one of his poems, "*Der Ring des Polykrates*":

*Des Lebens ungemischte Freude
ward keinem Irdischen zuteil.*[11]

In free translation: "Life's unmixed joy was never bestowed on a mortal."

The stewardess interrupted my thoughts as she walked through the aisle telling us, more through signs than with words, that we should fasten our seatbelts. We had passed the border and would land in Amsterdam for pass control in a few minutes.

I had to wake up Renatchen, who didn't like this at all. But a little cookie that the stewardess brought over to her helped a lot. The plane landed quite smoothly and finally came to a standstill. The stewardess told us to keep our passports and tickets ready and to follow her across the airport to the customs department. We would stay twenty minutes and then continue the flight to London.

Everything went quite smoothly. If the customs officer was wondering why my passport was made out for a few months only, he kept it to himself. Mrs. Tate, who had been standing right next to us through the whole procedure, just in case anything went wrong, went ahead to the exit and waited for us there. But just when we had joined her, Renatchen informed me a little anxiously that she had to go to the bathroom. I looked at Mrs. Tate, who hesitated for a moment, but then told me to go quickly; she would wait at the gate for us, but we had to hurry.

Well, that we did. As a matter of fact, we were so rushed that I did not even take the time to put my passport, which I was still holding in my hand, back into my handbag. After we accomplished our little errand, we rushed back to the gate, where Mrs. Tate was waiting for us. "You have everything, your passport, your ticket?" she asked. I stopped short. I had my ticket, which I had put in my coat pocket, but where was the passport? I remembered having it in my hand when we went into the restroom. My heart stood still for a moment—the passport gave me permission to enter England. At the moment, it was worth more than any amount of money! If it was lost, I would have been sent back to Germany!

I asked Mrs. Tate to hold on to Renatchen and raced back to the restroom, which was completely empty by now. And there on the windowsill was my passport! I remembered now that I had taken Renatchen out of the toilet so that she would not touch anything in there and had pulled up her little panties outside. To get my hands

Meeting Marvis Tate and Leaving Germany 153

free to do that as quickly as possible, I had put the passport on the windowsill, and in my anxiety not to miss the plane, I had picked up Renatchen and forgot all about the passport! I grabbed it and nearly kissed it, so happy to have it back. I rushed outside with my passport and waved it at Mrs. Tate. I picked up Renatchen, and we ran together to the plane, which took off as soon as the door closed behind us. And now in an hour or so, we would be in London!

I was kind of glad that the noise in the plane made a conversation impossible. I felt very ashamed about this little episode with the passport. But then these last few days I had lived like in a dream. Everything was so unreal to me. Everything had changed so suddenly. The unexpected release from the concentration camp, the two days with the Posses, Berlin, and now this trip. I looked over to Mrs. Tate, who was reading a book. I wished I could do that. I occupied myself with Renatchen, who had discovered my handbag and had started to unpack it and pack it again patiently. I let her play with it and only watched that nothing dropped on the floor.

And then I saw the seatbelt sign light up and the stewardess coming along the aisle to see if everybody had fastened their belts. I now felt the plane going down and looked out of the window. We were over the airport already. I took the handbag away from Renatchen. But this time I made sure that my passport was safely in there! Then I put Renatchen's coat on her, but to button it was not an easy task. All of a sudden, I felt so excited that my hands started to tremble. In a few minutes, we would be together with Opi!

Once Marvis Tate visited Ilse at the Posses' home, Ilse had to make a decision to leave Dessau for Berlin right away and then to leave Germany, her homeland, altogether. The emotional weight of such a decision was not insignificant, and she also had to leave without seeing or telling her parents, which only added to her unease. Tate also recognized the difficulty of persuading Ilse that she must leave Germany if permission was granted, as Tate recalled later in an interview in the *American Hebrew and Jewish Tribune*.[12]

Prior to visiting Ilse, Tate had a long meeting with Ernst Hanfstaengl in Berlin to persuade him to allow Ilse to leave Germany. Hanfstaengl was a German American businessman and intimate friend of Hitler who eventually became chief of the Nazi Foreign Press Bureau. He had an American education from Harvard, was fluent in English, and had many connections to higher society in the United Kingdom and the United States. It was his background, education, and influence over Hitler that led Tate to ultimately choose Hanfstaengl, after consulting with her British journalist friends, as the most likely agent to help with her request.[13] Hanfstaengl had called Dessau police commissioner Heisig in order to get Ilse and Renate released from Rosslau, and he also arranged for their passports, visas, and airplane tickets. Tate indulged Hanfstaengl's piano playing, dinner invites, and narcissism in order to make all this happen.[14]

Everything happened very quickly for Ilse, and she commented on how unreal it all felt. She had to say goodbye to Leni Posse, not knowing if she would ever see her again. The tenderness of this moment between Ilse and one of her best friends—and, at times during her traumatic experience, her sole support—can be felt even some forty years after the fact. Ilse's emotionality about leaving Germany, not knowing if and when she would see her parents again, and yet being reunited with her husband once again were palpable on her flight to London.

Notes

1. Rose, "Transnational Identities in National Politics," 80. For more on the connections Seger established between Social Democracy and pacifism, see chapter 3 of Rose's dissertation and Rose, "The Penumbra of Weimar Political Culture."
2. Seger, *A Nation Terrorized*, 200. The English version of his memoir has an additional chapter that does not appear in the German version. The chapter describes how he got his wife and daughter out of Rosslau and out of Germany with the help of MPs.
3. Seger, *Reisetagebuch*, 34–35. Seger also has a chapter in his second book, "Two Months in England," that further details how he got his wife and daughter out of Germany, including the larger political context.
4. Rose, "Transnational Identities in National Politics," 80.
5. Seger, *Reisetagebuch*, 35.
6. Ilse wrote this in 1970 and was referring to her release in 1934, so it had been thirty-six years.
7. Katharine Stewart-Murray was Duchess of Atholl from 1874 to 1960.
8. This translates to "This is the German Foreign Press Office. Is Mr. Seger there?"
9. Here, Hanfstaengl is referring to Nazi Party zealots.
10. It is unclear here if she went to the zoo again or if, more likely, she is talking about the same experience she had before meeting with Hanfstaengl.
11. *Polycrates' Ring* is a lyrical ballad by Friedrich Schiller, written in 1797.
12. Interview quoted and paraphrased extensively in Seger, *A Nation Terrorized*, 201–4.
13. Ibid., 201.
14. Ibid., 202–3.

7

Reunited with Gerhart and Living in Exile

This chapter picks up with Ilse's emotional arrival in London and her reunion with Gerhart, a very large press event that was atypical for the time.

I tried to look out the window, but I could not see anybody on this side of the plane. When the stewardess opened the door, I started to rush toward it, but Mrs. Tate held me back. "We will leave the plane last. There will be reporters and newsreel people for us out there; you are a celebrity today." She smiled. "We have to let the other passengers go out first."

Luckily, it did not take very long until the twenty or so passengers who were with us on the plane left. Finally, we could go. But we got only as far as the gangway of the plane. Loads of people were standing at the foot of it with cameras and notebooks and a big movie camera in the background. Everybody was shouting something, which I did not understand. I looked in vain for Opi, but could not find him in this sea of strange faces. Then far behind all these newspaper people, I saw someone waving a bunch of red roses—and there he was! I wanted to race down the gangway with Renate, but Mrs. Tate held on to me again. "Just a few more minutes. The movie cameras. . . ." But I did not hear her anymore because at that moment, the police or whoever was holding Opi back let him through, and he came running up the gangway, and then we were in his arms!

For a moment, both of us were not aware of all the people around us. But they did not give us much time. They asked questions, most of which I did not understand, and made demands: "Mr. Seger, kiss your wife and baby again." And the clicking of the cameras quickly interrupted that beautiful moment of our reunion.

News is news, and I, as the wife of a newspaper man, had to understand that. It was also a great moment for Mrs. Tate too, who had done so much for us. It would certainly be a great asset for her political career.[1]

Renatchen was quite bewildered by all the commotion around her. She looked very seriously at the strange man who smiled at her and kissed her tenderly on her cheek. But at least she did not cry as she had in Oranienburg a year ago, and I was very grateful for that. Maybe she saw some resemblance to the big picture that I had with me in Rosslau and that I had pointed to every so often and said, "Look, darling, this is your *Vati* [dad]," a word she had learned to pronounce by now. Finally, she got bored with all the strange faces and things that were going on around her, and she struggled to get down to the ground. I let her down, and she started to pick up little stones and walk away from us. There was no direct danger because our plane was the only one around there; the next one would be at night. After all, this was 1934. But just the same, I wanted to go after her when the stewardess of our plane came over to us and told us not to worry because she would look out for her.

There were more pictures, more questions, which Opi translated for me, and a long interview with Mrs. Tate, and finally, we could go. And then Mrs. Tate did something very nice. I had seen her talking to some people who did not seem to have anything to do with the press. She came over to us and told us that her friends would take her home and that her chauffeur would take us to her home, where we would have lunch with her and some friends, and then her chauffeur would take us to our hotel. I thought this was a very thoughtful gesture for her to give us her car, and we were certainly grateful for it.

We just wanted to get into the car when a man rushed over to us and greeted us in German like long-lost friends. I had never seen this man before, and Opi did not seem to recognize him either. But the man insisted that they had met at some press meeting years ago in Berlin. Now Opi seemed to remember him faintly and asked him what he was doing in London. He explained that he had lost his job and was now freelancing. At the moment, he was on an assignment for a German butcher-paper trade paper. "You can understand, one has to take everything that comes along, the way things are in Germany now," he said, laughing a little sheepishly. "We have to see each other. There is so much to talk about," he insisted. Somehow, I disliked this man very much. Opi seemed to feel the same way, and to get rid of him, he gave him the name of our hotel, and then we drove off and forgot about him completely.

The ride to Mrs. Tate's house seemed like a dream to me. I felt so beautifully secure and at peace. We did not talk very much. It was so good just to sit next to each other and hold hands. Renatchen sat in the corner next to me and played very quietly with the little stones she had picked up at the airport. From time to time, she gave Opi a shy look, but when he started to talk to her, she quickly looked away again.

Much too soon, we arrived at Mrs. Tate's house. The chauffeur rang the bell, and a very well-dressed man opened the door and greeted us seriously: "Welcome to England. Mrs. Tate is expecting you upstairs." So he knew who we were, but we could only guess that he might be the butler, which was correct. He took us upstairs, where he ordered a young woman in a pretty uniform to help us freshen up. She led Renatchen and me into the most extravagant bathroom one can imagine. It was as big as a regular room. The walls were covered with beautiful Delft tiles in that famous blue and white design. Everything was big—the washstands, two of them; the bathtub; all the bottles standing on the shelves—and all in matching blue, just beautiful. It was such a contrast to our way of life just a few days ago!

The maid, after inquiring if we needed anything else, left to wait for us in the hall. I looked around for a minute or so, and then I washed us a little, combed our hair, and powdered my nose, and, with a last look at that beautiful, big, tempting bathtub, we left, and the maid led the way to the dining room. Opi was there already, talking with Mrs. Tate and a group of people around him. When Mrs. Tate saw us coming in, she came over quickly, took my arm, and introduced me to these people. I remember only one of them faintly. It was a tall, very friendly woman who spoke very fast and temperamentally—a Mrs. Dugdale. As Opi explained to me later, she was a niece of Lord Balfour, the author of the famous Balfour Declaration (1917), which claimed British support of a Jewish national home (later called Israel), and she had been very active in planning for our freedom.[2]

Finally, we settled down to lunch at an endlessly long table with a very big, beautiful silver centerpiece and a lot of extra spoons and forks, salt and pepper bowls, and ashtrays all over the place. To me, it looked like a display of some sort. Two maids were serving under the watchful eye of the butler. It was like a movie, and everything seemed completely unreal to me. Opi was sitting far away from me between

Mrs. Tate and Mrs. Dugdale in a lively conversation, but from time to time our eyes met, and that was reassuring. Renatchen was sitting next to me, of course. I was very proud of her; she behaved like a little lady, ate very nicely, and tried to pick up some of the meat that I had cut into small pieces for her. But she soon realized that this was still a bit too difficult, and she put down the fork and took a spoon, the way she was used to still. I had to help her only a little from time to time. On the other side of me sat a good-looking young man who tried very hard to speak to me in German, and I tried to converse in the little English I knew. At least I understood that he was a member of Parliament too, and in the same party as Mrs. Tate. It was not much of a conversation, but he had such a nice smile that made me feel at ease.

Finally, the luncheon was over, and Mrs. Tate and the young man had to go to the Parliament for an evening session. But before Mrs. Tate left, she told us to wait. She would send her car right back to bring us to the hotel. It didn't take long, and I was glad because Renatchen was getting sleepy and was ready for her afternoon nap.

Finally, we were alone for the first time. Renatchen slept peacefully in the crib that the hotel had provided for her. We sat on a couch, and Opi had his arm around me. It was like a dream for both of us—to be together again! We hardly talked, just looked at each other, enjoying each other's presence. Neither of us really felt like talking. Just being near each other was enough. We would have all the time in the world now to fill in the gap of the endless time we had been separated, had not heard from each other, and had lived lives of our own. All this could wait—we were together!

The week in London was quite busy. We had little time for sightseeing, as much as I would have preferred that to the many lunch invitations from people I hardly remember any longer. Everybody wanted to be nice to us, and they really were, but I had to get used to people again, to all those little social niceties. I couldn't quickly forget what lay behind me. Besides, we had a problem that was very much on my mind. But more about that later.

Two things I remember very vividly. One was a visit by that man we had met at the airport, and the other was a visit to Lady Astor's townhouse, both on the same day. I think the name of the man was Dr. Wesemayer, but I am not quite sure.[3] He called very early the next morning and told Opi he would join us for breakfast. When we came down to the restaurant a little while later, he was already there, waiting for us. He was a fast talker and asked many questions about my release, about Opi's plans, and so on. He seemed to be quite nervous and tried to make jokes all the time, especially when Opi answered one of his questions rather vaguely. I disliked him even more than when we met him at the airport the day before. Besides, I didn't want company at breakfast already. I kept quiet most of the time and let Opi do the talking. I must have made a very unfriendly face because he finally gave up on me, and I concentrated on Renatchen and helped her with her breakfast. When we were half through with our meal, he got up, excused himself, said he had to make some urgent telephone calls, and rushed out of the restaurant. We finished our meal and waited a little while, but he did not come back, so we also left the restaurant. When we came out into the hall, I saw him running down the stairs, and he stopped—a little embarrassed, I thought—when he saw us. He looked reddish in his face, and I noticed that it was also wet with sweat. It was a nice warm spring day but certainly not hot. I wondered what he could have been doing upstairs since all the public phones were downstairs in the lounge. He wiped his face and came over to us and said he had to run and would call again. Then he left rather quickly without paying his breakfast bill, as we found out later. We did not quite know what to make of his funny behavior; it seemed a bit suspicious to us. We went up to our room and looked around, but everything was untouched. Opi's briefcase, which was lying on the desk, was not quite closed. But Opi was not sure if he had left it this way himself since he had looked something up in the morning before we went downstairs. Besides, he said, he had no secrets in there, just correspondence for future lecture engagements and things like that. But he agreed with me that he did not like the man, and he had no intention of making another appointment with him.

But the next day, Wesemayer showed up again. We were just leaving for a lunch engagement at the house of Lord and Lady Listowel.[4] I think I mentioned these people already. They had been in Germany before Mrs. Tate. They were interested in German political prisoners and tried to do something for them if they could. My name was on their list too. In Berlin, a high German official told them that Renatchen and I were free and living in our apartment. At first, they believed that, but then they decided to make sure and went to Dessau, where they found out the real story. Opi had mentioned these people's names the day before and that we would go to their house today. And that was the reason why Wesemayer came. He wanted to come with us. When Opi told him that was not possible, that we could not just bring another guest, he pleaded with him to take him too. He came onto the bus with us and tried again and again to convince Opi how important it would be for him to get in touch with people like this and have an interview with them. Opi finally got impatient and told him quite sternly that this was impossible, and this was final. We never saw him again. But a year and a half or so later, we read about him in a Swiss newspaper. He was really a Nazi spy. He had helped abduct a German Jewish journalist who had found asylum in Basel, where he [Wesemann] discovered him. He had drugged him, put him in a car, and, with the help of other Nazis, brought him across the Swiss border back into Germany.[5] So our suspicion was well founded. He just wanted to use us to get contacts with anti-Nazi groups.

That night was the evening at Lady Astor's townhouse. Through the manager of the hotel, we had secured the help of one of the maids, a nice elderly woman, to babysit. Since the invitation was for a rather late hour, we didn't have to leave before Renatchen was fast asleep, which made me feel better. The Astor house was even more impressive than Mrs. Tate's. It was like a little palace. Here, a well-dressed gentleman, the butler, welcomed us and led us into a tremendously big living room with an ornate fireplace. There were beautiful Oriental rugs on the floor and big gold-framed paintings on the walls. Beautiful flower arrangements were all around. When we entered, a small, slender, blondish woman dressed in a long, black velvet gown, a small pearl necklace, and a very long chain of red beads hanging down to her knees came quickly over to us—Lady Astor. She took one hand from each of us into hers, spoke first to Opi, and then turned to me and continued talking very lively and fast. All I really understood was something like "You must be very happy now to be safe here in England!" I nodded and smiled and said something like "Thank you" and hoped that would be all right with all she had said. Then, she asked me a question that I did not understand at all, and realizing this, she touched my cheek and exclaimed loudly, "You must learn English, young woman!" It sounded like a command. I still remember that at that moment I felt a slight resentment, like an unwilling child. Why could she not have learned German? Which of course was ridiculous. Opi took over and answered the question for me, and then she introduced us to the other guests. Mrs. Tate had been invited, of course, but she could not make it. She had an evening session in the House that night.

Everybody was talking now very animatedly. I just listened and tried hard to understand at least a little bit, but I understood only very little. I certainly could not participate at all in the conversation and would have felt very uncomfortable if it weren't for Opi, who sat next to me and reached over from time to time and pressed my hand reassuringly.

Then the butler came in again and opened both sides of the door to the hall for two male servants (footmen, as they are called in England) dressed in dark tailcoats with some gold trimming, black knee pants, and long white stockings and white gloves—an outfit similar to what was worn in France in the middle of the eighteenth century. The only thing missing were white wigs. They carried big trays with beautiful glasses, filled with either a green or pink liquid, which they offered to the guests. It was lemon and raspberry lemonade! That was all right, but I thought the elaborate way of serving it was rather funny. As Opi told me later, the Astors were both teetotalers and never served any kind of alcohol, not even with fancy dinner invitations.

Well, this was the social part of our stay in London. Of course, we did a little sightseeing too. We went to Hyde Park, which was beautiful in its spring colors, and we saw the changing of the guards at Windsor Castle, which Renatchen especially enjoyed, and saw the famous London Bridge. We very much wanted to visit the Tower, but somehow, we did not get around to it because we had a serious problem to solve, and that made these first days of our reunion not quite as happy as we had hoped for.

Opi had told me that he had accepted an invitation from the Norwegian Social Democratic Party for a two-week lecture trip, starting in Oslo and going all the way up to Hammerfest, nearly every night in another town. Naturally, he wanted me to come with him, but what to do with Renatchen? This would be impossible for a child of her age, traveling every day and sleeping in a different bed every night. She had already had enough emotional disturbances in her young life. So what to do? I could stay with her in London, a strange city, knowing very little of the language and certainly not very sure of myself at the moment, and be separated from Opi again so soon. On the other hand, Opi could cancel the trip, which had been arranged long before he had any idea we were coming. But this lecture trip was important. He felt it was his duty, since he had his freedom, to talk about what was going on in Germany, about the concentration camps. But one afternoon, sitting in a little park near our hotel, watching a group of small children playing happily under the supervision of two young ladies, he said, "There must be children's homes that would take a child for two weeks. We have to find out." So, when we got back to our hotel, Opi went to the manager, who was a very nice person and tried to help us whenever he could because he had read about us in the newspaper, and asked him about homes. The manager did not know of anything like this, but he gave us the name of a good agency that he thought would know about places like this, which, as we found out, were quite numerous in London. The reason for this was that a lot of British officials liked to leave their young children in England when the climate of the countries they were sent to did not seem to be healthy for young children from the Western part of the world. Pretty soon we had some addresses and used the "underground" to look at these places. Well, to make a long story short, these homes were beautiful, very well kept, and most of them were in the suburbs of London, surrounded by big gardens that contained beautiful playgrounds. They were certainly places where a child could be quite happy and in good hands. There were a lot of healthy-looking children playing under the watchful eyes of some nurses. As difficult as it was for me to leave Renatchen behind, even for a short time, I had to agree that she could be quite happy here. But then we heard the prices and found they were way above our means. Besides, most of them had a waiting list already, so that wouldn't work either. Quite depressed, we went back to our hotel.

When I put Renatchen down for her nap, the phone rang. An old acquaintance of Opi's, Rudolf Olden, a well-known journalist for one of the big Berlin newspapers, who had emigrated with his wife to England and who Opi had met already before Renatchen and I arrived in London, called to congratulate us on our reunion and asked if we could come for lunch the next day.[6] Opi accepted and then told him about our difficulties. He was quite sympathetic, but of course, he could not help us either.

The Oldens did not live very far from our hotel, and the next day we walked over to their flat. In the meantime, we had bought a little collapsible stroller at the Macy's of London, Selfridge, so that it was easy to take Renatchen with us everywhere without overtiring her. The Oldens lived in a small, furnished apartment. Mrs. Olden was his second wife; he was divorced, and his first wife lived in California now, as Opi had told me before we got there.[7] She was quite beautiful and much younger than her husband. We got along quite well right from the start. She was very interested in Renatchen and occupied herself with her quite a bit, and Renatchen seemed to like her too. And for me, it was so nice to have the opportunity to participate in the conversation instead of just listening. It was all together a very nice and relaxing visit. When we finally had to go, Renatchen put her arms around Mrs. Olden and gave her a kiss—something she seldom did with a stranger.

That night, after Renatchen was in bed, the phone rang. It was Mrs. Olden, who wanted to talk to me. She told me that she had a long conversation with her husband after we had left. They would love to take care of Renatchen for the time we would be in Norway if we would let them. They both liked the child and thought she would be better in a home than in one of the big nurseries. This was quite an unexpected solution for our problem. We both agreed that this would be best for the child. It would be difficult for me to be separated from Renatchen for so long. After all, we had been together constantly since she was born. But I knew Mrs. Olden would take good care of her; I could trust her. So, we thanked the Oldens profoundly and arranged to meet them again the next day to talk everything over and let Renatchen get more acquainted with her foster parents.

We still had a few days until our departure, and two days before that, we took Renatchen over to the Oldens' with all of her belongings. We had bought some clothes for her, and she was very proud of her new dresses. That afternoon, we left her there to find out how it would work out. Later in the evening, Mrs. Olden called us and reported that Renatchen had had her bath and had eaten her dinner, and everything had been all right so far. But when she had to go to bed, she had asked for *Mutti* and had started to cry a little when I did not show up. But then, after having her evening bottle in bed, she had fallen asleep right away. Mrs. Olden promised to call us again in the morning and tell us how it went.

That evening, we had dinner at a nice little restaurant somewhere near the Thames, and Opi did his best to take my mind off the separation from Renatchen. I understood his reasoning. Besides knowing that the child was in good hands, we needed some time for ourselves—so much had happened since that cold day in December in Oranienburg!

The next morning, we called the Oldens. Everything was fine. Renatchen was playing happily with some toys that Mrs. Olden had bought for her, and after a short question—*Mutti*?—at breakfast, she had taken everything in stride. It was good to hear this, but to tell the truth, it hurt a little too. I knew that children at that age (she was just twenty-two months old) have a short memory, and it proved that Mrs. Olden was the right person for her, but just the same! Mrs. Olden very carefully suggested that she thought it would be best if we did not come back again before our departure. She thought it would be the easiest way for Renatchen to get adjusted. Very reluctantly, we had to agree with her that this would be best. Of course, I called a few more times over the next two days. Everything was all right, and Renatchen was completely at home in her new surroundings. What else could I ask for? It would be for only a few weeks, and then she would be with us again.

The next day, we left London by train for Newcastle and from there, by ship to Norway. The trip was nice. Only the first night was quite stormy, and all the hatches had to be closed, which made the small cabin a little uncomfortable and made me feel a little nauseated, but that was over as soon as we went up on deck and enjoyed the beautiful sea breeze.

On board, we met the first American person we had ever met, a Canadian woman (at that time, Canada and America seemed the same to me; it was the same continent, after all) who was on a trip through Europe. As she told us, she had her own car on board, and whenever possible, she went by car. She intended to spend some more weeks in Europe before she returned home, and she invited us, whenever we would come to Canada, to visit her in Toronto, where she lived, and she even gave us her address. I was quite impressed. Having a car at that time was already something, but having it shipped to Europe was really something!

It was a beautiful sunny morning when we arrived in Oslo. A group of people was waiting for us when we came down the gangplank. Most of them were leaders and members of the Norwegian Social Democratic Party who had invited Opi for the lecture tour, and when they heard that I was with him now, they extended the invitation to me too. They welcomed us very warmly. Most of them even spoke German. There was, of course, a group of newspapermen and photographers, and after the welcoming and the picture taking was over, Opi was surrounded by the interviewers. I had stepped aside and looked at the nice houses that were built on the hills around the harbor in the distance, a bit envious. I must confess, all these nice homes—where would we have a home again and when?

As I turned to go back to the group that surrounded Opi, a young, good-looking man left the crowd and met me halfway. He introduced himself in fluent German as a correspondent of an Oslo paper and asked politely if I would answer some questions for him. Of course, I said yes, if I knew the answers. He wanted to know if I was ever maltreated during my stay in the concentration camp, which I honestly denied. Then he continued, "Did they molest you in any way?" or something like that. Again, I had to say no, they never physically harmed me. Then, he wanted to know if I had read Opi's book about Oranienburg. I told him that thus far, I had seen only the Dutch edition, and I had glanced through it, but not knowing the language, I did not understand very much of it, even if some words resemble German words a little. Before he could ask me another question, two of the people who had greeted us and who had been so friendly when we arrived came over to tell me that I should join their group. It astonished me that they did not talk to my interviewer and that he just said, "Thank you," to me and left very quickly. But when we walked over to Opi, they told me that this nice young man was an editor of a pro-Nazi newspaper, and I should not talk to any newspaper man without being introduced by one of them. I was quite shocked. This was Norway—I did not know that they had Nazi sympathizers there too. Of course, during the time I was in Rosslau, I had not read any newspaper; the only one I could have there was the *Völkischer Beobachter*, the Nazi Party newspaper, which I would not have touched for anything. So I had never heard of Vidkun Quisling, who had founded a Nazi Party of his own [in Norway]. It sounded so incredible to me. I quickly found out how much I had to learn. The next day, I was told that the young man who had interviewed me had put words into my mouth I never said. The headline in his newspaper was "Mrs. Seger Contradicts Her Husband, No Cruelty in Concentration Camp" or something like that. That was the first and last interview I have ever given. I was furious and depressed at the same time, and Opi had his hands full convincing me that there were more important papers in Oslo, and nobody in his right mind would really believe that I would have said that.

Well, this was the only unhappy experience during our trip through Norway. The people were overwhelmingly friendly and hospitable. Opi spoke nearly every night in another town before a big and very attentive audience. His speech was translated sometimes after a few sentences or after the whole lecture. That depended on if they had a stenographer there or not. But quite a few people did not need the translation. I never saw anybody leave. They listened attentively to Opi as well as to the translation.

After every lecture, I had to go up on stage, where some young woman took my hand, made a little speech, and then presented me with a beautiful bouquet of flowers. I felt a little awkward since I did not understand one word that she said, but I smiled, and she smiled, and everybody in the audience applauded wildly. But I was very grateful for all the friendliness these Norwegian people showed us. My only regret was that I had to leave these beautiful flowers in the hotel in the morning when we continued our trip.

We traveled by train, by car, by boat. Everything was arranged marvelously. We were always met by a whole group of people wherever and whenever we arrived, who were anxious to help, to show us around, to explain things. They were just wonderfully nice to us. We were invited to houses of party big shots as well as to the modest apartments of the workers and their families. I don't know how often we ate the wonderful salmon, which seemed to be the dish to honor and welcome guests with. We were really glad when once in a while we could eat in a restaurant and not have fish!

We had wonderful trips through the magnificent fjords in comfortable, small steamboats, and we were tremendously impressed by the beautiful, majestic landscape. We saw the fjords in mysterious fog and bright sunshine. I only wished I would have been better prepared for all this. Everything happened so fast; it all had a dreamlike quality for me. It was somehow unreal. I just could not cope with the contrast between my way of life just two weeks ago and now all this, a new impression every day; it left me in sort of a daze. I missed Renatchen too, and realizing that, Opi made me very happy when he called the Oldens in London to find out how she was. They told me that she was fine and was quite well adjusted, and they were very happy with her. This made us both feel good. Finally, we came back to Oslo, where we had a few days' rest before we left to make our way over Belgium to France, where Opi had a foreigner's permit to stay for a certain length of time and where we would be reunited with Renatchen.

We had most of the day for us, and we explored Oslo a bit on our own. Finally, we landed on a hill overlooking the harbor, and there, enjoying the warm sunshine, we started talking about our future. Somehow, we had both avoided doing that so far. We were so happy to be together again, and we didn't want to spoil this wonderful feeling. Opi had only told me that he had an opportunity to go to America in the fall on a visitor's visa for a lecture trip, and during his stay there he would try also to find an existence for us. But how to do this best? He knew he would have to travel most of the time, and the difficulties started here already. What would that mean for Renatchen and me? Was there any sense for us to go with him right away, and if he could not find a job, wouldn't it be a waste to spend the money for the ocean trip for nothing? Wasn't it better and less expensive if we stayed in Europe until he found out how it could work? But that meant another separation for at least nine months, and neither of us wanted that. I don't want to go into all the plans and ideas we discussed to avoid that, but in the end, we both agreed that this would be the only sensible way. Opi had made some money with his book, *Oranienburg*, which had come out in eight different languages, and lectures in France, Sweden, England, and, of course, this Norwegian trip had brought in some money too. He would need a ticket for the trip to America, and we figured, with some careful planning in the next months until October when he would have to leave, it should work out. There would even be a little money left so he would not have to worry about us for the first three months. He had one very well-paid engagement, which the famous Rabbi Abba Hillel Silver had arranged for him after he had heard him speak in Paris.[8] He not only gave Opi very good advice, but he also gave Opi the names and addresses of organizations and agents he should contact. This had been quite successful. He was confident that more would develop as soon as he was in the States, and the publicity in the newspapers would do the rest.

But the big question was where Renate and I should stay during that time. Opi thought about Prague first. He loved that town, which had given him shelter and where he had made friends. Life was not expensive there either. And he wanted us somewhere near Germany so that my parents could come see us and I would not feel so completely alone. But Prague was the refuge now for many anti-Nazis, which was well known to the German authorities. This would make trouble for my parents if they applied for a Czechoslovakian visa. (At that time, one still needed a visa for every European country.) So that was out. And then there was Switzerland or France. Well, we didn't solve that problem on the hills of Oslo that day, and we finally stopped talking about it. Luckily, there was still some time to make up our minds. Somehow, my thoughts went back to Germany. And for a moment, I dreamed what it would be like if all of a sudden, the Hitler regime toppled, and we could go back home again! To leave a country in which you had been quite happy until a short time ago, with a very unknown future ahead of you, was certainly not an easy task!

But Opi, a person of realistic and logical thinking, stopped my daydreaming and brought me gently back into reality. Soon, I found out how little I knew about what had happened around me during the four months we were in Rosslau. I remember that I became quite distressed and could hardly believe so many things that Opi told me about at first. For instance, the Reichstag fire: it was absolutely certain that the Nazis under Göring and Goebbels's order had started the fire themselves, that the young Dutchman was bought and used as a scapegoat, and that the Communists really had nothing to do with the fire, which would have brought them no gain whatsoever.[9] I certainly did not care for these two men, but to organize something like this—how could he be so sure? Where was the proof for that? There had been whispers and suspicions, I knew that, but are there not rumors all the time if something spectacular happens? I don't remember how he finally convinced me, certainly not right away, but he did, and it was that way with many other things that had happened and that I did not know anything about. But I understood now that there was no way to go back to Germany in the near future and that I had to prepare myself for a lot of changes in our lives, which had looked so promising and peaceful when we got married.

Late in the afternoon, after saying goodbye to many people who had come to see us off on the boat, we left this beautiful and friendly country and were on our way to Antwerp, Belgium, where we wanted to stay a day or two to see some friends who had found a new home there, at least for the time being. From there, we continued to Brussels to get a French visa for me so that we could go to Paris, where we would be reunited with our little girl again.

But in Brussels, we met some unexpected obstacles. After we settled down in a small hotel that our friends in Antwerp had recommended to us, we inquired about where the French consulate was and how to get there. Since it was too late to go there the same day, we walked a bit around Brussels, a very old town with beautiful medieval buildings, elegant stores, and nice restaurants. We had a nice dinner in one of them and decided to explore more of the city the next day after we were finished at the consulate. Well, it never came to that. The next morning, we walked to the French consulate as early as possible so that we could have the rest of the day to ourselves and then leave early the next morning for Paris. But it worked out quite differently.

When we entered the consulate, we were the first people there, and after telling the receptionist what we had come for, we were directed to an office where a very good-looking woman received us in a very friendly way. She did not speak any German, but that was all right since Opi's French was quite good. After giving her my passport and showing her his special Czech passport, which the Czech government had given him (the Czechs under the leadership of Dr. Benesch at that time had done so much to help the German refugees), and his special permit for a three-month stay in France, he asked her for a visa for me.[10] Of course, he explained to her our situation, about his and my stay in concentration camps, how the English had helped to get Renatchen and me out, the whole story. She listened without any interruption. But somehow her face had changed; it was certainly not friendly anymore. When Opi had finished, she took my passport, looked into it, gave it back to Opi, and said, "Your wife has to go back to the city where she came from or at least to Berlin and has to get her visa from the French consulate there. These are the rules."

As bad as my French was, I had understood perfectly what she had said, and I felt terrible. Opi bent forward and said slowly, "I think you did not quite understand, Madame. Maybe I did not make myself quite clear. My wife can't go back. The Nazis would never let her out again. She was in a concentration camp there, don't you see?" But she just repeated what she had said before—these were the rules, and there was nothing she could do about it. Opi tried again to explain that this was impossible. He nearly started shouting at her. But she insisted that there was nothing she could do, then got up and opened the door. We were dismissed!

We looked at each other. What was there to do? I tried very hard not to break out in tears. Opi took my arm reassuringly, but I could see on his face that he was upset too. When we were out of the building, we started walking in the direction of our hotel. Neither of us felt like talking. But suddenly, Opi stopped walking, turned toward me, gave me a kiss, and said, "Don't worry, darling. We will find a way."

Pretty soon, we arrived at our hotel, which we had left in such a good mood that morning, and went up to our room. I looked out the window. The city didn't seem to be interesting at all anymore. Opi walked back and forth through the room. "There must be someone who can help us. They cannot all be so idiotic as this woman," he muttered. And then he remembered the name of a Belgian member of Parliament, a Social Democrat, whom he had met at one of the international peace conferences when he was secretary general of the German Peace Society some years ago. Maybe he would have some idea or connections that could help. Opi looked up his telephone number and luckily found him in his office. After Opi gave him a short explanation, he asked us to meet him in his office as soon as possible since he had a meeting in the Parliament in the afternoon.

When we arrived there, his secretary ushered us in right away, and he greeted Opi like an old friend. He had read all about his escape from Oranienburg and also had bought his book. Finally, he asked how he could help us. After telling him about our experience at the French consulate, he agreed that the whole thing was ridiculous. "But you know the French bureaucracy," he said. "There is always a possibility to get around it," and he smiled. It so happened that he not only knew the French ambassador, but he was even a personal friend of his. He called him up right away and, after telling him a bit about our plight, got an appointment for us in the afternoon. We were certainly grateful to him and left this nice and helpful man in a more optimistic state of mind than we'd had when we'd arrived.

The ambassador was a very elegant and good-looking man. He listened to Opi's story, looked at our papers, and then smiled a little. "The young lady at the consulate only follows orders. But, of course, there are always exceptions possible to every rule, and certainly they are possible in your case. Madame should not be separated from you again. I will give you a personal note for the consulate, and you will get a visa for Madame. But I must warn you. This will be a visa only for a week. When you arrive in Paris, you have to go right away to the prefecture and ask for Madame's permit to stay, otherwise there can be serious consequences." Of course, we promised that. He wrote a little note for us to take to the consulate and assured us that everything would work out all right now. Then, he wished us a good trip, gallantly kissed my hand, and saw us to the door. What a difference from our first visit to the consulate!

It was too late to go to the consulate right now, which we would have loved to do, so we had to spend another night in Brussels. I don't remember any longer how we spent the rest of the day. We were both a little nervous and hated to wait until the next morning. But there was nothing we could do about that. We both didn't sleep very well that night and were relieved when it was time to go the next morning.

Again, we were the first people at the consulate. But this time, we had to wait quite a while until we were finally called into the office of the lady who had given us such a shock the day before. She gave us a very chilly greeting, and when Opi gave her the ambassador's letter, she read it quickly and then told us that he had already called and informed her to give me the visa. "But only for a week, you understand?" she said in a very unfriendly tone. We could really feel her hostility toward us. Later on, we often talked about this incident. Was she somehow connected to the secret police in Nazi Germany? Or was it just that a higher authority had overruled her judgment, maybe with some criticism? Whatever it was, I had my visa, and that was all that counted!

We went back to the hotel, quickly packed, and just managed to make the afternoon train to Paris.

Paris! The city nearly everybody wanted to visit. It was a strange feeling to be there all of a sudden, not just as a visitor but as a person without a home, not knowing where to go from there—certainly not the normal way to visit Paris. Maybe that was the reason that I never got any real feeling for Paris, any real impression of this beautiful city, and never felt at home there in any way. We even met some old friends there who were very good to us, but just the same, our whole stay was never real to me.

We arrived at our small hotel, which Opi had reserved from Brussels; it was the same hotel where he was staying when I spoke to him over the phone from Hanfstaengl's office. Then, Opi called our friends in London to find out when we could expect Renatchen. We were quite disappointed to hear that we would have to wait another three days since the young woman, a friend of our friends with whom Renatchen had stayed, who was supposed to bring the child to Paris, had a job for a few days and could not do it earlier. So we just had to wait.

On one of these three days, we made a trip to Versailles to visit the famous castle of Louis XVI and the beautiful gardens around it. This was the only day I really enjoyed our stay in Paris; at least it was the best memory I have of the weeks that we stayed there. When we were still in Dessau, just shortly after Renatchen was born, I read the beautiful biography of Marie Antoinette by Stefan Zweig, and now I saw the place that the author had described so vividly, and I felt like I was walking in her footsteps in the places where she had spent most of her married life. I was much more interested in the little summer cottages, the Petit and the Grand Trianon, which lie hidden in the big Versailles Park rather than in the grandiose main palace with its thousands of mirrors, its painted stucco ceilings, its silk-covered walls, its golden furniture, and its fantastic, glittering luxury. In the Petit Trianon, I felt as if I could see her sitting at her dressing table. There was the China powder box that she had used, the perfume bottles, a comb, and a brush. Next to an easy chair at the window stood a little table with a piece of needlework in a round frame, just as one still uses now. There was a needle with a long thread in it. It looked as if the queen had just left it there and would be right back to continue working on it. I relived the whole book while walking through the two houses, or at least the part in which Zweig talks about the early life of the queen. Since it was a weekday, very few tourists were there; we nearly had this peaceful place to ourselves, and it was easy to dream. Opi smiled a bit at my enthusiasm, but he understood how good it made me feel to be so far from reality for a short while.

Later, we had lunch in the small garden of a nice French country restaurant. I still remember, we ate a typical French dish, rabbit stew, but we could not quite make up our minds if we liked it or not. Perhaps the restaurant was not very good either, but it was cheap.

In the late afternoon, we went back to Paris and spent the evening in our small, not very attractive hotel room. Late that evening, we got a call from our friends in London with the good news that Renatchen would arrive the next day, very early in the morning. That was the best ending of a very nice day! We ordered a cot for her for our room, and since the train would be arriving in Paris at seven o'clock in the morning, we went to bed early.

In the morning, we were at the railway station long before the train was supposed to arrive. Finally, we saw it entering the huge station and coming to a stop. We ran along the cars and watched every door open. Finally, we saw a woman getting off a car not very far away from us, standing still and looking around. We both raced over to her, and there was Renatchen! I called out to her and opened my arms. She looked at me for a moment as if she had never seen me before. But that was only for a moment. Then a rather shy smile lit up her sweet face, and after hesitating for a moment, her arms stretched out to me, she bent over, and I had her in my arms. It was certainly a wonderful moment! It took a little longer for her to get familiar with Opi again. After all, she had been with him for only a week before we had to leave for Norway. But when we were back in the hotel and had her sitting between us on the bed, she was quite happy and not shy at all anymore.

Opi had rented a room for the young lady who had brought her [Renatchen] over from London, had paid for all expenses, and made sure that she did not need us anymore. She had been to Paris before, had friends there who would pick her up after she had rested for a while, and the next day, she would return to London. So we could concentrate on our little girl and make her feel at home with us again.

Then I remembered the big teddy bear that someone gave us for Renate in a little town called Drammen, where Opi gave his last lecture in Norway. There had been some excitement with this gift. The package was delivered to the stage door at the little theater where Opi spoke. The man who brought it backstage got a little scared when he put it down on a table. A funny deep sound came out of it—a bomb? As I said at the beginning of this memoir, there had been threats to the people who were responsible for the lecture tour when we arrived in Oslo. So the man talked to the people who were in charge, and instead of giving me the package on stage, as the sender had planned, they waited until after the lecture and told us about it when we came backstage. We opened it carefully. Nobody could hear any ticking, and out came a big, beautiful teddy bear, and the noise we all had heard was the tone every good teddy bear makes when one bends him over. So we all had a good laugh! I know the way things are today, one would probably call the bomb squad. But I have my doubts that something like that existed in that peaceful little town. The sender was a toy merchant, originally from Riga, a town in Russia where I had lived with my family for two years before the First World War broke out. There was a little note in the package: "For lille Renate Segerleben" (half Norwegian, half Jewish).[11] We were told he was the only Jew in Drammen and a very respected citizen. We were quite touched and glad to meet him later so we could thank him in person. And he enjoyed meeting someone he could talk to about his beloved hometown.

I unpacked the bear and put it down on one end of the bed, waiting to see Renatchen's reaction. The effect was quite unexpected. Renatchen gave the toy one look, then crawled away from it as far as she could and started to cry. She was scared of it, and it took quite a while to convince her that this was nothing to be afraid of. I put the bear on my lap and, with her hand in mine, let her touch it. After a little while, she started to touch the bear with one finger and smiled proudly at me. And finally, after a few more touches, she very carefully lifted the bear up and put him on her lap. And from then on, Renatchen and the bear became very good friends; she carried him around whenever she could, and he certainly had to sleep with her.

We spent the next days sightseeing and visiting and conferring with friends about where to live in the cheapest way possible during the summer months until we figured out where I would stay with Renatchen when Opi had to leave for America.

Renatchen already learned that other countries had other customs. She was used to going to Hyde Park with our London friends, where she could play happily on the green grass, often with other children. Here, every lawn was fenced in, and there were signs all over the place saying it was forbidden to step on the grass. She could not read the signs, of course, and the fences were no obstacle; she just crawled under them. We had quite some difficulty convincing her that she could not do that here. I still remember the difference between our healthy-looking child and the pale little boys and girls who walked very orderly with their mademoiselles, dressed very elegantly, all with hats and white gloves and rather pale faces. Poor kids—they didn't look as if they had much fun!

The most important thing we had to do now was renew my passport, which was valid only until August 31. It would have been impossible to get into another country without that. We also tried to get a permit of stay for me so there would be no trouble. We had already applied for it the day after our arrival in Paris. But since it had to go through all kinds of channels, and the French bureaucracy is famous for being very slow, every time we inquired about it at the prefecture, we got a polite regret that nothing had arrived from the department that issued these permits. We concentrated on getting my German passport extended. But under our special circumstances, that was not as easy as it sounded because I had to go to the German consulate. Opi was very hesitant and worried about that. Every embassy or consulate in a foreign country is the territory of the country it represents. So that meant the minute I entered the house of the consulate, I was on German soil again, so to speak. Opi was terribly afraid that the Germans might keep me there. There was, of course, the possibility that this could happen. The Reichsstatthalter for the State of Anhalt, the part of the country we had lived in, might certainly have been delighted to get me back, and since he could not get Opi, he could gladly hurt him by having me brought back to Germany.

Dr. Hanfstaengl had proved that this was a possibility in Berlin when he said he wanted to get me out of the country as quickly as possible.[12]

One of the people Opi got into contact with in Paris was an old friend and former colleague of his who now worked as a foreign correspondent and representative of the *Daily Herald* in Paris. This very helpful man, who understood quite well Opi's worries, wrote a letter for us to the German consul asking for an appointment to extend my passport. The connection with the English newspaper certainly helped. We got the appointment pretty quickly, and Mr. Schiff and I went to the consulate.[13] But Opi was quite nervous about this visit, and he waited outside the house with Renatchen, standing next to a French policeman who guarded the consulate. Opi was very determined to come into the building with the police if we were not allowed out within an hour. Well, all this was unnecessary. I got my passport extension without difficulty. When we wanted to leave, we were told to wait for a moment; the clerk who had given me my passport disappeared and came back a few moments later with a tall, military-looking man whom he introduced to us as the general consul. Without saying good day or greeting us, he turned to me and remarked in a very stern tone, "It was not necessary to trouble Mr. Schiff. You are a German citizen, and as such you are entitled to our help." With this reprimand, he turned around and disappeared into his office. Neither Mr. Schiff nor I believed that. The Nazis at that time still very much wanted the English on their side, and the publicity of our case was not at all to their liking. So, Mr. Schiff's mediation was certainly a big factor in this transaction. We left as quickly as possible, and I was certainly relieved to be out in the street and together with Opi and Renatchen again!

There was another event during our first weeks in Paris that is still very vivid in my memory. One evening, we attended a lecture in the German Club where Opi had spoken and where many refugees met. That evening, when we left the club with some friends, we heard loud cries: "Extra, extra!" I think I must explain a little. In 1934, not everyone possessed a radio, and there was no television, at least not in private households. As soon as some sensational news—a scoop—came out, the big newspapers printed leaflets or special editions with that news and sent them out on the street to sell them, which, of course, was very good business, especially for the paper that came out with it first. Opi and Max Brauer, who, after the war was over, went back to Germany and became the first mayor of Hamburg, and who was widely responsible for the quick restoration of this terribly bombed-out city, bought one. The news certainly was exciting, especially for people like us! It was a short report about the Blood Purge in Munich on the 30th of June in 1934! Röhm, the leader of the SA, and hundreds of SA troopers were killed in a surprise raid by the SS in the middle of the night in Munich, the headquarters of the SA![14] We could hardly believe this. It was no secret that the SS, the so-called elite troop of Hitler, never got along well with the SA. There had always been some sort of rivalry between these two groups. But this? We all became very excited. Did this mean that something had started in Germany to turn the tide?

We went into a little restaurant next to the club and found a large table in the background. After giving our orders and waiting until the waiter had brought everything, nearly everybody started to talk at once. What did all this mean for us? Was the Hitler spook over? Could we go home again? It took a little while until we all quieted down a bit and tried to analyze this disturbing news. The leaflet said very little. Maybe it was some kind of a hoax. Then we heard the cries of the newspaper boys, and Brauer went out into the street and came quickly back with another leaflet. The same story about killing SA leaders and men in Berlin! So that could mean the end of Hitler—there was a revolution starting in Germany! But those at the table who did not let their wishful thinking get in the way of their logical minds became more and more quiet, and I remember Opi saying very seriously, "The army will decide this. It all depends on whose side they are on. They have the weapons." Everybody became very quiet after that; there was no argument against it. The army was traditionally very conservative. They did not particularly care for Hitler, who, in their eyes, was an upstart, only a noncommissioned officer during the war. On the other hand, he wanted to make Germany strong again, and a great number of Germans were for him. We just had to wait and see what the next days would bring. We all got tired of debating the same thing back and forth and finally went home to our dingy little hotel room to try to get some sleep.

In the days that followed this exciting evening, we all bought every newspaper we could lay our hands on. What would happen now in Germany? But there were no signs of a revolution by the people. By and by, we found out that the events of June 30 were the result of the growing rivalry, at least partly, between Hitler and Röhm and the SS and the SA. If the army had stepped in at that time, maybe the terrible tragedy of the following years would have been avoided! It might have been the end of Hitler before he became the successor of President Hindenburg, who died a short time afterward. But the army evidently had other plans, and as history showed later on, they miscalculated the situation completely.

But all this came out much, much later, some of it long after the Second World War, when so many of the surviving Nazis were put on trial. Only one thing was very clear to us and our refugee friends. There was no revolution in Germany. The army was on Hitler's side. What could the German people have done, even if some of them would have wished to fight? They had no arms. The middle class was nearly completely for Hitler. The workers were divided between the Social Democrats and the Communists, who hated each other just as much as they hated the Nazis. It was quite hopeless. Only one thing was sure for us: there was no possibility for us to go back home in the near future.

It had become quite hot in Paris by now, and our little hotel room seemed to get smaller every day. Besides having to eat out so much, even eating only in very cheap restaurants, cost a lot of money, and I did not always get the food that I wanted for Renatchen, at least not the way I would have cooked for her. So we followed Mr. Schiff's advice, packed our belongings, and went by train to Normandy. We stayed one night there in the resort town Granville, and the next morning we continued our journey by bus to a little place called Carolles-Bourg. There, we went to a real estate agent who Mr. Schiff, who'd had some vacations in this neighborhood, had recommended to us. We looked at a few places and finally found a tiny house with two bedrooms, a big closed-in porch, and a nice kitchen—quite primitive, with an outhouse about fifty yards back in the garden. But it was clean, the beds were quite good, and, most importantly, the price was not too high. It was only a few minutes away from the beach on a very quiet dead-end street that ended at a very high wall that surrounded a monk's cloister. We could only hear the bell from the little chapel very early in the morning and all through the day when the monks went to mass. That was nearly the only interruption of the silence around us. The few houses on the little street were all surrounded by big gardens. A few of them were still closed, and the owners would not come before August, we were told. We didn't mind that a bit. We enjoyed the peaceful atmosphere after the heat and the noise in Paris. It was good for our strained nerves. And the big garden was heaven for Renatchen. It was not really cared for, so there was no "Forbidden" sign anywhere, and she could play wherever she wanted.

We unpacked and rearranged some of the furniture a little. With the books we had brought with us and with some flowers that I had picked in the garden, the place soon became home for us. There were some inconveniences—for instance, there was no running water, only a pump outside the kitchen door (something we had not noticed when we rented the place, and the real estate man had not told us), but we got used to that quickly. Opi filled the two pails we found in the kitchen for that purpose and the pitcher on the two washstands every evening, and I washed the vegetables and salad outside under the pump. A butcher and the country store were about ten minutes away from our place. That first evening, we had our first home-cooked meal together since that fateful day in March 1933, and a very happy one it was! Far away from all our troubles!

Before we went to bed that first night, we both stepped outside. But there was very little that we could see. It was a warm summer night, and the sky was cloudy, not one tiny star to be seen. Far away, we saw a light in one of the neighboring houses. Everything was very quiet and peaceful.

We must have slept for an hour or so when I woke up because a bright light was shining into my eyes. I sat up in bed and through the window, I saw the two very bright headlights of a car moving in the direction of our house. My heart started beating wildly. Who would come here so late at night? We were the last house on our street. Could it be some Nazis who had followed us here?

I woke up Opi. Somehow, he must have had the same thought. Without speaking, he rushed out of bed and over to the washstand and grabbed the water pitcher, the only weapon he could think of at the moment, the only thing that was heavy. We both crouched on the floor under the window and watched the headlights coming closer and closer. We were both trembling. Neither of us said a word; we just crouched there and pressed each other's hands. When the car was in front of our garden entrance, it stopped and a man got out, walked around for a moment, and stopped in front of our fence. Then, he went back into the car, and slowly the car turned and drove off. The room was pitch dark again. We sat for another moment on the floor, then we switched on the light, looked at each other, and started laughing. It took a little while until we could talk. But the whole scene made us realize how much we were still burdened by our past experiences.

Reunited with Gerhart and Living in Exile 179

It never occurred to us that the headlights we had seen could have belonged to a car whose driver was lost. So far, nobody knew our address; we had not written to a soul yet. But that would be a normal way of thinking in normal times. For us, our first reaction was always "This must be Nazis, and they are after us again!" Understandable?

Finally, we went to sleep again only to be awakened rudely by a terrific thunderstorm and rain gushing into our bedrooms through the open windows. We both got up quickly and started to dry the floor. Renatchen slept peacefully in her big double bed, which made her look as tiny as a baby again, completely unaware of all the commotion around her on the first night in our home. I was on my way to the kitchen to make us a sandwich—all this excitement had made us hungry—when a terrifying thunder and lightning at the same time seemed to make the house shake. Then the lights went out, and we stood in complete darkness. In that deep silence that surrounded us, the storm seemed to have ended with this last strong performance, and we heard a loud thump from Renatchen's room. Opi quickly lit a candle that stood on a small table near the washstand (as we heard the next day, nearly every thunderstorm produced such a blackout, so people were prepared for it), and we rushed into Renatchen's room. I ran over to her bed, and it was empty! I raced around it and there she was, lying in front of it on the floor, fast asleep! She must have rolled over in her sleep and just fell off. The bed was rather high, and I still cannot understand how she did not get hurt or at least wake up! I picked her up without waking her and put her between us in our bed, and finally we got some well-deserved sleep without further disturbances until the morning sun woke us up to a beautiful bright summer day.

After this eventful first night, our stay was quite peaceful and enjoyable in Carolles-Bourg. In the mornings, Opi worked on his book, *Reisetagebuch eines Deutschen Emigranten* (*Travel Diary of a German Emigrant*), which would be published by a Swiss publisher. Besides that, he had a lot of correspondence in preparation for his American trip to attend to. I did the little housework and laundry that was necessary. I really enjoyed that after being without a home for such a long time. Renate played in the garden whenever we were home. We had brought beautiful white sea sand up from the beach and put it under a shady tree. She played there every day with a little spoon and some little sand forms that we had bought for her in the village store, and she was completely happy. The big teddy bear leaned against the tree next to her, and from time to time she interrupted her playing, picked him up, hugged him, and talked to him in her own language. Shortly before lunch, we went to do the necessary shopping, and since there was no icebox or refrigerator, we had to do that nearly every day. We spent the afternoons at the beach. We usually sat down near a group of big rocks. At low tide, small water-filled shallow channels appeared between them, and Renatchen played very happily with all sorts of small shells and little stones. Sometimes a little French boy joined her, and it was fun to watch them. The language difference was no problem. Neither could speak very well yet, but once in a while we heard an energetic *"nein"* from Renatchen or a strong *"non"* from the little boy when either one picked up a shell or stone that the other thought belonged to her or him.

If the weather was not so good, we took long strolls in the dunes or walked along nice, shaded country roads, where we saw some very old well-kept farmhouses, mostly built with fieldstones, covered with vines or climbing rosebushes, all very beautiful. In the yards there were chickens, and in the meadows around them there were cows and horses—all very interesting for Renatchen, who had never seen those animals before. She always wanted to touch them, and we had a hard time getting her away from them or making it clear that it would be dangerous to do that. To our delight, we found a lot of blackberries and raspberries on the bushes along these picturesque country roads that nobody seemed to care for. I made some jam from them, and Renatchen loved them with a bit of sugar and milk. Since every kind of fruit was quite expensive in the village store, this was a welcome addition to our food budget.

The first five weeks passed by very quietly, and we were very happy in our little cottage. I tried not to think about our separation in the fall and to live in the present. But then some new difficulties arose. We had decided that Renatchen and I should stay in Switzerland during Opi's America trip. But for that, we, of course, needed visas and a residency permit for Renatchen and me. We had chosen a nice little old town, St. Gallen, not far from Lake Constance. The widow of a Jewish journalist who was killed by the Nazis had found refuge there.[15] She had very much recommended St. Gallen. It was a small town, very beautifully located in the mountains. She quoted us some prices, especially for apartments, and it was certainly less expensive than Basel, the city we had thought about at first. She was very helpful and even offered for us to stay with her until we could find an apartment in order to save the cost of a hotel room. I had never met her, but Opi had remembered her from some years back when he had been in Munich and had spent an evening with her and her husband in their home. So that decision was easy, and since she had three children, the youngest one a little older than Renatchen, our little girl might find a friend there.

So Opi wrote to the Swiss government in Bern and applied for a permit for me and Renatchen. He explained our situation in detail. He also told them that he needed only a transit visa for a month or so to get us settled, and then he would continue to America for his lecture tour. He told them that we would not require any support from the Swiss government, that we had some money, and that, of course, he would provide for us. He explained that neither he nor I would do any political work, that we just wanted to make our home there for the time being.

The answer came soon, and the decision was quite unexpected. Renatchen and I could stay for a certain time, but the permission for a few weeks' stay for Opi was denied due to his political background. And that from free, democratic Switzerland! We were quite upset and disappointed. What now? But then, Opi started writing letters to a lot of important Swiss people explaining our situation. The answers were mostly very sympathetic letters, but there was nothing they could do about this. Finally, Opi wrote to the president of the Swiss National Council (the Swiss Parliament), who was a Social Democrat by the name of Johannes Huber, a lawyer by profession and a wonderful person who became a very good friend of ours.[16] Renatchen and I spent many nice hours in his beautiful home. His wife was very fond of Renatchen, and we never went home without a bag full of *Gutzele* (cookies) for her. As he had helped many other people, he helped us too, and Opi got the permit to stay for four weeks with us in St. Gallen.

But now another problem arose. Would we get our furniture, or should we look for a little furnished apartment right away? As I said before, our furniture, what was left of it, was in a warehouse in Dessau. Was it still ours, or had the Nazis confiscated it? First, we thought the Posses could maybe find out. But then, we thought we might get them in trouble, so we dropped that idea. We chose the direct way. I wrote a very carefully worded letter to Commissioner Heisig, not mentioning Opi at all, explaining that I would like to live in St. Gallen, Switzerland, with Renatchen and asking if it would be possible to arrange for my furniture to be shipped there as soon as I found an apartment in a few weeks. We really did not have much hope, but Opi was right: why not try? To our pleasant surprise, we got an answer from Heisig. The furniture would be shipped as soon as I provided the bill for the warehouse and the transport to St. Gallen in advance. He said I should do this in the next four to five weeks, otherwise the furniture would be confiscated by the German state. Both bills came together with his letter. It sounded too good to be true—was it a trick? But we had to take the chance.

As I said before, when Opi was transferred from the Dessau jail to Oranienburg, I had sent all the money in our savings account to my parents in Freiburg for safekeeping, following the good advice of our friends, the Posses. So we sent the bills to them right away and asked them to take care of them as soon as possible.

Now we had to go back to Paris, where Opi had to get his boat ticket for America and then continue as quickly as possible to St. Gallen. Luckily, Opi's American visitor visa had arrived already; he had applied for it before we went to Carolles-Bourg, so we had to stay only a very short time in Paris.

We packed our few belongings in Carolles-Bourg very quickly. It was not quite so easy to leave the little house. We were really quite happy and at home in it after our first exciting night. And the thought of soon being separated from Opi again for quite a long time made the departure even more difficult. But that was the way it was, and the sooner we would be in St. Gallen, the more time we had to find the right apartment and get settled again before Opi had to leave. And the thought of seeing my parents again in the near future also helped me feel not quite so desperate about the long, lonely winter ahead of me.

Opi settled the things he still had to attend to in Paris more quickly than we'd thought. By the way, I never did get my permission for residence in France. We had tried again and again. I had really never needed it for anything. But when we crossed the French border in Basel, we saw that some people ahead of us had to give that little card to the French customs officials. We got a little nervous, but we had to go through. Opi marched ahead of me, showing them his passport and giving them his stay permit. I walked very close behind him, carrying Renatchen and holding my passport, and rushed through the gate. The French official shouted after me furiously, but there was nothing he could do because I was on Swiss soil now. I went to the Swiss customs official quite composed and gave him my passport with the

Swiss entrance visa—everything was all right now. I felt very good. We passed through the Swiss pass control, and everything, thanks to Mr. Huber, went smoothly and fast.

We had about four hours before the departure time of our train to St. Gallen. At that time, the Rosenbergs still lived in Freiburg, and we didn't know anybody in Basel.[17] It was long past lunchtime, and we were just deciding to go to a restaurant when we heard a woman's voice calling, "Ilse, Gert." We turned, and there was my mother running over to us! That was certainly a wonderful surprise! I had not seen her since she had visited me in Dessau, and so much had happened in the meantime. My father had wanted to come too, but he had a performance in the evening, and it would have been impossible for him to be back in time.

I can barely describe the next few hours. You can imagine how we all talked at the same time. We just stood there, surrounded by our luggage, and talked and talked. Finally, Renatchen brought us down to earth. She was hungry and thirsty and not very interested in the family reunion. She had said, "Guten Tag" very politely, but she saw no reason why she should kiss this strange woman. Mother understood that it would take a little time. We saw a nice-looking restaurant just across the street from the railway station, and after checking our suitcases at the luggage counter, we went over there. It was a nice, clean place, and after giving Renatchen her lunch, we put her on the small sofa in the booth; in a few minutes, she was fast asleep. We could now continue our conversation without her feeling neglected. And there was so much to talk about. Of course, I had written to my parents a few times, and they had responded. But we could not be sure that the Nazis had not opened our letters, so we did not dare to say too much or ask any questions about the things we were most interested in. The slightest criticism could be dangerous for them or my brothers.

So far, the Nazis had left my family in peace. But just the same, life was not very pleasant for people who were not convinced Nazis. Mother told us that quite a few people whom they never had expected to be Nazis were running around now, wearing the swastika on their lapels and shouting, "Heil Hitler!" at the slightest provocation. So my parents kept more and more to themselves, seeing only the very old friends they really could trust. My younger brother, Wolfgang, was now an apprentice of a very well-known cameraman at the time, Sepp Allgeier, who specialized in skiing and mountain movies.[18] And Joachim had a good and interesting job in the radio department at the University of Freiburg. All this was new to us. My parents only mentioned in their letters that the "boys" were well. This way, they hoped to prevent any connection between my brothers and Opi. It sounds a little naive now, but at that time, one could not be careful enough. Whatever the reason, luckily, my family never had any difficulties during that terrible time, even though they were related to us.

The few hours that we were together passed very quickly, and it was time to go to our trains. Mother's left a little earlier than ours, so we could still see her off. Then, we picked up our luggage and went to our train. The trip was only two hours, and it was still daylight when we arrived in St. Gallen. I had been standing at the window for the last twenty minutes to get the first glimpse of the town that would be Renatchen's and my home for the next ten months or so. I really liked what I saw. St. Gallen is situated in a valley on the outskirts of the Alps, a very old town of about seventy thousand inhabitants. Since the railway station was in the middle of the city, I already got a glimpse of the town from the train, and I liked what I saw.

When we stepped off the train, a woman waved to us and came over quickly. It was the lady who had written to us, a Mrs. Fechenbach. Opi introduced me to her. She welcomed us very heartily and helped us bring our luggage to a taxi. I left the conversation to Opi and tried to see as much as I could on the short trip to Mrs. Fechenbach's apartment. There, her three children greeted us, and they tried very hard to make friends with Renatchen. That wasn't so easy at first. The children were very temperamental and scared her. She was not used to so much going on around her. She just looked at them with big eyes and held tight onto my skirt. But then the little girl went and got her doll, and that broke the ice; after a little while, the two little girls started playing with the doll together.

Finally, it was bedtime for the children, and Mrs. Fechenbach, Opi, and I sat together and talked things over. She had already looked up some ads in the newspaper and marked them for us. She had a very good map of the city for us, so we could start with the apartment hunting the next morning. She offered to keep Renatchen with her, and we gratefully accepted that offer.

Well, it took a few days, but we found a very nice apartment with a bath and a beautiful balcony on one of the hillsides of the city. The small apartment was well kept, and the owners seemed to be very nice and friendly. On the ground floor was a tiny little restaurant, or rather a *conditorei*, as it is called in Europe, where one is served coffee, tea, and all sorts of wonderful cakes. It was connected to a bakery and small grocery store, so whatever I needed besides meat I could purchase right there instead of going down to the city. A three-car electric train had a stop in front of the house, so if one did not feel like walking up and down to the city, transportation was easy.

On the other side of the street was a long and very high wall with a small entrance door at one end of it. Only some old trees and a small church steeple could be seen from the street. We were told that a very old nun's cloister was behind the wall. The nuns belonged to one of those very strict orders where nuns, after they have entered the cloister grounds and taken the veil, are never allowed to see the outside world again. I don't know if these orders still exist. Over the years, the Catholic Church has become more modernized and more liberal in many ways. These nuns' entire lives took place behind the wall. Whatever food they needed, they produced themselves. They cultivated the garden and fields; they had chickens and some cows. Whatever products they did not need, they were allowed to sell. I bought all my vegetables and eggs there, but I never saw a nun. When I wanted something, I had to ring a tiny bell outside the door on the wall. A long chain, which was operated from inside the house, opened the door. The door to a rather dark and cold hall (even in summer) opened. On one side of the wall, there was a big opening in which a metal cylinder was turned around until an opening with shelves in it was in front of me. In the back of the cylinder wall, there were a few small holes, through which a woman's voice asked me what I wanted. When I had given my order, she asked me to put the money onto one of the shelves, and then the cylinder was turned around again. After a short time, the cylinder was turned again, and my eggs or vegetables I had asked and paid for appeared, and I could take them out. The voice said a friendly "God bless you," and the cylinder turned again. The nun could see me through the little holes, but I never saw her. But I found all this out much later. I was very much intrigued by this old cloister right away, especially when I found out that one could see over the wall into the garden of it from the balcony of the apartment. When we moved in, I watched the nuns very often on Sundays when they walked in the garden, enjoying the sunshine. It looked like a beautiful painting of the Middle Ages—these women in their black habits and their big white starched caps, walking between flowerbeds and high old trees.

The apartment was very nice, with beautifully kept parquet floors. The living room was especially attractive, with birch paneling from floor to ceiling. It made it so warm looking, even without any furniture in it. The landlady and her two daughters, who were about my age, were very friendly, and when we told them a little about the reason we had come to live in Switzerland, they became very sympathetic in such a nice way that I had the feeling I would really be at home there. The neighborhood was very attractive, only a few well-kept private houses with big gardens around them. A beautiful forest with comfortable footpaths was just five minutes away from the house. The only inconvenience was the distance from the city. But I would not have to go down there very often. Most of the things I needed I could get in the little grocery store or in the bakery. I was told that a farmer came around twice a week with fresh vegetables, and what I could not get at the cloister, I could buy from him, so I had my choice. And if I wanted meat, the landlady told me I should just let her know what I wanted, and she would have it sent up from the butcher together with her order. Otherwise, I had not much money to spend anyhow, certainly not in the first few months, so I really did not have to go to the city very often. So after we had figured out what we could spend, we rented it. Opi felt good about it too since there were those two young girls, and he hoped I would have some company this way. Renatchen, who usually didn't make friends with strangers very quickly, already got along quite well with them. But then they had bribed her with a big piece of chocolate cake.

When we returned to Mrs. Fechenbach's, we found a letter from the freight department of the railway: our furniture had arrived! They had enclosed the list of the moving company, and to Opi's delight, it mentioned six boxes of books. But Opi was greatly disappointed when we went to the depot. There were no boxes with books. The Nazis had confiscated them at the last moment, as well as Opi's desk, which had some sentimental value for him since he had inherited it from his father after his death. Most of our personal documents and papers were in this desk, so they kept all that too. But otherwise, everything else seemed to be there, even the boards of our bookshelves, which our friends had taken apart when they moved me into the small apartment when I could not afford the big one anymore. But before we could order a moving van for our furniture, we had to sign a paper that obliged us not to sell any of the furniture in the next five years; otherwise, we would have to pay customs duty, which was rather high.

Our next step was to get a mover. But that took a few days since most of them were fully booked. Finally, we were lucky, and we could move in. In the meantime, we had brought nearly all of our luggage to the apartment. Opi had started to work on an unfinished table to use as a desk. He had sanded and varnished it, so we already had a piece of our "own" furniture there. The few books we had were put in a pile on the floor. It sounds funny, but to us, it started to look a little bit like a home.

The day our furniture was supposed to arrive, we went to the apartment with the rest of our things very early in the morning. A few minutes later, our bell rang, and when I opened the door, the two girls, Mia and Pia [the landlady's daughters], stood there. They looked a little embarrassed and seemed a bit excited. Then Mia, the older one, told us that they'd had to go into the apartment after we'd left the day before. The electrician had to fix something. When they looked around, they had seen Opi's book, *Oranienburg*, on the floor and picked it up. When they saw his name as the author, they had taken it downstairs with them and read it together. They had become so excited that they had hardly slept the night before. Of course, they had heard a little bit about what was going on in Germany, but this? They were so happy that we all were out of Germany and now in Switzerland and that we would live with them! While we were talking and answering a few questions, the mother came up too. And without saying a word, she came over to me and took me in her arms. It was a heartwarming moment, and I had the good feeling to have gained some real friends.

A little while later, our furniture arrived; the next few days were filled with unpacking and arranging our things, and we enjoyed every minute of it. Renatchen was quite excited with so many boxes standing around, and we finally found the one with most of her toys in it. We let her unpack them, and she had a wonderful time in a corner of her room playing with them, quite oblivious to all the commotion around her.

The next two weeks were restful and happy. It was the end of September, and the leaves started to change color a little bit. But the days were still sunny and warm. I remember the beautiful walks we took along the meadows or through the forest to the mountaintop, from which we had a great view. Renatchen, who was only a little over two years old, walked bravely with us. From time to time, we put her into her little stroller so that she could rest a little, but never for long because there were too many interesting things to be picked up—pine cones, tiny little flowers, mushrooms—everything was interesting. She had now learned to talk a lot, and being very proud of this new achievement, she very seldom stopped.

We enjoyed our apartment, and we had a home again! It had been very nice in the little cottage in France. But now we were surrounded by our own things, and that made a big difference. Besides, we appreciated having a bathtub again and not taking long walks to the outhouse, especially Renatchen, who could now have a bath every evening again. Only our empty bookshelf looked sort of strange to us after we had put the few books we had on it. I started to fill in the empty spaces with vases; the three empty bottom shelves I hid behind a dark curtain, and we both felt that was an improvement.

Ilse's and Gerhart's reunion on Saturday, May 26, 1934, was a big press event in Britain, likely because of the uniqueness of their story amid the rise of the antidemocratic Nazi Germany in the middle of Europe. One paper described their dramatic reunion as a "love story from a novel" (red roses and all) and equated it to a "[triumph] not only over imprisonment under the Hitler regime, but over an extraordinarily cruel attempt to make the wife believe that her husband was no longer faithful and had no desire to see her again."[19] Their reunion also received a lot of press because MPs were involved in Ilse's and Renate's release. *The Daily Telegraph* described Mrs. Tate as "the fairy godmother."[20] Mrs. Tate also received a bouquet of spring flowers that had been sent "by a number of wives and mothers who admired her energy in the cause of a family reunion."[21] Even Ilse mentioned above how this would benefit Mrs. Tate politically. After their reunion, Gerhart and Ilse spent their week in London meeting with several important MPs. They also had to be aware of people who were Nazi spies—people like Hans Wesemann—who were trying to find out more about German refugees or trying to use them for their access to these MPs; after all, Nazi Germany was still trying to win over Great Britain.

After a week in London, Ilse and Gerhart left for Norway, where members of the Norwegian Social Democratic Party had invited Gerhart for a lecture tour. They were constantly on the move, and everything about their trip was very positive with the exception of the encounter that Ilse had with a pro-Nazi journalist, Vidkun Quisling.[22] Leaving Renate with friends of friends in London, Gerhart and Ilse had some time to themselves to discuss their future plans—namely, his lecture tour in the United States, which would result in another long separation. They had to figure out where she and Renate would stay while he was in America, and they considered several options. She was quite resistant to the idea of leaving Germany permanently at that point and even thought she might be able to return. In these moments, Ilse provided insight as to why more Jews or political opponents did not simply leave Germany immediately after Hitler came to power. Even after having been imprisoned by the Nazis, she still said it was difficult to leave a country one loved his or her whole life and live somewhere else without a known future. Additionally, there was also the question of if one could even emigrate elsewhere. This was at the height of the Depression, and most countries did not want refugees. This was a problem for some Jews but probably not for well-connected people who were relatively financially stable, like Gerhart and Ilse. In order to convince Ilse that they could not go back to Germany, Gerhart told her that it was the Nazis who had started the Reichstag fire.[23] She had trouble being convinced at first, but he used this information and other things the Nazis had done to persuade her that Germany was no longer a safe place for them.

Gerhart clearly had an advantage with his European-wide political connections, and relied on many German Social Democrats living in exile. They helped him escape from Germany and get quickly established in Czechoslovakia. They helped him facilitate the release of his wife and daughter through transnational attention and intervention. They aided him in creating a life in exile for his family in France and Switzerland, and they helped him earn a living in various European countries (for example, through invited lectures).

While in Paris, Gerhart encountered other German exiles and SPD members, including Victor Schiff and Max Brauer. It was alongside these other German refugees that Ilse and Gerhart learned about the Night of Long Knives. Also known as the Röhm Purge, it was a series of murders that took place between June 30 and July 2, 1934. This was when Hitler ordered the purge of the SA, which he saw as a threat to his power because of how large they had grown. The SS carried out the murders of top SA leaders, including the head of the SA, Ernst Röhm, and used the opportunity to kill other political enemies.[24]

After hearing the details of the purge shortly after it happened, Gerhart and Ilse debated with their friends and other refugees what this meant for the Nazi regime and for Germany. They thought it could result in the toppling of Hitler's regime or the beginning of a revolution of the German people. They speculated how the army would react, recognizing that this would have a large impact on the path Germany took moving forward. This certainly coincided with the message that Gerhart preached on his antifascist speaking tour throughout the United States just a few months later. Instead of seeing the Night of Long Knives as a final consolidation of Hitler's power (which is the view that many historians held much later on), Gerhart saw the blood purge as "a confession of weakness."[25] In front of several hundred people at the University of Texas in Austin, he claimed that the Nazi Party may be disintegrating, initiated by the fact that Hitler had disappointed so many of his followers by "not carrying out the many promises that he had made when he was ascending to power." The June 1934 purge, in Gerhart's opinion, was one such example of the "internal decomposition of the Nazi group."[26]

It was only later that Gerhart, Ilse, and the rest of the world would realize that the purge only cemented the relationship between the Nazi regime and the army and enabled Hitler to claim absolute power, especially after the death of President Paul von Hindenburg a month later (August 2, 1934). A day before Hindenburg's death, Hitler proclaimed that upon Hindenburg's death, the offices of chancellor and president would be combined. Thus, when Hindenburg died, Hitler assumed the powers of the president without ever assuming the office itself and took on a new title: *Der Führer* (the leader).[27] Hitler held a referendum on the merging of the offices of chancellor and president on August 19, 1934, and received overwhelming positive support for this from the German people.[28]

After realizing that the army was on Hitler's side, Ilse recalled some of the other reasons why uniform resistance against Hitler seemed futile. As a whole, she claimed there was little the German people could do because they lacked arms. The middle class overwhelmingly supported Hitler, and the workers were still divided, with some supporting the Communists and some supporting the Social Democrats, who still hated each other. With all this in mind, Ilse became engulfed in a sense of hopelessness. And it was at this point that she realized they could not go back to Germany anytime soon.

They spent the rest of summer in Carolles-Bourg on the coast of France, which was a very peaceful time for them. Gerhart prepared for his trip to America and started a new book. Meant to be a sequel to *Oranienburg*, *Reisetagebuch eines deutschen Emigranten*, which was published in 1936, was about his life in Europe and America after he escaped Oranienburg. The book discussed his time in Czechoslovakia, England, Norway, Belgium, France, and Switzerland and then his antifascist speaking tour throughout America. Other than that, it was a lot of quiet family time that summer. For some time after they left Germany, even when they were in this serene village, they always thought the Nazis were coming for them. Clearly, their past experiences still haunted them. They spent the end of their time in Carolles-Bourg making arrangements for Ilse and Renate's longer stay in St. Gallen, Switzerland. This, of course, required acquiring the appropriate documentation, which meant Gerhart once again took advantage of his connections among Social Democrats in Switzerland to help them.

Once they moved to St. Gallen, they immediately gained the sympathy of their landlord and her daughters, who read *Oranienburg* after finding it in Ilse's apartment. Like many people living abroad, they did not realize the full extent of things going on in Germany, but after reading his account, they were more than willing to help. This was perhaps a premonition of how most people they encountered might act once they left Germany and then Europe.

Notes

1. Tate went on to have a long career in Parliament, serving from 1931 until 1945. She spent much of her career advocating for women's rights.

2. Blanche Elizabeth Campbell Dugdale was a British Zionist and the niece of Arthur James Balfour. For more, see https://www.jewishvirtuallibrary.org/dugdale-blanche-elizabeth-campbell-xoobo.

3. Based on the details Ilse provided about "Wesemayer," she was talking about Hans Wesemann, who was a German journalist in the 1920s, when Gerhart was also working as a journalist. Whether or not Wesemann and Seger had crossed paths in Berlin at a press meeting is unknown, but it is certainly possible based on the timeline.

4. William Francis Hare, 5th Earl of Listowel, or Lord Listowel, was a member of the Labour Party in the House of Lords.

5. The timeline and location Ilse described here also further confirmed that she and Gerhart likely met Hans Wesemann. Wesemann had become a Gestapo agent—a spy, according to Ilse. He fled Germany in 1933 to Britain and agreed to provide the German embassy in London with information about other refugees—people like Ilse and Gerhart. He kidnapped a German pacifist journalist, Berthold Jacob, in Basel, Switzerland, on March 9, 1935. He was arrested in September 1935 by local police in Basel, which would have been approximately a year and a half after the Segers met him in May 1934. In May 1936, Wesemann confessed to this kidnapping and was found guilty by a Basel court and imprisoned until 1938. After his release, he was deported from Switzerland. See Palmier, *Weimar in Exile*, 432–33 and "Nazi Agent Admits Kidnapping Writer: Says in Basle That the German Embassy in London Was Base of Nazi Secret Police," *New York Times*, May 6, 1936, 19. See also Barnes and Barnes, *Nazi Refugee Turned Gestapo Spy* and Bernard Degen, "Jacob-Affäre," *Historisches Lexikon der Schweiz*, January 30, 2014, https://hls-dhs-dss.ch/de/articles/017338/2014-01-30.

6. Rudolf Olden worked as a journalist for a number of publications in the Weimar Republic, including *Berliner Tageblatt*, one of the most important liberal German publications of the era. He escaped Germany to Prague the day after the Reichstag fire, and eventually settled in London where he oversaw the German PEN (Poets, Essayists, Novelists) Club in exile. See Palmier, *Weimar in Exile*, pages 93, 144, 150.

7. His second wife was Ika Olden (née Halpern) and they were married in 1933.

8. Abba Hillel Silver was an American rabbi in Cleveland, Ohio, and an avid Zionist.

9. Joseph Goebbels was the Reichsminister for Public Enlightenment and Propaganda during the Third Reich.

10. Benesch is likely Edvard Beneš, whom Ilse mistook as being the president of Czechoslovakia at this time. See endnotes of chapter 2.

11. I am unsure what she meant by this or why the sender may have written this other than to indicate his own background.

12. Ilse misused Dr. here to refer to Hanfstaengl.

13. Victor Schiff worked as a foreign policy editor for *Vorwärts*, a daily newspaper published by the SPD, between 1920 and 1933. This was likely when he befriended Gerhart, who was also working as a journalist at this time. After the Nazis came to power, Schiff was arrested twice and thus emigrated to Great Britain and then France in 1933. When Ilse and Gerhart met up with him again in 1934, he was working as a correspondent for the *Daily Herald* and for various German exile newspapers. He was also the representative for the Sopade in Paris, which was why he would have been in contact with Gerhart once he arrived there. See "Schiff, Victor," in *Biographisches Handbuch der deutschsprachigen Emigration nach 1933–1945*, 645.

14. Ernst Röhm was a close friend of Hitler's and cofounder and leader of the SA.

15. The Jewish journalist who was killed by the Nazis was Felix Fechenbach. He was also a Social Democrat and editor of a Social Democratic journal in Detmold, so it is not surprising that he and Gerhart had crossed paths in Germany. The Nazis arrested him in March 1933 and placed in "protective custody." He was shot and killed in a car on the journey to Dachau concentration camp on August 7, 1933. His widow, Irma Fechenbach (née Epstein) managed to escape to Switzerland with their three children. See "Felix Fechenbach," Gedenkstätte Deutscher Widerstand, https://www.gdw-berlin.de/en/recess/biographies/index_of_persons/biographie/view-bio/felix-fechenbach/?no_cache=1.

16. Johannes Huber was a Swiss politician who had at one point promised his support to the Communists on trial for the Reichstag fire. See Palmier, *Weimar in Exile*, 316.

17. It is unclear who the Rosenberg's were, but presumably, they were friends of Ilse's from Freiburg. Ilse also refers to a Werner Rosenberg who lived in Basel with his wife and son in chapter 8.

18. Josef "Sepp" Allgeier was a German cinematographer. He went on to become Leni Riefenstahl's lead cameraman for *Triumph des Willens* (*Triumph of the Will*), a propaganda film that Hitler commissioned in 1935 about the Nazi Party Congress in Nuremberg. See Reimer and Reimer, *The A to Z of German Cinema*, 57.

19. "Woman from Nazi Prison Camp Free by Efforts of Mrs. Tate, M.P., Reunion in London with Husband," *Daily Telegraph*, May 28, 1934.

20. Ibid.

21. "Wife's Release from Germany, Reunion with Refugee Husband," *Daily Sketch*, May 28, 1934.

22. At the time that Ilse encountered Quisling, a decorated Norwegian army officer and politician, he had recently founded the Norwegian fascist party *Nasjonal Samling* (National Union). On April 9, 1940, the first day Norway entered the Second World War, Quisling attempted to seize power in the world's first radio-broadcast coup d'état, but the German occupiers refused to support his government, and the British press overwhelmingly condemned this as an act of treason. From 1942 to 1945, he jointly administered the Norwegian state with the German Reichskommissar, Josef Terboven. His pro-Nazi puppet government, known as the Quisling regime, collaborated with the Nazis, including in the Final Solution. See Dahl, *Quisling*.

23. See my comments on the debate about who set the fire in chapter 3. Gerhart's circle would have been among the group that gave weight to the idea that the Nazis had started the fire.

24. "Röhm Purge," *Holocaust Encyclopedia*, United States Holocaust Memorial Museum, https://encyclopedia.ushmm.org/content/en/article/roehm-purge.

25. "Assails Hitler: German Here Hits Nazis," *New Orleans Item*, April 9, 1935.

26. William Weeg, "Dr. Seger Declares Nazi Decomposition Has Already Begun," newspaper unknown, April 13, 1935.

27. See "Gesetz über das Staatsoberhaupt des Deutschen Reichs," August 1, 1934, http://www.documentarchiv.de/ns/stobrhpt.html, and Shirer, *The Rise and Fall of the Third Reich*, 226–27.

28. Zurcher, "The Hitler Referenda," 91–99.

8

Another Separation from Gerhart and Planning for America

At the beginning of this chapter, Gerhart's departure day for America has arrived.

The time passed by so quickly, and the day of Opi's departure arrived. It was not easy for both of us. We had already lost nearly a year out of our life together, and now there would be at least another ten months until we could be together again. Of course, this separation was different. We were both in friendly countries, no Gestapo, no SA, no SS. We could go wherever we pleased, and we could write to each other as often as we wanted to. Nobody would censor our letters. I told myself all that, but it didn't help very much. We both would be very lonely again!

I had told Renatchen that her father would have to go on a long trip. It did not mean very much to her until we were at the railroad station, and Opi picked her up to give her a last goodbye kiss. She absolutely wanted to go with him into the train and started to cry bitterly when he didn't take her and the train started moving slowly away. It took all my willpower not to do the same at that moment. We stood and waved until the train was out of sight. Then we went back to the little electric train to get up to our place again. The train ride consoled Renatchen a bit, and soon her mind was occupied with what she saw from the window, and she told me all about it.

When we arrived at our stop, which was just in front of our apartment, both of the landlady's daughters were standing in front of their store, waving to us. They insisted that we had to come inside and have some coffee and cake with them before going up to the apartment. I think they knew exactly how I felt and that it would be good not to be alone at the moment. We really became very good friends, just as Opi had hoped, and we had quite a few nice cozy evenings, sitting in my living room around the big, warm tile stove. We had long discussions about Nazi Germany and the Catholic Church, which was also in trouble since most of the members of the clergy were much more outspoken than their opponents from the Protestant Church. Since the Thalmanns were very strict Catholics, I learned a lot about the Catholic Church in those interesting debates we had.[1] Both girls were quite intelligent and much more liberal than their mother, who was one of the most religious people I have ever met. So absolutely sincere. Her strong, unwavering faith had helped her through many difficult times in her life, and through her strength, she helped her children and nearly everybody around her. She really was kindness in a person. I really was lucky to find a home in her house. It helped a lot to get through that long winter a little easier.

The girls were very interested in Opi's experiences and impressions of America and waited for a letter from him nearly as eagerly as I did. I always read them the parts of his letters I thought might interest them. They had started to pick up books about America in the public library, and quite often we read them together in the evening and discussed their contents. I remember that none of us could really imagine what a drugstore was. For us, it meant an apothecary, and that was the way it was translated in those books, where one had a prescription made up or bought ointments or cough medicine, headache pills, things like that. But ice cream, frankfurters, soft drinks? We really couldn't imagine all this together in one store. Besides, our drugstores always smelled of some medication or disinfectant. How could one be tempted to eat in there?

There were other things that seemed funny to us. From time to time, Opi sent me some magazines and newspapers. They were also different from those we were used to in Germany and Switzerland. For instance, one difference was that an article started on the front page and then continued ten or more pages back in the newspaper so that one had to wrestle with the paper if one wanted to finish the story. There were also some funny misunderstandings. For instance, there were sales of closets advertised. Of course, I translated *closet* with the German word *Klosett*, which means toilet, and couldn't understand why one had to build one's own toilet in America when one rented an apartment! And there were more of these little misunderstandings, but these are the ones I remember best.

I tried very hard to improve my English during that time, but there was nobody who spoke the language fluently. Since Mia and Pia knew just as much or as little English as I did, and it had been nearly ten years since I had left school, I didn't have the feeling that I had made much progress.

In November, my parents came to visit us, and that was a wonderful time for all of us. Mother came first, and my father, whom I had not seen since he had visited me in the concentration camp, came for a weekend since he could not be away from the theater for a long time. But later on, they came quite often, and one day, my two brothers came too. They had made the whole trip from Freiburg to St. Gallen on their bicycles—quite a trip![2]

Renatchen got along fine with my parents, and it was always a very sad day when they had to leave again. Mother was a great help to me just by her being there, which certainly was appreciated; after all, she had my two brothers to care for, and I knew she never liked to go anywhere without my father. But she knew I needed her too. She made a whole new wardrobe for Renatchen, who by now had outgrown nearly all of her clothes and certainly needed new things. She always brought some material with her when she visited, and Renatchen became a very well-dressed young lady who was proud of her new clothes. I especially remember one dress that Mother made for her out of an old dress of mine. I had bought it for our honeymoon trip. It was now completely out of fashion, and I was delighted that it could still be useful and that it became one of Renatchen's favorites.

In spite of the frequent visits from my mother—or, when possible, from both of my parents—the winter was quite long, and I had the feeling that the end of June, the time Opi hoped to come back, would never come. Whenever the weather permitted, Renatchen and I took long walks in the afternoon, and once in a while we went down to the city or visited with Mrs. Fechenbach, or she visited with her three children. But that was always a bit difficult; the children were very wild and noisy, and Renatchen did not care very much for them. She was not used to their wild games. And when they left, I had to straighten out the whole apartment; there was not one toy in its place, and quite frequently something was broken and pushed under the bed. So, I did not encourage her visiting too much. Besides, we were very different in our ways; we just could not warm up to one another! I think I now know why. Deep down in her heart, she resented me. We had gone through the same hard experiences, but she had lost her husband,

and mine was still alive and was coming back to me. I am afraid I was too young at the time and too occupied with myself and with our future to give much thought to her feelings, to try to understand her better. It was always easier when we met at a mutual friend's house, the Hubers', for instance, or another couple I had met through the Hubers.

One day shortly before Christmas, I had an exciting and unexpected visitor. It was a rainy, cold, unfriendly day, and we could not go out of the house. I was looking forward to a boring afternoon and felt quite low when the doorbell rang. I opened the door, and there stood an old friend from Dessau, a construction worker from the Junker factory with whom we had worked through all the election campaigns, one of those people who had visited me in the concentration camp at Rosslau. He greeted me with a big grin and a hearty "Guten Tag, Genossin Seger, wie geht es Ihnen denn?"[3] I was so surprised to see someone from Dessau that I nearly embraced him, which I guess would have embarrassed him quite a bit. We shook hands for a while, and I nearly cried, I was so excited. So many memories came back all of a sudden. I asked him in and was glad that Renatchen was still napping so that we could have some time without being interrupted. He told me that he worked at the Dornier factory, another German airplane factory, in a sort of exchange program. This factory was in Konstanz am Bodensee, not very far from the Swiss border and St. Gallen. The Posses had given him my address, and on his first day off since being in Konstanz, he took the train to St. Gallen to visit me.

My first question, of course, was about Leni and Otto. Were they all right? I had heard so little from them, just a few very short letters telling me that they were well, saw very few people, and stayed home most of the time. Now our friend told me a little more about them. So far, they had been unmolested. The only setback Otto had suffered since I had left was that he did not get the position as principal of his school, which normally would have been due to him. Instead, they promoted a younger teacher at the same school to this post, who was known as a very active member of the Nazi Party. Otto was transferred to another school, far away from where the Posses lived, and certainly not as a principal. They were very disappointed for two reasons: first, it hit his pride because Otto was a good and very devoted teacher, and second, they had counted very much on the raise in salary. But they took it in stride; there was nothing they could do about it. A complaint to the new rulers would only bring trouble. They did not want me to mention anything about this in my letters because they were not sure if their mail was read in the post office; the letters sometimes looked that way. They had asked our mutual friend to tell me all about this, and they asked me to understand why their letters were so short and few, and that I should be very careful about everything I wrote to them. As a matter of fact, they would rather correspond with my parents and hear about us this way, for they felt this would be safer. They wanted me to know that they missed us very much but were glad for us to be out of Germany. I missed them very much too. I would miss their letters, short as they were, too. But I could understand their uneasiness quite well—in Germany at that time, one never knew what to expect!

Our friend brought me a book that the Posses had borrowed from us a long time ago, which I then put into our empty bookshelf—one more book! But he also brought the first edition of Hitler's *Mein Kampf* from the year 1932. He had lent these two books to a former editor of the *Dessauer Volkszeitung* shortly before he was put in jail. Opi was very delighted when I wrote him about that because it became quite useful for him later on in his work at the *Neue Volkszeitung* here in New York and for his lectures too.

I heard a lot about Dessau that afternoon. Mostly sad things. Quite a few members of our party were now in the Rosslau concentration camp. Some of the people I was there with were discharged now. But they kept very much to themselves. They always felt watched. Nobody trusted anybody. Life was not very amusing in Nazi Germany now, unless you were a full-fledged Nazi and very loud about it too. Since my visitor was a bachelor, he did not mind being in Konstanz for a while. Nobody knew him there, and he could go wherever he wanted to.

Something else he told me—all our books had landed in the Dessau paper mill! He had a friend working there who had told him that some weeks ago, a truck had arrived there with boxes and boxes of books. The workers were told to unload the boxes, bring them into the mill, and unpack them right away so they could be processed as soon as possible. One calls it "recycling" today. Naturally, nobody dared ask any questions since the driver of the truck was in full SA uniform. When the driver left, the men started to unpack the books and, of course, opened some of them. They found Opi's name in every one they opened, so they knew whose books they had to destroy. My visitor's friend, an old Social Democrat, let one or two books disappear in his overalls to keep them as a souvenir.

After my visitor had gone and Renatchen was in bed, I wrote a long letter to Opi about this eventful day. I was very sad, not only about the loss of our books. We were rather resigned to that already. Of course, we had still thought that there might be a chance to get some of them back sometime much later. Now, that was settled once and for all. But what made me even more sad was the idea that in a country of high cultural standard like Germany, books were destroyed not because of their content (there were so many books that had nothing to do with politics—books about art, philosophy, classics, history) but just because they belonged to a man who had fought against the ideas of the Nazis because he felt they were wrong and would do so much harm to the country! This narrow-mindedness, this stupidity, was so hard to understand! If the Nazis took them to punish us, why could they not give them to a library, at least those that had nothing to do with politics? I remembered the SA man, a man of about forty or so who came to me shortly before I moved into my little apartment. He was interested in our apartment. I told him that if he could use the bookshelves, I would sell them to him for a very reasonable price. He looked at me with contempt. "I would have no use for them," he said. "We National Socialists have no time for books. We have more important things to do." Well, that was not only the opinion of this man. There was a lot of hatred for intellectuals in the speeches of lower-class party leaders; the remark of this man fit into the overall picture. Be a good Nazi, and there is no thinking required!

It was now the day before Christmas. I had bought a little Christmas tree for us and some small gifts for Renatchen. My mother had sent a Christmas package with very good Christmas cookies and a piece of Stollen and some gifts.[4] She added a big fir branch to the package so the whole thing smelled like Christmas. But I did not feel very Christmassy. This was now the second Christmas without Opi. I knew he would be in Los Angeles, but that did not mean anything to me, nor did the people he might be with.[5] Or would he be alone in a cold, unfriendly hotel room? I knew that his thoughts would be with us as mine would be with him. But that did not help either of us very much! I just went to look for the box with the tree trimmings to have it handy for the next day and to see if I needed anything when the doorbell rang. Who could that be? I opened it. Two men were standing at the front door, one carrying a very big box. The older man, a very well-dressed gentleman, took off his hat and asked if I was Mrs. Seger. When I confirmed that, he smiled at me and said, "Mrs. Seger, I bring you the very best regards from your husband. This package here is his Christmas gift to you. May we come in and unpack it?" I showed them into the living room, and there the younger man opened the big box, and out came a beautiful radio! "Where would you like to have it? We would like to connect it for you and try it out," the older man said. I quickly took the gramophone off my little music table, and the younger man put the radio there. Luckily, there was a plug in the wall right behind it, and in a few minutes, I heard music floating through my living room! The radio not only looked beautiful, but its tone was no comparison to my little gramophone—the "Rührmusik" (stir music) as Renatchen had named it. It was one of those that one still had to turn on with a handle, just like the starter of an old-fashioned car. The two men explained to me how the radio functioned, how to get different stations, how to regulate the tone, and so on. I really was overwhelmed. That radio would bring a lot of the outside world to me. There would be concerts from Rome or London, lectures, all sorts of things to which I could listen—it certainly would make my life less monotonous, especially during these long winter evenings!

Finally, I asked how this had come about. The older man explained to me that he was the owner of the biggest music store in town. I knew this store. I had passed by it quite often when I was down in the city with Renatchen. I had stood in front of its show windows and looked at the beautiful radios among the other instruments there, and now I had one in my own living room. I could hardly believe it. But now, I turned my attention back to my visitor. He told me that Opi had come into his store shortly before he left for America and had looked around in the store and picked this model. He told the owner that he would send a check to him shortly before Christmas, and he would like to have the radio delivered on the 23rd or 24th of December. The owner agreed, and since he thought that this was such a nice idea, he decided to come himself and bring me Opi's greetings in person. Well, if he wanted to see a happy person, he certainly saw one! I thanked him profoundly and wished him and the young man a very Merry Christmas too. When I closed the door behind them, I rushed into Renatchen's room. She just started to wake up. I took her out of bed and ran with her into the living room and turned on the radio. I don't remember what kind of music I heard, but I danced around the room with Renatchen in my arms. She looked a bit bewildered at her funny-acting mother but finally smiled and gave me a big kiss—just what I needed. It became a very nice Christmas after all!

During our stay in Switzerland, I remember one political event in Germany that became another great disappointment for all those who still had hopes that there might be some change in the political structure of Germany, something that might help to turn this tide and show people in other countries that not all Germans were followers of Hitler's doctrine. This event was the vote for or against the status quo in the Saarland, a province of Germany situated at the French and Luxembourg border. After the end of the First World War, this province was separated from Germany and put under the command of a Commission of the League of Nations. In January 1935, there was a plebiscite held under international supervision, and the citizens of the Saarland had to decide to go back to Germany or to stay with the Commission of the League of Nations.

Now that day had arrived. Of course, France, which had the right due to the Treaty of Versailles to exploit the coal mines of the Saarland as a reparation for her own mines that were partially destroyed by the Germans during the war, had tried to get the Saar population on her side. So did Nazi Germany, naturally. And there was a third party very hard at work: those people who were not anti-German, but they were anti-Hitler and what he stood for. Many of these men were Social Democrats who had left Germany, and the Saarland was their first stop into emigration. They tried very hard to explain to the Saar people what was going on in Germany, fearful of what it would end up like. They pleaded for a prolonged stay under the status quo, at least for the time being. I had heard quite a few of these passionate speeches over my radio. I had also read a lot about it in a very good refugee newspaper that was printed in Paris in the German language. It was called the *Pariser Zeitung* and was published and edited by a former well-known Berlin newspaperman, Georg Bernhard, who had emigrated to Paris.[6] I had a subscription to it and was always looking forward to receiving it in the mail. From this paper, I learned a lot more about Germany and what was going on there than from my St. Gallen newspaper. So, I followed this plebiscite quite closely.

All this gave me the feeling of hope that there was now a chance to show the world that not every German wanted the Nazi regime. The Saar people had the opportunity to hear both sides. They could read foreign newspapers. They must have heard about concentration camps and about the persecution of the Jews! They would vote for the status quo! Oh, was I wrong!

On the morning of January 13, 1935, I turned on the radio as soon as we had finished breakfast so that I would not miss any news bulletin that might come through. Of course, there would be no news that early. But I was much too excited to do anything else, so I listened to everything—music, city news, whatever came through. Finally, there was the report: the voting was very heavy; all voting places were very crowded. That was good, I thought. People wanted to show their opinion, and here they could do that, as there was no personal danger for them. Every voting place was under international control.

Finally, late in the afternoon, the usual program was interrupted, and the first results came through. Only a few small villages were finished with their counting. I had paper and pencil ready. The first results were certainly not very good. I told myself these were only small villages, and farmers were never very much interested in politics. It would be different when the results from the cities were announced. I listened all evening. Mia and Pia came up after dinner, and we listened together. But the trend didn't change. It got worse and worse. We had long given up on marking the votes. The last complete results would not be out before the next morning, but the outcome was already quite clear.

I didn't sleep very much that night. It was so unbelievable to me. I might have understood the result if it had been a question of choosing between becoming French citizens or staying with Germany. But just to stay with the status quo for a few more years instead of becoming part of what was going on in Germany! But then I remembered the long talks I'd had with Opi in Oslo, when even I, who had seen so much and went through a lot, found it hard to believe everything in the beginning.

The next morning, the complete results were in the newspapers—90 percent had voted for Germany and only 8 percent for the status quo! I think the whole thing hit me so hard because somehow, I still had a tiny bit of hope that there might be a change for the better, that it might not be necessary that we would have to move so far away. My parents, my brothers, and my friends were in Germany—it was not easy!

I don't remember very much of this long winter. It certainly was a very quiet one. We had a lot of snow, which was very beautiful to look at but made it very difficult to make long walks through the forest. I had bought a little sleigh and dutifully went out with Renatchen every afternoon. I spent the evenings with my radio, reading, and mostly writing letters to Opi. I was much better off than he was since I was always in the same spot. Sometimes my letters arrived after he had already left and had to be forwarded to him. But as a whole, it worked quite well considering that there was no overseas airmail at that time.

Finally, it was spring, and Opi's homecoming drew nearer. He also waited impatiently for the end of his tour. But he had to change the date of his departure for home quite a few times because every extra lecture fee counted. The trip as a whole did not bring as much money as we had hoped for. For publicity's sake, he had to do quite a few lectures without an honorarium, just expenses paid. It was quite true what an old friend of ours used to say: "America is the land of the unexpected possibilities, but of the unpaid ones as well!" After all, Opi came to the United States as an unknown person. He had a few lecture engagements to start out with, but that was all. In New York, he had some interviews with reporters at the big newspapers, which was very important. And he had the help of the small Social Democratic Party, which really did all it could. From there, he had to make his own contacts. In France and in St. Gallen, he had already started corresponding with some union leaders whose names he had gotten from the very helpful Rabbi Hillel Silver, whom he had met in France and who had helped start Opi's whole trip.

Finally, Opi wrote me the exact date of when he would arrive in St. Gallen. It seemed as if the last few weeks would never end. I cleaned the little apartment from top to bottom and then all over again. There always seemed to be something I could do again; the floor was not shiny enough, or the few books looked better arranged in a different way. The anticipation was wonderful!

At last, on a beautiful June day, a few days before our seventh wedding anniversary, I got the cable with the exact time for his arrival in St. Gallen. Mr. Huber had offered to pick us up in his car and take us to the station. During these last days of waiting, I had talked a lot to Renatchen about *Vati* now coming home again, and she was excited and asked a lot of questions.

The great moment came, and the train rolled into the station with a beaming Opi hanging out of the railway car window, waving to us. Minutes later, we were in each other's arms. This time, Renatchen was not as shy as she had been in London. She looked at her father with a very serious face, then her eyes lit up, and without any coaxing by either of us, she went over to him, and when he picked her up, she gave him a shy kiss. Mr. Huber watched this scene with an amused smile. It was his influence again that got Opi his entrance visa and permission to stay until he could take us back with him to America at the end of September, when we hoped that Renatchen and I would have the immigration visas for the United States. Opi had, of course, already started to work on that in America and had brought some very good affidavits for us with him.

When Opi finally turned to him [Mr. Huber] to thank him for all he had done for us, he just waved his hand and said we'd better get going and that he had to go back to work. We picked up Opi's luggage and went to his car. Opi took Renatchen on his lap. She sat there very quiet without saying a word, as if she had something on her mind. Suddenly, she turned around, looked very seriously at Opi, and said, *"Herr Vati bleibst Du nun bei uns?"* (Mr. Daddy, are you staying with us now?)

She had recognized her father, but of course, after ten months of separation, she had to get used to him again. But luckily, that did not take very long. Opi had brought a beautiful doll for her, which was soft to the touch, something quite new that had just come out in America. The doll could drink out of a tiny little bottle, wet her diapers, and, best of all, could be taken into the bathtub without any trouble at all. That doll and a perfectly fitting, very elegant little sun suit with matching hat won her heart completely. All strange feelings that she might have had in the beginning disappeared very quickly, and she took Vati by the hand to come look at all her possessions. She hardly left his side until she had to go to bed, and he tucked her in. We certainly were a happy family again!

The next few weeks went very fast. We had so much to talk about. I wanted to know so much about New York and about the people Opi had met and had made friends with. Some were Americans; some were refugees like us. So, there were at least some people I could talk to and who could give me some advice as far as household items were concerned—things about which Opi naturally knew very little. Opi tried to convince me that everything would work out fine, but I could not help feeling a little scared. After all, this was not just another country—this was another continent. That meant a lot more in the year 1935 than it does today, when it takes only a few hours to be in another part of the world. The thought of going to America was very exciting but a bit frightening too, especially because Opi told me that he already had a few new lecture engagements for the coming winter. That meant Renatchen and I would be alone in New York from time to time. But these speaking engagements would very much be needed. One of the first things Opi told me the day he had come home was that he had a job. When he was back in New York in September, he would start as editor-in-chief at a small weekly German-language newspaper, the *Neue Volkszeitung*. This was fine, but they could not pay very much. They were desperately looking for a new editor because the one they had was old and wanted to retire as soon as possible. They were sure Opi would be just the right man for the job, so they made a special agreement with him. He could take on speaking engagements throughout the country but had to write reports from his trips for the paper and edit material that they would send him when he was not in New York. Of course, it would not be easy, and since at that time he would have to travel mostly by car, it often meant some late-night hours so that he could make the deadline for printing every week. Naturally, the news about his traveling dampened my enthusiasm a bit, but then I told myself it would be only short trips, and then he would be back again. And sometimes we might even be going with him too. After all, we would be in the same country now!

During the first week of Opi's stay in St. Gallen, we traveled to Zürich and went to the American general consulate to get a reentry permit for Opi, which would not be difficult since he had a job when he returned and an emigration visa for Renate and myself. A very friendly, good-looking young American official, who spoke German quite well, took care of us. The only thing that seemed to be difficult was that neither Renate nor I had a birth certificate. These were with all our papers in Opi's desk in Dessau, which the Nazis had confiscated. Luckily, I had that little family book with me that I packed into my suitcase at the last moment when we were taken to the concentration camp. After Renatchen was born, I had asked the official to enter it in our family book too. The American looked at it, but then he asked us to try to get copies of our birth certificates as soon as possible. They would be needed for the files. I promised to do it, but I also told him that I had my doubts that I would get the copies with the way the things were now in Germany. And I was right. I did write and enclosed three marks with each letter to the city halls of Elberfeld, where I was born, and Dessau. I never got an answer or my money back. But as you can see, we made the grades just the same! The certificates were the only objection the American had; otherwise, everything seemed to be all right, and we were told that we would be notified in a few weeks.

We left the consulate very optimistic. This was still June, and we would not have to leave until the middle of September anyhow. We took a nice long walk around part of the very beautiful Lake Zürich, which was very enjoyable. But we had a hard time convincing Renatchen that she could not make *bade bade* in it because it would be much too deep for her.[7]

A Swiss publisher whom Opi had already made contact with before he went to America and who suggested Opi write *Reisetagebuch eines deutschen Emigranten* invited us for lunch. We had great hopes for the book, which was supposed to be a follow-up to *Oranienburg*. Opi had started to write it in America and had promised to finish it during the summer, which he did. But the book never became the success it could have been. He finished it in August 1935, and it was finally published in the second part of 1936. As far as we could find out, the publisher had hardly advertised it, and by then, the excitement over *Oranienburg* had died down. So much more had happened in the meantime. There may have been some pressure from the Nazis, who may have closed the German book market for a publisher who brought out a book by Gerhart Seger, the author of *Oranienburg*, but of course, this was only an idea. We never found out why the publication took so long or why the publisher gave it so little press, especially advertising the fact that the author was the same one who had written the first authentic report about a concentration camp in Germany. It should have been successful! But fewer books were sold than we had hoped for.

But back to our very nice visit with Opi's publisher and his very charming wife. They lived in a beautiful old house on one of the hills around the lake. From their terrace, one had a wonderful view over the lake and part of Zürich with the Alps in the background. When we arrived, the publisher introduced us to another guest whom he thought Opi should meet. He was the program editor of the Zürich radio station, a very good-looking elderly man. Over a glass of very good sherry, a lively conversation soon started. Renatchen sat quietly at the other end of the room, occupied with some picture books our host had given to her, whispering about the things she saw to her doll, which she held on her lap. I guess the time passed quicker than we thought. Suddenly I felt a little hand slipping into mine, and a plaintive, tiny voice said quite distinctly, "Don't we get anything to eat here?" Everybody laughed, and our hostess rang a bell; a maid came in and served a very good luncheon and the dessert—something we very seldom had at home—allowed Renatchen to quickly forget any resentments she might have still had about the delayed meal.

After we had our coffee, the lady of the house took Renatchen and me into another room and, showing Renatchen the couch in there, asked her if she would like to try to have a little nap. Without the slightest protest, Renatchen climbed onto the couch, her doll right next to her, and when I covered her with a blanket, she gave me a kiss, turned to the wall, and was asleep even before we had left the room.

When we came back into the living room, Opi and the two other men were conversing very animatedly. When Opi saw me, he got up and came over to me to tell me that the program director of the radio station had just asked him to do a broadcast lecture about his American trip. That was certainly good news! Every extra income was a very welcome addition to our rather tight budget. I had to restrain myself very hard from asking how much it would bring in. But finally, we had to leave after picking up our well-rested little girl, for whom our friendly hostess had prepared a little bag with cookies for the "long way home." When we were a few yards away from the house, Opi pushed me behind an old tree, gave me a big kiss, and held me. It was good that we were on a quiet street with hardly any people in sight. The very reserved Swiss would have been quite shocked at our behavior.

Well, it was certainly a wonderful summer! My parents came often to visit us over the weekends, and when the summer vacations started, my brothers came too. One of our neighbors rented a room to my parents only three houses away from us, and my brothers slept in our living room, using the cushions of our easy chairs as mattresses. Renatchen had a lot of fun romping with them on the floor in the morning. We took nice, inexpensive trips with the little mountain railroad higher up into the mountains, and on the way home, we put my mother and Renatchen on the little train, and the rest of the family walked down. My favorite aunt and uncle came to visit us too and promptly fell in love with their little great-niece, who could get away with anything with them.

Even my mother-in-law came for a week. Since the farthest she had been away from Leipzig was Dessau, this was quite a decision for her. But she made it with the help of a friend. We were glad that she did. Of course, we did not know it then, but that was the last time that we ever saw her. Her visit was a little difficult. She was much older than my parents and very set in her ways. Renatchen didn't take to her at all. And my mother-in-law was not used to children at all anymore. She talked to her as if she were a grown-up. And her very strong Saxon dialect made her even stranger to the little girl. I felt very sorry for my mother-in-law, but there was very little I could do about this. I even tried to bribe Renatchen, telling her that she would get a piece of chocolate if she gave her grandmother a kiss without being asked to do so. But that was quite wrong. Renatchen went into the room where my mother-in-law was sitting with her friend and, without a word, climbed into her lap, planted a quick kiss on her cheek, climbed just as quickly down again, came over to me, and said, "Can I have my chocolate now?" Luckily, my mother-in-law, who was a bit hard of hearing, didn't understand what she was saying, and I quickly took her out of the room, mumbling something about the bathroom. Outside, I gave her the promised piece of chocolate and only hoped that my mother-in-law really had not understood what Renatchen had said to me.

While my mother-in-law was staying, we were on the go quite a bit. We even rented a car and made a trip to one of the higher mountains in the neighborhood, the Säntis, which Opi's mother treated us to and which we all enjoyed very much, especially Renatchen because this was something very new and quite exciting.[8] When we came home, I asked her to thank her grandmother for this nice trip. She went over to her right away, hugged her, and gave her a kiss on both cheeks. This time no coaxing was necessary!

A few days later, Opi got a letter from the Zürich radio manager with a contract for his lecture there and the date and time. I would have liked to go with him, especially since my aunt and uncle were still with us and could have taken care of Renatchen. But we decided against it because only Opi's travel expenses would be paid.

On the day of the broadcast, we were all sitting around the radio long before the time the lecture was to begin, just in case there might be a change in the program. We had not told Renate anything about what would happen, and she played with her blocks and did not pay much attention to whatever came out of the radio. Finally, after some music, there was a longer pause, and then the announcer came on and gave a short introduction, and when he mentioned Opi's name, Renatchen came quickly over to me. But before she could say anything, Opi's voice came clearly and distinctly over the radio.

Renatchen ran quickly over to it and looked intensely into the loudspeaker. Then she turned to me and said, "Daddy is in here, but I cannot see him" with a very astonished expression on her face. I made a sign with my finger over my mouth to prevent her from talking and whispered in her ear that I would explain later. She really stood quite motionless through the whole lecture with a very serious face. When the lecture was over, she turned to me and asked a little anxiously, "Can Daddy get out of the box now?" I tried to explain to her that her father was not really in the box. But how can one explain the wonder of a radio to a three-year-old child? I no longer remember exactly what I said, and I was very glad when my uncle made up a little story about Opi speaking into one end of a hose and the other end coming out of the loudspeaker of the radio behind the little piece of cloth that covered it. She finally started playing with her blocks again, but she stayed very quiet the rest of the day, not at all the talkative little girl she usually was. When Opi finally came home that night, she rushed into his arms and didn't want to leave his side for a moment. She even insisted that he had to give her a bath and put her to bed. Opi and I were a bit worried about her behavior. What was going on in her mind? I went into her room a few times during the night, but she slept peacefully through, and the next morning she was her happy self again. Whatever had been bothering her the day before, after the radio experience, seemed completely forgotten.

We were very happy that beautiful summer in St. Gallen. As excited as I was about America, if there would have been the slightest possibility of us making a living there, I would have loved to stay. But there was no possibility of this, and I think it would have not been the same for Opi. He was looking forward to going back to the States. Besides, in Switzerland, we were only refugees and had only a limited permission to stay, which could be revoked at any time. It was nearly impossible to become a Swiss citizen unless you had a lot of money or brought your own business, and even then, it was not easy. It was understandable when one took into account that the whole country had a population of only about 4.25 million people—about half the size of New York's. They didn't need any immigrants, so I tried to concentrate on our future in America.

But we were in for quite a shock! One beautiful morning in August, we got a letter from the American consulate. Opi's immigration visa—his first visa had only been a visitor's visa—was granted, but mine was not! We both could not understand what had happened.

There must have been a mistake. This was not possible! We decided to travel to Zürich the next day to clear this up. After a rather sleepless night, we took the earliest train to Zürich the next morning. I still remember us walking back and forth along the lake near the American consulate until the office finally opened. We had left Renatchen with our landlady and the two girls, which Renatchen didn't mind a bit, and we were grateful to know that she was in good hands.

At the consulate, we asked for the young American, who had given us his name when we were there the first time, just in case we had some questions—only to find out that he was back in the States. Then we asked for the consul general, but he was on vacation somewhere out of the country! When we stated our case, we were referred to another official, evidently his deputy. This man was quite unfriendly and short, just the opposite of the one we had talked to the first time. He told us that my visa could only be granted after Opi was back in the States and could prove that he had started a job there and made enough money to support us. As soon as he could prove that, I would get my visa too. And that was that!

Opi tried to explain to him that he had already lived nearly a year in America, and he supported us from there, and he knew his way around and would start a job as soon as he got back. The answer was, "If you have proven that, there won't be any difficulties in about a quarter of a year or so. I am sure you wife will get her visa then too." When Opi tried to convince him that it would be very difficult for me to do all the moving business without any help, his cool reply was, "Mrs. Seger, one can have any help one needs. There are people whose job it is to do these things." We knew there were many things that were just a matter of money, of which we had very little. Well, we knew we were licked. Bureaucracy is the same everywhere. We had seen this at the French consulate in Belgium, at the Swiss one, and now here. There were always officials who didn't want to see the human side of each case, who went by the book and that was that. But then, of course, there were exceptions too, as the French ambassador in Belgium had proven.

Our trip home was quite different from the one to Zürich in the morning. We were both very depressed. There would be a separation again, and would it really be only a quarter of a year or so? Opi assured me that the moment he was back in New York, he would start working on my permit. He had met people during his lecture trips who had all sorts of connections and certainly would be helpful. With his wonderful optimism, he could see some positive sides to our dilemma. He would have enough time to look at apartments and could rent one as soon as he knew when we would arrive. I could still be with my family a little while longer. In short, he tried very hard to help me get over my disappointment and his as best as he could. When we got home, a tired but happy little girl greeted us, and she had so much to tell us. The sympathy of our landlady and her daughters was touching. And their joy at having Renatchen and me a little longer was heartwarming.

The few weeks before Opi's departure passed rather quickly. Opi tried to prepare for our later move as much as possible. He found a mover who did overseas transport and who satisfied him. He arranged everything with the mover so that when the time came, I just had to notify the man, who would then send an experienced packer for most everything, and I really would only have to pack our clothes and the linens. He would deliver special boxes for that. This man would do everything else. And besides, we did not have much. Everything would be taken down to the company's warehouse and from there transferred to a large lift, a tremendous wooden box, which then went by freight car to the next harbor, where it would be shipped over to New York. All of these prearrangements certainly made things easier for me, and I was not so afraid of the moving business anymore. Of course, the transport would cost quite a lot. But there was nothing else we could do because we had to sign an agreement when our furniture had arrived not to sell anything in the next five years; otherwise, we would have had to pay a lot of customs duties. This was the condition under which the Swiss let our furniture into the country without any taxes. I am sure we could have bought most of the furniture we needed here in America for the money we had to pay for the transport, but the familiar things would help us to feel at home quicker in the new and strange surroundings. I experienced that in St. Gallen, and I was sure it would be even more true in America, where everything would be so much stranger and different than it was in Switzerland, only a few hours away from our homeland.

It was now September, and in a few days, Opi would have to leave again. We both dreaded the new separation, and we both hoped that the consul in Zürich did know what he was talking about when he told us that I would get my immigration visa in four months, when Opi could prove that he earned enough money to support us. Opi's immigrant visa with the intention of becoming an American citizen, rather than his visitor visa, as he'd had the year before, would also help speed things up, we hoped.

Renatchen was very upset that her daddy was going away again, and it took some effort to convince her that the time when we would go to the Merka, as she called the States, would arrive much sooner than she thought. Only the promise that Omi would be coming soon and staying with us a little while and could maybe make her a new dress helped her get over her distress.

The time really passed faster than I anticipated. My family came to visit a few times. I started to freshen up my English a little bit every day with the self-teaching method that Opi had used to successfully teach himself during the three months he spent in the Dessau prison. It helped a little. But there was nobody with whom I could practice what I had learned and who could correct my pronunciation. Besides, I did not have the fantastic energy and perseverance of your grandfather.

And then, on one of the rare sunny days at the beginning of November, instead of the expected letter from Opi in my mailbox, I found one from the American consulate in Zürich! I raced up the stairs. What could the contents be? Only two and a half months had passed since Opi was back in the United States. The consul had said it would take four months. I had the letter in my hand and could not bring myself to open it. I just stood there staring at it until my mother, who was staying with us for a few days, bent over my shoulder; reading the name of the sender on the envelope, she put her hand on my shoulder and gave me a friendly little push. "Go ahead, open it. Whatever it is, you have to find out."

She was right, of course. So I opened it slowly. It was only a short note, written in English, of course, which was initially a little frightening. But then I started to translate and found out that my studying had done some good after all. Reading another language always seemed easier to me than speaking it. I understood that I should come to Zürich as soon as possible and bring my passport in order to receive my immigration visa for the United States of America!

This was certainly a great moment! My mother took me into her arms. She had tears in her eyes. I understood that for her, it was a double-edged sword. Of course, she wanted us to be united with Opi, to live in a country where we really would belong and could build up an existence again. In Switzerland, we were only guests and not very welcome either. But my parents and I would be separated for a long time—America was far away! She tried to overcome her emotion as quickly as possible, just as I did. I decided to travel to Zürich the next day, and Mother and Renatchen would go with me.

We left on an early train the next morning and seemed to be the first visitors at the consulate. Everything went very smoothly. The official again asked for Renatchen's birth certificate. I told him that I had written to Dessau but had not gotten any response or my money back, which I had put in the envelope. He looked at us for a moment and then said with a smile, "Well, she is here, so she exists." And then he stamped my passport with that precious visa for the United States of America, gave it back to me, and wished me a friendly good luck in the States. We could then leave, which was fine with Renatchen, who was quite hungry and a bit bored by now. Going to a restaurant was much more important for her than the process for becoming an American citizen!

We had a nice lunch at a small restaurant, and I looked up the address of the French consulate to get my transit visa in order to travel through France, which we would have to do to get to Boulogne-sur-Mer, where the Holland-America Line stopped to take passengers to England and America. I called up the French consulate, and there was still enough time to go there before we had to catch our train back to St. Gallen. A friendly waiter described to me how I could get there, and since it was only ten minutes or so away, I left Mother and Renatchen at the restaurant and walked over to the consulate alone. I got the transit visa without any difficulties, paid the ten francs they asked for it, and left the consulate as quickly as possible, remembering the nasty experiences we'd had in the French consulate in Belgium. I picked up Mother and Renatchen, and we went to the railway station, and after a short while we were settled comfortably in our train home.

That night, I wrote a long letter to Opi. Now he could get the ball rolling with everything—buying the tickets for our trip and sending the money for the transport of our furniture to the shipping agent. It suddenly occurred to me that if everything worked out according to our expectations, we would be together at Christmas, the first one Renatchen would spend together with her father since she was a four-month-old baby!

Mother left a few days later with the promise to come back soon with my father for a weekend. Before she left, we went down to the city, where she bought a beautiful winter coat for Renatchen, which was a very welcome and necessary gift since she had certainly outgrown her old one.

Now a very busy time started for me. First, I got in touch with the mover, and he promised to come soon and give me some advice about my own packing and to look over the things his packer would pack for me, such as china and all the breakable things like lamps and pictures. The moving date would be set as soon as I had the tickets and knew which day the boat would leave. When Opi and I had visited them one day in the summer, my friends in Basel had already offered me and Renatchen to stay a few days with them before we left for the States. This, of course, was very helpful. We had to get the express train to Paris, and we would have to go over to Basel anyhow. This was only a two-hour trip, and we could leave as soon as the last piece of furniture was taken out of the apartment. This way, we would have to stay only one night in a hotel in Paris, from where we would have to take the boat train to Boulogne-sur-Mer. All this, as Opi had already written to me, would be arranged by the travel agent of the Holland-America Line, who would send me the ticket with the hotel reservation.

It was all very exciting, as you can imagine. I had very seldom traveled alone, and this was not only from one city to another but from one country to another—and then on top of it, from one continent to another! I envied Renatchen, who trusted me implicitly and had no idea how insecure her mother felt inside! In addition, the thought came that I would have to leave my family soon, and none of us had any idea when we would see each other again. All this dimmed my joyful anticipation to be together with Opi, and my thoughts went from one extreme to another.

It was good that I had so much to do and to arrange since there were only a few weeks left before the departure. Opi's letter had arrived only a few days before the agent sent the ticket and the date of the departure from Boulogne-sur-Mer. I think it was the 12th of December, and the date for the movers could be set now. Since our landlady knew that our stay would only be short after Opi had gone back to the States, there were no difficulties getting out of the apartment. Besides, she already had a young couple waiting to move in as soon as I moved out, which made me feel better. Even better, these young people had seen my radio when they came to look at the apartment and had asked me if I would sell it to them. They offered a very good price for it, and since Opi had written that it would be quite useless in America without a very costly repair (America has a different frequency than Europe), I gladly sold it to them. I knew it would be in good hands. I hoped they would get as much pleasure out of it as I had since the Christmas I had received it.

Finally, the day of our departure arrived. The week before, we spent some time seeing the few friends we had made during our year and a half stay in St. Gallen. But the most difficult parting was with our landlady and her two daughters, who really had become very dear friends. They all came down with us to the railway station, and we all had tears in our eyes when the train started moving. We waved as long as I could see them from the open window of the train. Even Renatchen, without understanding everything, was quite subdued, and it took a little while to get her interested in the picture book that the girls had given her as a goodbye present. I felt quite depressed myself. It was not only the people I had to leave behind; I had grown quite fond of St. Gallen, the little peaceful town and the beautiful mountains around it. Now, a completely strange and different world lay ahead of me. Would I adjust to it? How long would it take to feel at home in a completely strange country with a different language, which I knew a little of, but certainly not enough to feel at home as quickly as I had in St. Gallen? But then, Opi would be there, and the thought of him helped me overcome my sadness a bit. And there was my little girl, who had a lot of questions about the pictures in the book, and I occupied myself with her, and that helped too.

In Basel, our friends, the Rosenbergs, picked us up at the station, and Renatchen and their young son quickly became good friends. The few days we stayed there passed rather quickly. To my pleasant surprise, I found out that my friend had to go to Paris on business, and he had put it off until now so that we could travel together, which made me feel quite relieved. He stayed in a different hotel, but he promised to come back to mine after he checked into his so that we could have dinner together in my hotel. When I arrived in my hotel and showed the desk clerk my reservation, he gave me a note that the travel agent had left there. It said that I should be in the hotel lobby at eight o'clock the next morning with all my luggage, and he would pick us up there to take us to the train. I felt my nerves settle down with all these arrangements made.

When we got upstairs to our room, I asked for room service and ordered something to eat for Renatchen. The very nice young maid who brought my order up even spoke a little German with a nice

French accent. She promised to check in from time to time to see if everything was all right. I was quite sure it would be. Renatchen was so tired—it was long past her bedtime—that she fell asleep as soon as I tucked her into our big double bed, long before the phone rang and the desk clerk told me that Werner Rosenberg was downstairs, waiting for "Madame."

We had a very pleasant dinner together, topped off by a good bottle of champagne to give my last evening in Europe some sparkle and to drink to our future. When I went upstairs, I saw the maid closing the door to our room. *"La petite est tres charmant,"* she said, *"nicht aufgewacht die ganze Zeit."*[9] I had been quite sure of that, but since I knew someone was looking after her when I was downstairs, it made me feel better. I gave her a *pourboire* (tip) and asked her to tell the night clerk downstairs to wake me at seven o'clock the next morning, just to be on the safe side. In the end, it was not necessary because I woke up at six o'clock all by myself, which was fine; this way, I had plenty of time to have a nice bath, to pack everything, and to leisurely dress Renatchen and myself, and we had still plenty of time to have a little breakfast downstairs.

When we got to the lobby later on, there were already about twenty people waiting, and the agent arrived pretty soon after we had got there. I found out they all had the same destination—namely, the *Statendam*. Some went only as far as England, but most of them went all the way like we did. As I found out later, most of them were refugees too and hoped to find a new home in America. The agent started to read their names from a list, and I waited for mine. He repeated it twice before I realized that *"Madame Seger et enfant"* was me.[10] Finally, we were herded into a little bus, the luggage was stowed away on top of it, and we rode through the still very quiet streets of Paris to the train where the agent brought us to the train car that was reserved for us, wished us "bon voyage," and left us.

I don't remember how long the train ride was, but it must have been a few hours because we all were quite hungry when we finally arrived in Boulogne-sur-Mer. Luckily, I had some chocolate with me, which made Renatchen very happy and helped her over the next hour. At the station, a young man in a sailor's uniform greeted us, and a group of sailors took care of our luggage. We then walked over to the pier, which was very close to the railway station. Here a customs cutter awaited us, which brought us to the beautiful white ship, the *Statendam*, which waited for us at the entrance to the harbor. I found out later that it was much cheaper to bring passengers on board this way; otherwise, the big liner would have been brought in with the help of tugboats. But it would have been a little more comfortable for the passengers, especially on a stormy day like this one! It was in the middle of winter and icy cold. The only shelter was a very small cabin that had only enough room for the women. The men had to brave the icy wind outside. The closer we got to our boat, the higher the waves got. One poor woman already got seasick on that little trip. Renatchen and I felt fine. But when we got next to the ship, I became quite worried. How would we get up there? I saw a big ship's ladder hanging down from the first deck, but how could we get up there? The little cutter was much lower and really danced on the high waves. How would I ever get Renatchen up there? I was quite scared, and when I looked around at the other passengers, I didn't see very much courage on their faces either.

But it all worked out miraculously well. These young sailors knew their jobs. One of them took Renatchen in his arms and stood on the railing of the cutter, and at the moment a big wave lifted it, he jumped onto the ladder. Renatchen looked anxiously down at me, but before she could utter any protest, she was already up and safe on the board of the *Statendam*. With the next big wave and the help of another sailor, I went up there too and had my happy, smiling little girl in my arms, and everything was all right! We were welcomed on board, and a stewardess brought us to our cabin. She told us that in about ten minutes' time, food would be served in the big recreation room on deck, which was quite welcome news. In the meantime, our luggage would be brought to our cabin. When she had left, I looked around. It was a beautiful outboard cabin with two comfortable looking beds, two easy chairs, a small closet and chest, and a washstand. It had two big hatches through which I could see the harbor in the last rays of sunshine—my last look at the continent of Europe!

Gerhart left for his speaking tour in America in October 1934, which meant another prolonged separation from Ilse. This was very difficult for both of them, even if the circumstances were much improved. They communicated by letter; Ilse saved many (if not all) of the letters, and they survive in the Gerhart and Ilse Seger family collection. Gerhart often shared his impressions of and experiences in America in his letters, which Ilse enjoyed alongside her landlady's daughters. Like anyone who imagines life in a different country, she commented on the strangeness of something as innocuous as an American drugstore and snickered about the use of foreign words. Gerhart sent press articles about him speaking from magazines and newspapers (most if not all of which also still survive in the family's collection), but she seemed more interested in the odd layout of American newspapers. Their ability to send letters back and forth was hampered only by Gerhart's tour schedule, which had him moving around a lot. Although Gerhart did not always receive an honorarium for his lectures, he was able to support Ilse and Renate while they lived in St. Gallen—information that he could later use to secure permanent visas for them once they were ready to immigrate.

The winter of 1934–35 was long and lonely for Ilse. She passed the time taking walks with Renate, writing to Gerhart, and learning English in anticipation of immigrating to America at some point. Highlights included frequent visits from her parents, seeing an old friend from Dessau, and receiving a radio as a gift from Gerhart on Christmas Eve.

The visit from her old friend in Dessau got her thinking and talking about books once again—something that she commented on frequently. In earlier chapters, she mentioned books that she was reading, Gerhart's books being confiscated after he was first imprisoned in Dessau, and the Nazi book burning on May 1, 1933. Ilse and Gerhart were certainly intellectuals, which was why the empty bookshelves in her St. Gallen apartment felt so strange to her even though she was surrounded by the familiarity of their furniture from Dessau. The warmth of books helped her house feel more like a home, and this was perhaps why she was so overjoyed when this visitor brought her one more book for her bookshelf. After catching up with her friend about how the members of the SPD (Sozialdemokratische Partei Deutschlands; Social Democratic Party of Germany), including Otto and Leni Posse, were faring in Nazi Germany, he also informed her that workers at the paper mill in Dessau had destroyed all of Gerhart's books. She had been holding out hope that they might get some of them back, so this upset her greatly. The destruction of books for no good reason and the Nazi hatred for intellectuals and critical thinking caused Ilse great distress and shame for her country. She was especially disturbed by the fact that there was a lack of thinking or questioning of the Nazis in such a highly cultured place as Germany. Gerhart commented on this as well in *Reisetagebuch*, claiming that the cultural collapse of Germany, even more so than the Nazi atrocities, had done the most damage to its reputation and had provoked such a passionate rejection of Hitler and the Nazis among Americans.[11] This is perhaps part of the reason why the rise of Nazism in a modern, cultured Western country like Germany still elicits such fascination from Americans.

Another moment of disgrace Ilse felt for her country came in January 1935, when she followed the Saar plebiscite closely via her radio. In this referendum, the German population living in the Saar region, which the League of Nations had administered since the end of the First World War, voted whether they wanted to be reunited with Germany. She thought that this was Germany's chance to show the world that not everyone was enthralled by Hitler. The people living there also had the opportunity to think critically, to read foreign newspapers, and to hear from all sides, including from many Social Democrats who had fled Germany and could tell the truth about what was going on there. Ilse revealed some of her own urban background and class biases, dismissing the early returns from small villages and farmers as people who did not pay attention to politics and who could not have possibly been representative of her country. This was perhaps also why she was so shocked and disappointed when over 90 percent of the voters voted to reunite with Germany. She was holding out hope that the people of Germany would turn against Hitler through this plebiscite and that she also did not have to leave her parents, her brothers, her friends, and her home.

Ilse and Gerhart were reunited in June 1935 and spent the summer together in St. Gallen before they planned to immigrate to America. They spent some time that summer working toward securing emigration visas for Ilse and Renate. Ilse claimed that she would have happily stayed in Switzerland because she really liked it there, but there was not much possibility for Gerhart to make a living there. Besides, Switzerland was not the most receptive toward immigrants and frankly did not need them, according to Ilse. Her visa to America was also initially rejected, which led Ilse to remark on how unfriendly America was to immigrants in the 1930s. America immigration quotas at that time were very restrictive, and American public opinion did not support increased immigration, even in light of the large number of individuals who sought a safe haven from Nazi persecution in Europe.[12] As a result of her experiences attempting to secure temporary or permanent visas in Belgium, France, and Switzerland, Ilse became very critical of the bureaucratic system and especially of bureaucrats who, as she claimed, did not always see the human side of immigration stories but just went by the book. One wonders if she became friendly to immigrants later in life because of her past experiences.

Even once she had her visa, and after all the moving arrangements had been made, she still felt very uncertain about immigrating to a new country and continent and leaving her family, not knowing when she would see them again. She had a difficult time parting with her landlady and her landlady's daughters because they had become good friends of hers, and she had grown to enjoy St. Gallen. All of her insecurities were mixed with the anticipation and excitement of being with Gerhart again and the possibilities for them in America. This vacillation of her emotions—so characteristic throughout the entire memoir—was how we leave her as she took one last look at the continent of Europe.

This chapter especially offers insight to the subjective experience of dislocation and exile. Living in exile in Switzerland and anticipating immigrating to America, Ilse navigated the domestic task of setting up her family in new homes and foreign contexts, including a small child who needed constant care and attention. She faced the issue of making friends in Switzerland, which was why her landlady and the landlady's daughters grew to be such important companions; finding friends in America was also something she may have pondered. She learned the importance of Gerhart's transnational connections and support for facilitating their living in exile in the first place. She also learned to value her own personal connections and support, which was why she commented on how important the visits were from her parents and her old friend from Dessau. She had to learn new languages—enough French to survive her time in Carolles-Bourg and then English, which she taught herself, in anticipation of her permanent exile. She constantly worried about her financial situation, even if her perception of finances did not necessarily meet reality, especially compared to others at the time; having enough money and finding employment in America were also something she certainly thought about, and the abysmal economic situation of the Great Depression likely only compounded her uncertainty. She navigated and overcame the problem of accessing official documents from a hostile state when she was trying to obtain a visa and made other practical arrangements for her move to America. Perhaps most importantly, her emotional attachment to her home and family made decisions about when to leave very difficult. Most of what Ilse experienced and overcame during this year and a half period were individual, lonely experiences because Gerhart was absent for the majority of it.

Ilse's descriptions of maintaining normality for her daughter during such upheaval—not only before the move to America but throughout Renate's short life—and remaining true to her own convictions while struggling with huge existential dilemmas and the loneliness of separation make clear the courage needed for survival. Ilse had no formal education and none of her own foreign connections. And yet, she managed all of this alone during what was a relatively long, unsettled period of life, demonstrating tremendous diligence, bravery, and resilience—characteristics that certainly enabled her to succeed in America.

Notes

1. The Thalmanns were the family she and Renate lived with in Switzerland.
2. The distance between Freiburg and St. Gallen is approximately 172 kilometers or 106 miles.
3. This translates to "Good day, Comrade Seger. How are you?"
4. Stollen is a traditional German fruit bread eaten during the Christmas season.
5. Based on his letters to Ilse, his tour schedule, and the press coverage from the time in the Gerhart and Ilse Seger family collection, located in Terra Haute, Indiana, he was in Los Angeles giving several lectures during Christmas 1934.
6. Bernhard, who was Jewish, had been editor-in-chief of the *Vossische Zeitung* of Berlin. He immigrated to Paris in the spring of 1933. The newspaper he started in Paris in December 1933 was called the *Pariser Tageblatt*, later renamed to *Pariser Tageszeitung* (Ilse made a mistake with the name), and it was an exile newspaper of the German opposition published until 1940. See "Georg Bernhard," *Holocaust Encyclopedia*, United States Holocaust Memorial Museum, https://encyclopedia.ushmm.org/content/en/article/georg-bernhard.
7. Renate wanted to bathe in the lake.
8. Säntis mountain is one of the highest summits in the Alps.
9. This translates to "the little one is quite charming—never woke up once."
10. This translates to "Mrs. Seger and infant."
11. Seger, *Reisetagebuch*, 110–11.
12. "Immigration to the United States, 1933–41," *Holocaust Encyclopedia*, United States Holocaust Memorial Museum, https://encyclopedia.ushmm.org/content/en/article/immigration-to-the-united-states-1933-41.

Epilogue

Mark Brandt, June 2022

Of course, although she chose not to write it down, Ilse Seger's story did not end with the voyage across the Atlantic to America. She liked to say that Renate learned English while playing with the other children on the *Statendam*. While this was probably not really true, as is the case with many young children who move to a new country, Renate was able to learn to speak English fluently with a standard American accent. For Ilse, learning English in her thirties was more of a challenge, but it was one that she approached with the energy and diligence that she wrote about in her memoir. She listened to the radio, watched movies, and, most importantly, read many books.

She wrote about how important their library in Germany had been and how much it hurt when those books were destroyed. She and Gerhart began creating a new library, with an extensive collection of books. One of her favorite books was *Gone with the Wind*, which she read several times, dictionary in hand, underlining words and making comments in the margins. Although she never finished high school, Ilse had been well read while she lived in Europe, and she continued to read widely for the rest of her life.

As a woman born in 1903, Ilse had somewhat limited opportunities, made worse by the Great Depression. When she arrived in the United States, besides learning English, she had to take care of Renate. Furthermore, Gerhart spent much of the 1930s traveling around the United States, because in addition to his work as an editor for a New York German-language newspaper (*Neue Volkszeitung*), Gerhart earned honoraria by giving talks to a wide variety of audiences, trying to warn them about the dangers of Nazi Germany. While he was away, often for months of each year, Ilse had to take care of the finances and the house, including dealing with any necessary repairs. She was a resourceful individual, although in later conversations, she would downplay her role and pretend that Gerhart took care of everything.

Shortly before the start of World War II, Ilse's parents came to visit. The outbreak of the war meant that they were not able to return to Europe for about eight years. Although their daughter had been exiled, and although they were not Nazi supporters, Ilse's parents were German patriots. Renate (my mother), in the rare instances that she would talk about her childhood, described walking around New York trying to look as unconnected as possible to the two older people talking loudly in German on the sidewalks of a US city at war with Germany.

When Renate finished high school, she had to decide what to do next. The fact that her parents had moved to New York City gave her an opportunity that she might not otherwise have had: the City University of New York system did not charge tuition. She took and passed the difficult entrance exam and began attending Queens College, majoring in political science. Among other activities, she joined a service sorority. While working a service event, she met a member of a service fraternity working the same event—Richard Brandt, my father. Richard was born in New York. His parents had limited formal education, with his father not finishing high school and his mother not finishing grammar school. But Richard, like Renate, had been able to take advantage of the educational opportunities open to New York City residents and, after graduating from high school, also gained admission to Queens College.

When Renate brought Richard home to meet her parents, Gerhart apparently was impressed, while Ilse was not. Richard described himself as "rough around the edges," having grown up in largely lower-class neighborhoods and having gone to the all-male Brooklyn Technical High School. He was also two years younger than Renate, in a time when women largely married older men. In later years, Richard pointed out that had the Nazis not arrested Gerhart and then held Ilse and Renate hostage, he would never have met Renate because Renate and her parents would likely have never left Germany. He also explained that even if they had met, the social class differences between a lower-class New Yorker and the daughter of a prominent German politician would have prevented a relationship. By prominent, I mean both that Gerhart had been a member of the Reichstag and that Richard thought Gerhart would likely have continued his political career and might have become chancellor eventually, based on Gerhart's intelligence, charisma, drive, and political skills.

Renate married Richard in Gerhart and Ilse's house in Queens, New York, in September 1956. Initially, both Richard and Renate found employment in New York, with Richard doing chemical analyses and Renate working at a publishing house. Richard then went to graduate school. While he was in graduate school, Renate and Richard had three children: Mark (me, their oldest child), Andrew, and Jennifer, all born between 1960 and 1965. Raising three children on a graduate student stipend was a challenge, especially because Renate had to quit her job to raise the children. Renate earned some money typing dissertations for graduate students. The documents had to be perfect, without typographical errors, and errors could not be repaired because each required three copies made from the original with carbon paper. Mistakes near the top of a page Renate would shrug off, but mistakes toward the bottom of the page represented a considerable amount of stressful effort, so her children learned to be very quiet as she was getting close to the end of a page.

Richard's time in graduate school resulted in his earning a master of science in chemistry and a PhD in biochemistry. His doctorate opened the possibility of working as a faculty member at a university, and he accepted an offer from the Medical College of Virginia (MCV) in Richmond. Richard was a faculty member at MCV until his retirement twenty-seven years later. He then went on to work for more than fifteen years as an adviser for two charitable trusts and one scientific trust, making recommendations for the distribution of grants to applicants. The applicants for the charitable trusts included Monticello, the preserved home of Thomas Jefferson, and several museums in Richmond, while the scientific trust applicants included scientists across Virginia.

When my sister, Jennifer, began elementary school, Renate decided to take the courses necessary for certification as a school librarian. She then worked as the librarian of J. E. B. Stuart Elementary School (which was renamed Barack Obama Elementary School in 2018, a change that overjoyed my parents) for about twenty years, helping to encourage a generation of students to appreciate books. For years after she retired, former students would meet her and thank her for how she had inspired them as a teacher.

Like her husband, Renate did not stop making contributions when she retired. Instead, she acted as an adviser to other school librarians and spent years as a docent at the Virginia Museum of Fine Arts, while also volunteering at the arboretum at Maymont in Richmond for many years. Eventually, however, her declining health made further work impossible, and she, and then my father, had to fully retire. They moved to Indiana in 2016—Richard liked to say that their children had voted 3–0 that they needed to move near one of their children, and I lived in Indiana—and lived there for the last years of their lives. Renate died in 2020 at the age of eighty-eight; Richard died a little over a year later at the age of eighty-seven.

During their last few years in Virginia, Richard and Renate decided that something should be done with Ilse's manuscript. Richard, through his work at the charitable trust, had many contacts, one of whom recommended that he talk to Melissa Kravetz, who is the main editor and source of historical context for this memoir.

I think that writing this memoir, as my mother had suggested after Gerhart's death and after my family moved to Richmond, made Ilse somewhat happier; Ilse seemed to find revisiting the events of her last years in Germany cathartic. On a personal note, I regret not more forcefully encouraging her to continue her writing beyond the trip to America. By then, I was a teenager and not always reasonable.

In the summer of 1974, Ilse visited Europe to see her brothers while all three of them were still alive, and she brought me along. I had a wonderful time visiting places I had only read about, and she showed me some of the places that she wrote about in the memoir. She could not show me Dessau, however, because that city was in what was then East Germany, which was under the Soviet sphere of influence at that time. We once went to the border and saw the barbed wire fence and machine gun towers that the East German government maintained to keep East and West Germans separated.

Ilse finally moved to Richmond, Virginia, in the summer of 1978. By that time, some of her friends had died, and both she and her remaining friends were getting old. As I mentioned earlier, she never learned to drive, so she had to walk or use public transportation to go anywhere. In New York City this is possible, but as she got older, the four-block walk to the closest bus stop became more of a challenge. Reluctantly, she sold the house in New York and moved to an apartment in Richmond. She still lived alone, although she was getting somewhat weaker. Ilse Seger died in June 1979, aged seventy-six.

I miss her. She was a wonderfully warm and caring individual who had not let her experiences embitter her. She had a broad range of interests. I was never bored when I was with her, and she had a major role in shaping the person I am. Her broad interests influenced mine and especially sparked my interests in history and politics.

Ilse, in part because of her association with her husband, but even more because of her own strong sense of what was right, was an astute political observer. I learned from her how easy it can be for people to simply allow events to happen and then to accept the changes. She thought that many people seemed to be happier if someone else was making the decisions for them. The Nazis told people what to think, and for many people in Germany, that gave them a surprising level of comfort. As she told me, and as she wrote, Ilse wanted to think for herself. Her story is a compelling one about how people survived human-inflicted adversity while remaining true to their own principles—one reason I wanted to help publish her memoir.

My father and I had many arguments in which he, who lived through World War II, and I, born fifteen years after the war ended, disagreed about whether Nazi Germany was unique. I pointed out that the United States had concentration camps during World War II. For years, he viewed those as aberrations and as being somehow different from the concentration camps in Germany. While the US camps such as Manzanar were not involved in industrial-scale murder, a number of American citizens died, and most of the inmates had their possessions confiscated for no reason other than their Japanese ancestry. Eventually he began to agree, possibly because his logical mind overcame the years of propaganda from the war years, but also because of how the political situation in the United States has changed over my lifetime.

My father and I agreed on many other topics. One such topic that has become more relevant over the past few years in the United States is immigration. Historically, the US population has frequently objected to immigration, with each immigrant group being criticized by the previous one. My father was born in the United States, with his grandparents being the immigrants—also from Germany in the nineteenth century. He liked to point out that I was a first-generation US citizen. He also pointed out that Gerhart, Ilse, and Renate had all been net contributors to their adopted country. I like to think that my siblings and I are also net contributors; my brother and I are university professors, and my sister is a successful artist. His view, with which I strongly agree, was that immigrants tend to be highly motivated individuals, which is why they actually managed to leave their former countries to move to the United States. The story of Gerhart and Ilse is a common one, not in its details but in the difficulties that immigrants had to overcome in order to restart their lives. This raises a question: does the rhetoric criticizing immigration arise from economically disadvantaged US citizens afraid of competition, or from politicians creating an out-group to help themselves gain political power in the same fashion that the Nazis used the Jews in the 1930s? Why have anti-immigrant speeches become acceptable in the United States with little, if any, discussion of the possible consequences?

Like my father, my views are colored by my experiences; my experiences include growing up hearing about how Germany went from a parliamentary democracy to a dictatorship in a few years. Watching certain state governments attempt to strip the right to vote from some of their citizens, watching some US political figures attempt to set aside an election by inventing their own reality, and watching US citizens attempt to overthrow the government by force has brought back vivid memories of my grandmother telling me about disturbingly similar events occurring in Germany in the early 1930s.

Some commentators have suggested that since the January 6, 2021 coup attempt in the United States was inept, it should not be a matter of concern. The 1923 Beer Hall Putsch in Germany was inept also, and yet a decade later, Hitler was dictator of Germany. We do not know how events in the future will unfold, but there is reason to be concerned.

Some commentators have objected to statements by US politicians calling the prisons holding newly arrived asylum seekers concentration camps. Their point was that the purpose of those prisons was not industrial murder. However, their objections miss the point. Oranienburg and Rosslau were not death camps, but they were concentration camps. They were the first stage of a process that eventually resulted in the murder of millions of people. Germans in 1933 and 1934 did not know what would happen in the 1940s. The consequences that the current US anti-immigrant rhetoric will have in the future are not yet certain, but the trends are similar.

Ilse Seger would have been horrified by what has been happening. Her story illustrates how easily a country can become a fascist dictatorship while the people trying to warn their fellow citizens are ignored. Many in the United States seem not merely accepting of the possibility of fascism but are actually seeking to transform the United States into a fascist state. Ilse's autobiography is a description of a past event, but it is also a cautionary tale about how rapidly democracy can evaporate.

BIBLIOGRAPHY

Aycoberry, Pierre. *The Social History of the Third Reich, 1933–1945*. New York: New Press, 1999.
Barnes, James J., and Patience P. Barnes. *Nazi Refugee Turned Gestapo Spy: The Life of Hans Wesemann, 1895–1971*. Westport, CT: Praeger, 2001.
Bergen, Doris. *War and Genocide: A Concise History of the Holocaust*, 3rd edition. New York: Rowman & Littlefield, 2016.
Berger, Stefan. *Social Democracy and the Working Class in Nineteenth and Twentieth Century Germany*. New York: Pearson, 2000.
Berghahn, Volker. "Defiance and Resistance to Nazism from the Perspective of Gender, Class, and Generation." In *Women Defying Hitler: Rescue and Resistance under the Nazis*, edited by Nathan Stoltzfus, Mordecai Paldiel, and Judy Baumel-Schwartz, 77–85. New York: Bloomsbury Academic, 2021.
Bessel, Richard. *Life in the Third Reich*. New York: Oxford University Press, 1987.
Biddiscombe, Perry. *The Denazification of Germany: A History, 1945–1950*. Stroud: Tempus, 2007.
Blackbourn, David. "The Political Alignment of Centre Party in Wilhelmine Germany: A Study of the Party's Emergence in Nineteenth-Century Württemberg." *Historical Journal* 18, no. 4 (December 1975): 821–50.
Braskén, Kasper. "'Aid the Victims of German Fascism!': Transatlantic Networks and the Rise of Anti-Nazism in the USA 1933–1935." In *Anti-Fascism in a Global Perspective: Transnational Networks, Exile Communities, and Radical Internationalism*, edited by Kasper Braskén, Nigel Copsey, and David Featherstone, 197–219. New York: Routledge, 2021.
———. "'Make Scandinavia a Bulwark against Fascism!' Hitler's Seizure of Power and the Transnational Anti-Fascist Movement in the Nordic Countries." In *Anti-Fascism in a Global Perspective: Transnational Networks, Exile Communities, and Radical Internationalism*, edited by Kasper Braskén, Nigel Copsey, and David Featherstone, 96–114. New York: Routledge, 2021.
Braskén, Kasper, Nigel Copsey, and David Featherstone, eds. *Anti-Fascism in a Global Perspective: Transnational Networks, Exile Communities, and Radical Internationalism*. New York: Routledge, 2021.
Buchholz, Marlis, and Bernd Rother. *Der Parteivorstand der SPD im Exil. Protokolle der Sopade 1933–1940*. Bonn: Dietz, 1995.
Caplan, Jane. "Political Detention and the Origin of the Concentration Camps in Nazi Germany, 1933–1935/6." In *Nazism, War and Genocide: Essays in Honour of Jeremy Noakes*, edited by Neil Gregor, 22–41. Exeter, UK: University of Exeter Press, 2005.

Chickering, Robert Philip. "The Reichsbanner and the Weimar Republic, 1924–1926." *Journal of Modern History* 40, no. 4 (December 1968): 524–34.

Crew, David. ed. *Nazism and German Society, 1933–1945*. London: Routledge, 1993.

Dahl, Hans Fredrik. *Quisling: A Study in Treachery*. Translated by Anne-Marie Stanton-Ife. Cambridge, UK: Cambridge University Press, 1999.

Diels, Rudolf. *Lucifer Ante Portas: Es Spricht der erste Chef der Gestapo*. Stuttgart: Deutsche Verlags-Anstalt, 1950.

Dörner, Bernward. "Oranienburg." Translated by Stephen Pallavinci. In *Encyclopedia of Camps and Ghettos, 1933–1945. Volume I, Part A: Early Camps, Youth Camps, and Concentration Camps and Subcamps under the SS-Business Administration Main Office (WVHA)*, edited by Geoffrey P. Megargee, 147–49. Bloomington: Indiana University Press, 2009.

Edwards, M. Jean. "Lessons of the Bauhaus." *Journal of Interior Design* 44, no. 3 (September 2019): 135–40.

Evans, Richard J. *The Coming of the Third Reich*. New York: Penguin, 2003.

———. *The Feminist Movement in Germany, 1894–1933*. London: Sage, 1976.

"Everyday Life in Nazi Germany," *German History* 27, no. 4 (October 2009): 560–79.

Fitzpatrick, Sheila, and Robert Gellately. "Introduction to the Practices of Denunciation in Modern European History." In *Accusatory Practices: Denunciation in Modern European History, 1789–1989*, edited by Sheila Fitzpatrick and Robert Gellately, 1–21. Chicago: University of Chicago Press, 1998.

Fladhammer, Christa, and Michael Wildt, eds. *Max Brauer im Exil: Briefe und Reden aus den Jahren 1933–1946*. Hamburg: Hans Christians, 1994.

Gellately, Robert. *Backing Hitler: Consent and Coercion in Nazi Germany*. New York: Oxford University Press, 2001.

Geyken, Frauke. *Wir standen nichts abseits: Frauen im Widerstand gegen Hitler*. Munich: C. H. Beck, 2014.

Goeschel, Christian, and Nikolaus Wachsmann. "Before Auschwitz: The Formation of the Nazi Concentration Camps, 1933–9." *Journal of Contemporary History* 45, no. 3 (July 2010): 515–34.

Grunberger, Richard. *A Social History of the Third Reich*. London: Weidenfeld and Nicolson, 1971.

Gurewitsch, Brana, ed. *Mothers, Sisters, Resisters: Oral Histories of Women Who Survived the Holocaust*. Tuscaloosa: University of Alabama Press, 1998.

Haffner, Sebastian. *Defying Hitler: A Memoir*. New York: Farrar, Straus and Giroux, 2002.

Harsch, Donna. "The Iron Front: Weimar Social Democracy between Tradition and Modernity." In *Between Reform and Revolution: German Socialism and Communism from 1840 to 1990*, edited by David E. Barclay and Eric D. Weitz, 251–74. New York: Berghahn, 1998.

Hett, Benjamin Carter. "'This Story Is about Something Fundamental': Nazi Criminals, History, Memory, and the Reichstag Fire." *Central European History* 48, no. 2 (June 2015): 199–224.

Holl, Karl. *Pazifismus in Deutschland*. Frankfurt am Main: Suhrkamp, 1998.

Horn, Gerd-Rainer. "The Social Origins of Unity Sentiments in the German Socialist Underground, 1933 to 1936." In *Between Reform and Revolution: German Socialism and Communism from 1840 to 1990*, edited by David E. Barclay and Eric D. Weitz, 341–55. New York: Berghahn, 1998.

Hunt, Richard N. *German Social Democracy, 1918-1933*. Chicago: Quadrangle, 1970.

Kaplan, Marion A. *Between Dignity and Despair: Jewish Life in Nazi Germany*. New York: Oxford University Press, 1998.

Kay, Antony. *Junkers Aircraft and Engines, 1913–1945*. London: Putnam Aeronautical, 2004.
Kershaw, Ian. *Hitler, 1889–1936: Hubris*. New York: Norton, 1998.
Kienle, Marcus. "Gotteszell." Translated by Lynn Wolff. In *Encyclopedia of Camps and Ghettos, 1933–1945. Volume I, Part A: Early Camps, Youth Camps, and Concentration Camps and Subcamps under the SS-Business Administration Main Office (WVHA)*, edited by Geoffrey P. Megargee, 83–4. Bloomington: Indiana University Press, 2009.
Kramer, Hilde. *Rebellin in München, Moskau, und Berlin. Autobiographisches Fragment, 1901–1924*. Berlin: BasisDruck, 2011.
Krohn, Claus-Dieter et al. *Frauen und Exil: zwischen Anpassung und Selbstbehauptung*. Munich: Text + Kritik, 1993.
———. *Handbuch der deutschsprachigen Emigration, 1933–1945*. Darmstadt: Wissenschaftliche Buchgesellschaft, 2008.
Lower, Wendy. *Hitler's Furies: German Women in the Nazi Killing Fields*. Boston: Houghton Mifflin Harcourt, 2013.
Luban, Ottokar. "Die Novemberrevolution 1918 in Berlin. Eine notwendige Revision des bisherigen Geschichtsbildes." *Jarbuch für Forschungen zur Geschichte der Arbeiterbewegung* 8 (January 2009): 53–78.
Mann, Thomas. *Ein Zeitalter wird besichtigt*. Stockholm: Neuer, 1946.
McKelway, St. Clair. "A Reporter at Large: Their Country Right, But Not Wrong." *New Yorker*, September 30, 1939.
Miller, Michael D., and Andreas Schulz. *Gauleiter: The Regional Leaders of the Nazi Party and Their Deputies, 1925–1945, Volume 2: Georg Joes to Bernhard Rust*. San Jose, CA: R. James Bender, 2017.
Palmier, Jean-Michel. *Weimar in Exile: The Antifascist Emigration in Europe and America*. Translated by David Fernbach. New York: Verso, 2017.
Peterson, Larry. *German Communism, Workers' Protest, and Labor Unions: The Politics of the United Front in Rhineland-Westphalia, 1920–1924*. Dordrecht: Springer Netherlands, 2012.
Peukert, Detlev. *Inside Nazi Germany: Conformity, Opposition, and Racism in Everyday Life*. New Haven, CT: Yale University Press, 1997.
Pine, Lisa. *Hitler's 'National Community': Society and Culture in Nazi Germany*, 2nd edition. London: Bloomsbury, 2017.
———, ed. *Life and Times in Nazi Germany*. London: Bloomsbury, 2016.
Potthoff, Heinrich, and Bernd Faulenbach. *Sozialdemokraten und Kommunisten nach Nationalsozialismus und Krieg: zur historischen Einordnung der Zwangsvereinigung*. Essen: Klartext, 1998.
Rabinbach, Anson. "Paris: Capital of Anti-Fascism." In *The Modernist Imagination: Intellectual History and Critical Theory: Essays in Honor of Martin Jay*, edited by Warren Breckman, Peter E. Gordon, A. Dirk Moses, Samuel Moyn, and Elliot Neaman, 183–209. New York: Berghahn, 2009.
Reed, Douglas. *The Burning of the Reichstag*. New York: Covici, Friede, 1935.
Reimer, Robert C., and Carol J. Reimer. *The A to Z of German Cinema*. Lanham, MD: Scarecrow, 2008.
Ringelheim, Joan. "Women and the Holocaust: A Reconsideration of Research." In *Different Voices: Women and the Holocaust*, edited by Carol Rittner and John K. Roth, 373–405. New York: Paragon, 1993.
Rittner, Carol, and John K. Roth, eds. *Different Voices: Women and the Holocaust*. New York: Paragon, 1993.
Rose, Shelley. "The Penumbra of Weimar Political Culture: Pacifism, Feminism, and Social Democracy." *Peace and Change* 36, no. 3 (July 2011): 313–43.

———. "Transnational Identities in National Politics: The SPD and the German Peace Movements, 1921–1966." PhD diss., Binghamton University, 2010. https://engagedscholarship.csuohio.edu/cgi/viewcontent.cgi?article=1032&context=msl_ae_ebooks.
Sagner, Reinhard. *Gerhart Seger: radikaler Pazifist und konsequenter Sozialdemokrat, Gerhart Seger in Deutschland bis 1933*. Dessau-Rosslau: Funk, 2012.
Schad, Martha. *Frauen gegen Hitler: vergessene Widerstandskämpferinnen im Nationalsozialismus*. Munich: Herbig, 2010.
Scheck, Raffael. *Love Between Enemies: Western Prisoners of War and German Women in World War II*. Cambridge, UK: Cambridge University Press, 2021.
Schildt, Axel. *Max Brauer*. Hamburg: Ellert & Richter, 2002.
"Schiff, Victor." In *Biographisches Handbuch der deutschsprachigen Emigration nach 1933–1945: Band I: Politik, Wirtschaft, Öffentliches Leben*, edited by Werner Röder and Herbert A. Strauss, 645–46. Berlin: De Gruyter, 1980.
Seger, Gerhart. *A Nation Terrorized*. Chicago: Reilly and Lee Co., 1935.
———. *Oranienburg: Erster authentischer Bericht eines aus dem Konzentrationslager Geflüchteten*. Karlsbad: Verlagsanstalt Graphia, 1934.
———. *Reisetagebuch eines deutschen Emigranten*. Zurich: Europa, 1935.
Seger, Gerhart Heinrich. *The Reminiscences of Gerhart Heinrich Seger*. Interview by Wendell Link. December 1950. Oral History Archives at Columbia, Rare Book and Manuscript Library, Columbia University in the City of New York.
Sender, Toni. *The Autobiography of a German Rebel*. New York: Vanguard, 1939.
Sharp, Ingrid. "Dangerous Visionaries and Revolutionary Transformations: Women's Political Cultures in the Aftermath of War." *Oxford German Studies* 40, no. 4 (2020): 401–19.
Shirer, William. *The Rise and Fall of the Third Reich*. New York: Simon and Schuster, 2011.
Steinberg, Swen. "Should I Stay or Should I Go? Regional Functionaries, Political Networks, and the German-Czechoslovakian Borderlands in 1933." In *Vorstufen des Exils/Early Stages of Exile*, edited by Reinhard Andress, 82–94. Boston: Brill, 2020.
Stiefel, Elisabeth. *Sie waren im Getriebe: Frauen im Widerstand*. Marburg: Franke, 2015.
Stoltzfus, Nathan, Mordecai Paldiel, and Judy Baumel-Schwartz. "Women Defying Hitler: An Introduction." In *Women Defying Hitler: Rescue and Resistance under the Nazis*, edited by Nathan Stoltzfus, Mordecai Paldiel, and Judy Baumel-Schwartz, 1–13. New York: Bloomsbury Academic, 2021.
Stoltzfus, Nathan, Mordecai Paldiel, and Judy Baumel-Schwartz, eds. *Women Defying Hitler: Rescue and Resistance under the Nazis*. New York: Bloomsbury Academic, 2021.
Strobl, Gerwin. *The Germanic Isle: Nazi Perceptions of Britain*. Cambridge, UK: Cambridge University Press, 2000.
Wachsmann, Nikolaus. "The Dynamic of Destruction: The Development of Concentration Camps, 1933–1945." In *Concentration Camps in Nazi Germany: The New Histories*, edited by Jane Caplan and Nikolaus Wachsmann, 17–43. New York: Routledge, 2010.
White, Joseph Robert. "Introduction to the Early Camps." In *Encyclopedia of Camps and Ghettos, 1933–1945. Volume I, Part A: Early Camps, Youth Camps, and Concentration Camps and Subcamps under the SS-Business Administration Main Office (WVHA)*, edited by Geoffrey P. Megargee, 3–16. Bloomington: Indiana University Press, 2009.
———. "Moringen-Solling (Women)." In *Encyclopedia of Camps and Ghettos, 1933–1945. Volume I, Part A: Early Camps, Youth Camps, and Concentration Camps and Subcamps under the SS-Business Administration Main Office (WVHA)*, edited by Geoffrey P. Megargee, 128–31. Bloomington: Indiana University Press, 2009.

———. "Rosslau." In *Encyclopedia of Camps and Ghettos, 1933–1945. Volume I, Part A: Early Camps, Youth Camps, and Concentration Camps and Subcamps under the SS-Business Administration Main Office (WVHA)*, edited by Geoffrey P. Megargee, 157–58. Bloomington: Indiana University Press, 2009.

Winkler, Heinrich August. *Germany: The Long Road West, Volume II, 1933–1990*. Oxford: Oxford University Press, 2007.

Zurcher, Arnold J. "The Hitler Referenda." *American Political Science Review* 29, no. 1 (February 1935): 91–99.

INDEX

Page numbers in *italics* refer to photos
Ilse refers to Seger, Ilse
Gerhart refers to Seger, Gerhart

Allgeier, Sepp, 184, 193n18
America, life in
   Gerhart, America antifascist lecture tour, 167–68, 203–4, 217–18, 222
   Gerhart, editor of Neue Volkszeitung, 222
   Ilse memoir, Renate and Richard encouraging to write, 224–25
   Ilse on limited opportunities for women, 222
   Ilse responsibilities, Gerhart on tours, 222
   Ilse's death, 225
   Ilse's parents' visit, prior World War II, 223
   Meinicke (SS officer), Ilse's support through denazification, 127, 140n10
   move to Richmond, VA (1978), 225
   Renate, marriage to Richard, 223–24
   Renate, school librarian, 224
   Renate and Richard, at Queens College, 223
   Renate and Richard, move to Indiana, 224
   visiting brothers in Europe (1974), 225
   See also Brandt, Mark
American Hebrew and Jewish Tribune, Marvis Tate interview, 154
antifascism
   centers of, 8–9, 78
   Gerhart on speaking tour in US, 1, 3, 190, 191
   movement in Paris, 9
   struggle under, 7
anti-Hitler parties, 23–24
Anti-Socialist Laws, 4
arrests, public knowledge of, 50

Article 48. *See* Weimar Constitution
Astor, Nancy
   Ilse's release orchestration, 142, 145, 159
   Ilse's visits, 154, 161–62
Atholl, Duchess of, 145, 155n7

Balfour, Arthur James, 158, 192n2
Bauhaus, 19, 34n7
Beer Hall Putsch, 5
   and January 6, 2021, Mark on similarities, 227
Beneš, Edvard, 46, 52n11, 170, 192n10
Bergen, Doris, definition of resistance, 12, 78, 103
Bernhard, Georg (publisher, *Pariser Tagesblatt*), 201, 221n6
Bismarck, Otto von (first German chancellor), 3–4
Black-Red-Gold Banner of the Reich
   Dessau demonstration, 30
   formation, 23–24, 33–34
Blood Purge in Munich, 176–78
   See also Night of the Long Knives; Röhm Purge
book burnings, 140n6
   forbidden list, 119, 140n6
   Leipzig, 46–47, 50
Borchardt department store, boycott day, 68–69, 79
Brandt, Andrew (Ilse's grandson), 1, *106h*
Brandt, Jennifer (Ilse's granddaughter), 1, *106h*

Brandt, Mark (Ilse's grandson), 1, *106h*
   and father (Richard), agreements and disagreements, 226
   on Ilse and Renate learning English, 222
   on Ilse's influence, 225
   on importance of German library to Ilse, 222
   on January 6, 2021 and Beer Hall Putsch similarities, 227
   on US politics, 226–27
Brandt, Renate (Richard's wife, Ilse's daughter, Renatchen), 1, 2, 25, *106e–f*
   birth, 24
   marriage to Richard, 223–24
   See also America, life in; Seger, Ilse
Brandt, Richard (Renate's husband), 1, 2, *106f*
   marriage to Renate, 223–24
   and Renate, move to Indiana, 224
Braskén, Kasper, on antifascist movement, 9
Brauer, Max, 9, 15n36, 176–77, 190
Brown Book of the Hitler Terror, The (Münzenberg), 78
Brown Shirts. *See* SA
Bruno, Walter (conductor), cancelled radio concert, 46

Caplan, Jane
   on collaboration, local and state agencies, 37
   on political detention acceptance, 50–51
Centre Party, 5, 6, 15n16, 33, 35n15
Christmas amnesty 1933, 73, 80, 84
Communists, and Social Democrats, 137–38
comrades (Genossen), 66–67
concentration camps, 50
   See also specific concentration camps

DDP (German Democratic Party), 33, 35n15
detention sites, opening of, 50, 51
   See also specific concentration camps
Deutsche Demokratische Partei (DDP). *See* DDP
Deutsche Friedensgesellschaft (DFG). *See* DFG
Deutschnationale Volkspartei (DNVP). *See* DNVP
DFG (German Peace Society), 18, 34n3, 74, 142, 171
Die Freiheit (Freedom), Gerhart as editor, 17
Diels, Rudolf (first Gestapo chief), 80n1
DNVP (German National People's Party), 7, 15n22, 28, 45
Dugdale, Blanche (niece of Lord Balfour), 158, 192n2

Ebert, Friedrich (President 1919-25, Weimar Republic), 4, 15n17
émigrés
   early stories, 7–8
   German, settling in Prague, 9
Enabling Act, 36–37
exile, France
   Brussels, French visa application, 169–72
   Carolles-Bourg, summer in, 178–83, 191
   Paris, 172–78
      German passport extension, 175–76
      Renate arrival, 173–75
      visit at Versailles, 172–73
exile, Switzerland
   American visa application, 205–6, 209–13
   Christmas, 199–200
   entry at Basel, 183
   Fechenbach visits, 196
   furniture, from Dessau, 182–83, 187–88
   Gerhart
      America tour, 203
      broadcast lecture on Zürich radio station, 206–9
      departure to America, 194
   Ilse
      comments on America, strangeness and newspaper layout, 195–96
      on going to America, 204–5
      leaving for America, preparations, 213–15
      mother, meeting in Basel, 184–85
      on Nazi destruction of books, 199, 218
      parents' and brothers' visit, 196, 207–8
      on Saarland plebiscite, 201–2
      and Thalmanns, friendship, 194–95
   Mein Kampf, gift of first edition, 198
   news about the Posses, 197–99
   radio, Gerhart's Christmas gift, 199–201
   Renate and father, reconnection, 204
   Renate and grandparents, 196
   St. Gallen, settling in, 185–89
   Thalmanns' daughters, interest in America, 195
   visas and resident visas, 181–82
   visit at Gerhart's publisher, 206
   visitor from Dessau, 197–99
   winter 1934-1935, passing time, 196, 202–3
Exile Research—An International Yearbook (Society for Exilforschung), 7
exile studies (Exilforschung), 7
Exilforschung—Ein internationales Jahrbuch (Society for Exilforschung), 7

family arrests (Sippenhaft), 107
Fechenbach, Felix, 193n15
Fechenbach, Irma (widow of Felix), 185, 193n15, 196
Fitzpatrick, Sheila, on denunciations to Gestapo, 12
France, exile. *See* exile, France
Frauen im Exil (Society for Exile Studies, working group), 7
Freikorps, Luxemburg and Liebknecht murder, 4
Führerprinzip (leader principle), 5

Geheime Staatspolizei. *See* Gestapo
Gellately, Robert
  Nazi control, 80
  on Oranienburg prisoner life, 53–54
  on public knowledge of arrests, 12, 50
German Centre Party, 5, 6, 15n16, 33, 35n15
German life, change of, 50
German Republic, proclamation 1918, 3
Germany
  flag, unofficial, 23, 34n9
  Great Depression, effects, 5, 33, 139–40
  Jewish emigration, 190
  newspapers, political coordination (Gleichschaltung), 59, 81n12
  unemployment in, 6, 49
  See also Jews, in Germany
Gesellschaft für Exilforschung (Society for Exile Studies), 7
Gestapo (German Secret State Police)
  Rudolf Diels, first chief, 80n1
  Sheila Fitzpatrick, on denunciations to, 12
  Helmut Heisig (commissioner), 71, 80, 82n22, 93, 126, 147
  Rosslau concentration camp, control, 136–37
  Wesemann, agent of, 192n5
Gleichschaltung (political coordination of newspapers), 59, 81n12
Goebbels, Joseph, 169, 192n9
Gone with the Wind (Mitchell), importance to Ilse, 222
Göring, Hermann, 82n22, 120, 140n8, 169
Gotteszell concentration camp, KPD women in, 8
Great Depression, effects, 5, 33, 139–40
Groener, Wilhelm (General), deal with Ebert, 4
Gurewitsch, Brana, 12

Haffner, Sebastian, on Hitler as chancellor, 10
Hanfstaengl, Ernst (chief of Nazi Foreign Press Bureau), 154–55
  Ilse's release, assistance in, 145–46, 148–50, 176
  meetings with Marvis Tate, 145, 148, 154
Hart, Ernst (father of Ilse), 1, 106b
  visiting Ilse, 95–96, 133–34
Hart, Joachim (brother of Ilse), 1, 106b, 184
Hart, Margaret (mother of Ilse), 1, 106b
  and father visits, Switzerland, 196, 207–8, 212
  meeting Ilse in Basel, 184–85
  Renate's birth, visiting Ilse at, 24, 26
  visiting Ilse in Dessau, 71
Hart, Wolfgang (brother of Ilse), 1, 106b, 184
Heisig, Helmut (commissioner, Gestapo), 71, 80, 82n22, 93, 126
  passport delivery, 147
  Rosslau detention of Ilse, notification, 107–8
  See also Seger, Ilse
Hilversum radio station, Gerhart on, 98, 100, 106n7
Hindenburg, Paul von (President), 5
  Article 48, invoking, 5–6, 15n17, 15n19, 36
  death, 191
  Hitler appointment as chancellor, 7, 12, 36, 38
  reelection 1932, 6
Hitler, Adolf, 19, 120
  absolute power, claim of, 191
  antisemitism under, 23
  chancellor, appointed as, 7, 12, 36, 38
  and changing life in Germany, 23–32
  Der Führer, assuming title of, 191
  growing support, 33
  Jewish artists, performance denial, 46
  leader principle, 5
  League of Nations, vote on leaving, 69, 79, 81n18
  Mein Kampf, 5, 19, 119
  power consolidation 1933, 50
  Reichstag majority (1932), 7
  rise to power, 5
  and Röhm rivalry, 177–78
Hoesch, Leopold von (German ambassador to the UK), 142, 145
Huber, Johannes, 182, 193n16

Independent Social Democratic Party (USPD). *See* USPD

Jews, in Germany
    artists, performance denial, 46
    emigration, 67, 81n16, 190
    first boycott day, 67–68
    hatred of, 23, 25

Kaplan, Marion, on memory and gender
    relationship, 2–3, 9, 14
Kershaw, Ian, on Reichstag fire originators,
    78, 82n30
Kommunistische Partei Deutschlands (KPD).
    See KPD
KPD (Communist Party of Germany)
    election gains (1930), 6
    formation, 4
    and Reichstag fire, 36, 78
    and SA skirmishes with, 33
    and Social Democrats, division and united
        front, 137–38
    suppression, 37
    USPD, union with, 4
    women, detention in Gotteszell, 8
    working-class inmates, Oranienburg, 53
Kramer, Hilde, political memoir, 10
Kupsch, Käthe, Ilse visit, 74, 83

labor unions. *See* trade unions
Law for the Restoration of the Professional
    Civil Service, passage, 50
League of Nations, vote on leaving, 69–70, 79,
    81n18, 81n20
Leipzig School of Journalism, 17
Liebknecht, Karl (co-founder of KPD), 4, 137
Listowel, Lord and Lady, luncheon with Ilse
    and Gerhart, 160, 192n4
Loeper, Wilhelm Friedrich (Gauleiter, later
    Reichstatthalter)
    Ilse's detention as safety protection, 107–8
    reaction to Gerhart's escape, 93, 105n2
    revenge actions, 134
London, reunion
    activities in, 159
    arrival, 156–57
    care for Renate, during Norwegian trip,
        162–64
    lecture trip, Norwegian, 162
    lunch at Oldens, 163–64
    luncheon at Tates' house, 157–59
    luncheon with Lord and Lady Listowel, 160,
        192n4
    Wesemayer interactions, 157–58, 159–61, 189,
        192n3

Lower, Wendy, 79, 140
Lubbe, Marinus van der, 82n30
Luxemburg, Rosa (co-founder of KPD), 4, 137

Majority Social Democratic Party of Germany,
    4, 14n13
Mann, Heinrich, on émigrés welcome, 9
Marx, Karl, 3
Marx, Otto (commander, Rosslau
    concentration camp), interactions with
    Ilse, 111–13, 127, 131, 135, 137
Masaryk, Tomáš G. (Czech President), asylum
    policy, 52n11, 104
Mehrheitssozialdemokratische Partei
    Deutschlands, 4, 14n13
Meinicke (SS officer), Ilse's support through
    denazification, 127, 140n10
    See also Rosslau concentration camp
Mein Kampf (Hitler), 5, 19, 119, 198
Münzenberg, Willi, 9, 78
Münzenberg network, 9
Mussolini, Benito, 5

National Socialists. *See* Nazis
Nationalsozialistische Deutsche
    Arbeiterpartei (NSDAP). *See* NSDAP
Nation Terrorized, A (Seger), 3, 7, 32, 77, 155n2
Nazis (National Socialists), 20
    aggressiveness, growing, 24
    Anglo-German partnership, attempt to
        create, 106n3, 143, 145
    opposition to, 25
    political party inroads, 21
    rise to power, 5–7
    sympathizers in Norway, 166
newspapers, political coordination
    (Gleichschaltung), 59, 81n12
Night of Long Knifes, 9, 190, 191
Night of Long Knives
    See also Blood Purge in Munich; Röhm
        Purge
Norwegian lecture tour. *See* Seger, Gerhart;
    Seger, Ilse
Norwegian Social Democratic Party, 9, 162,
    165, 189
November Revolution, 3, 4
NSDAP (National Socialist German Workers'
    Party), 4–5, 138
    gains, 1933 elections, 37
    growth, 19
    only legal party, 50
    Reichstag, rise in, 6–7, 21, 37

Twenty-Five-Points, platform, 5
Weimar Republic, overthrow, 5
See also SA; SS

Olden, Rudolf (journalist), 163–65, 192nn6–7
150 percenters, 150, 155n9
Opi. *See* Seger, Gerhart
Oranienburg concentration camp, 227
  Gerhart in
    account of, 77
    arrival, 53–56
    books about, 3, 7
    depression, at, 70, 73
    escape to Prague, 1, 85, 103, 142
    on life conditions, 60
  Ilse and
    Gerhart's escape, hearing about, 85
    smuggling money into, 12–13, 79
    visits at, 56–62, 83
    prisoners' life in, 53–54, 57–58, 60, 77, 80
    torture at, 77
    transitions, prisoners, 80
  Oranienburg: Erster authentischer Bericht eines aus dem Konzentrationslager Geflüchteten (Seger), 3, 7, 32, 77
    international editions, 9, 53, 168
    secret circulation, 127–28

Palmier, Jean-Michel, on antifascist Germans (1933-1945), 7
Papen, Franz von (chancellor), 6, 7
Paris (France)
  antifascist capital, 9, 78
  Ilse and Gerhart in, 172–78
  See also exile, France
Pariser Tageszeitung (refugee newspaper), 201, 221n6
People's Observer (Völkischer Beobachter), 59, 77, 81n11, 166
Persilscheine, 140n10
political detention acceptance, 50–51
political meetings, SA disturbances of, 24
Posse, Otto and Leni
  Czech visitor, message from Gerhart, 97–98
  Ilse release from Rosslau, Leni accompanying, 142, 143–47
  and Ilse's mother-in-law, 89–92, 103
  last goodbye to Ilse, 151, 155
  Otto, school transfer, 197
  and Renate, care for, 68, 75, 84, 95, 129–30
  supporting Ilse, 63–64

visiting Ilse in Rosslau, 121–22, 124
  See also Seger, Ilse
prisoners. *See* Oranienburg concentration camp; Rosslau concentration camp
protective custody camps, 50, 105, 137

Quisling, Vidkun (Nazi journalist, Norway), 166, 189, 193n22

Reed, Douglas (London Times), on Reichstag fire, 39
Reichsbanner Schwarz-Rot-Gold. *See* Black-Red-Gold Banner of the Reich
Reichstag
  dissolution and elections, 26, 36–38
  election cycle (1930-1932), 6–7, 20, 26, 32–33
  elections 1930, 5–6
  Hindenburg dissolving, 5–6, 36
  KPD, rise in, 6
  March 23 session, aftermath, 45–47
  member arrests, 80
  NSDAP, rise in, 6–7, 21, 37
  Toni Sender, on legislative work in, 32–33
  SPD in, 4
  See also Weimar Constitution
Reichstag fire, 10, 38–39
  arrests, 51
  consequences, 78
  discussions by Ilse and friends, 12, 67, 71, 78
  originators, 36, 169
  responsibility for, 78, 169, 190
  trial, 67, 71
Reichstag Fire Decree, Hitler's use of, 36–37, 51n5
Reisetagebuch eines deutschen Emigranten (Seger), 3, 143, 180, 191, 206, 218
resistance, 138–39
  definition by Bergen, 12, 78, 103
  definition by Gurewitsch, 12
  by Ilse, 10–13, 67–70, 78–79, 103–4
  infrastructure, 9
  women, to National Socialism, 11
  See also women
reunion, Ilse and Gerhart. *See* London, reunion
Röhm, Ernst (SA leader), 177, 193n14
Röhm Purge, 190
  See also Blood Purge; Night of the Long Knives
Rose, Shelley, on Gerhart's transnational connections, 143

Index   239

Rosslau concentration camp, 1, 227
  camp control, 97, 106n6, 136–37
  Ilse in
    camp layout, 13, 110–13, 136
    Czech newsroom man, camp visit, 130–32
    denial of divorce, 127
    depression and escape thoughts, 134–35
    Dessau apartment, evacuation, 128–30
    discharge, 135–36
    "escape" suitcase and move, 128, 129–30
    father's visit, 133–34
    first day, 113–17
    Gerhart's book, news about, 127–28
    guards' sympathy, 114–15
    hostage, detention as a, 107–8, 118, 131
    hostage, emotions as a, 138
    hostage, realization of being, 113, 139
    humor, turning to, 138
    kindness, experience of, 138–39
    leaving with Leni Posse, 142, 143–47
    letter to parents, 117–18
    letter to Posses, 116
    library visits, 123
    meeting prisoners, 122
    Meinicke interactions, 120, 132–33, 136, 139–40, 140n7
    Meinicke's prevention of transfer, 124–26
    mental torment tactics, experience of, 138
    nurse encounters, 108, 109–10, 119, 140
    outside friends, 123
    Posses' Thursday visits, 121–22, 124
    preparation for move to, 108–10
    privileges, 112–13, 139
    release, 142
    Renate and Great Dane, 115
    Social Democrats, greeting arrival, 110
  opening, 97, 105, 106n6
  prisoners
    beatings and torture, 125, 137
    interviews, by Czech journalist, 131
    life as, 97
    outside work and privileges, 13, 122
    population fluctuations, 126, 137
    Social Democrats and Communists, alliances, 137
  See also Seger, Ilse

SA (Storm Troopers)
  Brown Shirts, 5
  elections, monitoring of, 37
  members, murdered by SS, 9, 177, 190
  paramilitary NSDAP branch, 33

  political meetings, disturbance of, 24
  and Reichsbanner, similarities, 34
  SPD offices, ransacking of, 77
  See also SS
Saarland plebiscite, Ilse on, 201–2
Sachsenhausen camp, 54
Schäfer, Werner (commander, Oranienburg), 56–57, 81n10, 105
Schiff, Victor (journalist), 176, 190, 192n13
Schleicher, Kurt von (chancellor, 1932), 7
Schutzstaffel (SS). See SS
Seger, Gerhart ("Opi," Ilse's husband), 106a–g
  arrest in Leipzig, 40–43
  background, 17–18
  book and paper confiscation, 77
  at DFG, 18
  editor-in-chief at Neue Volkszeitung New York, 205
  efforts to reunite with Ilse, 142–42, 155n3
  election campaign, 19–20
  election to Reichstag, 1, 5–6, 19–21
  escape plans, 73–76, 80
  escape to Prague, 103
  leaving for Leipzig, 39–40
  lecture tours
    American antifascist, 167–68, 203–4, 217–18, 222
    in England, 142
    in Europe, 168, 190
    in Germany, 20
    Hilversum radio station, 98, 100, 106n7
    Norway, with Ilse, 9, 162, 165–69, 189–90
    Zürich radio station, 206–9
  Mein Kampf, gift of first edition, 198
  mother's visit, 207–8
  about Nazi Party, at University of Texas Austin, 190–91
  Neue Volkszeitung New York, editor-in-chief, 205
  Norwegian lecture tour, with Ilse, 9, 162, 165–69, 189–90
  Oranienburg, distribution, 9, 127–28
  political connections, help from, 190
  in "protective custody," Dessau, 37, 51n5
  reelection 1933, 37
  return from America tour, 203–4
  SA threats, 27–30
  SPD, becoming member, 1
  transfer to Dessau jail, 43–44
  transnational connections, 142, 143, 220

Volksblatt für Anhalt, chief editor, 32
See also America, life in; exile, France; exile, Switzerland; London, reunion; Oranienburg concentration camp; Seger, Ilse
Seger, Hedwig (Ilse's mother-in-law), 17
   Gerhart and Ilse visiting, 39–44
   Gerhart's arrest at, 40–43
   and Posses, 89–92, 103
   visiting Ilse, 89–93, 97–100, 103–5, 207–8
Seger, Ilse ("Ilse," née Hart), 1, *106a–h*
   America, interest in, 22
   Blumberg, visits at, 69–70, 81n19
   Christmas in Freiburg, 25
   on comrades (Genossen), 64, 66–67, 78
   death, 225
   election cycle, affected by, 32
   escape attempt
      Czech messenger, meeting Gerhart's, 97–100
      failed escape, 101–5
      Gerhart's divorce idea, 96, 100
      planning, 99–100
   father's visit, 95–96
   financial condition, 62
   Gerhart in Prague, notice, 95
   Gerhart leaving for Leipzig, 39–40
   Gerhart's departure to Oranienburg, 53–56
   Heisig support, 71–73, 116, 133, 135, 139, 145, 147, 182–83
   history of daily life, 13–14
   house arrest, 84–95
      conversation with police guards, 93–94
      Gerhart's message of safety, 92–93
   kindness, acts of, 12, 138–39, 148
   League of Nations, vote on, 69–70, 79, 81n20
   leaving Germany
      in Berlin, 147–51
      British support, 142–43, 145
      flight to London, 151–54
      Hanfstaengl, visit to office of, 149–50
      meeting Marvis Tate, 144–45
      permit to leave for England, 148, 150
      phone call with Gerhart, 149–50
      Leni Posse, last goodbye, 151, 155
      reunion with Gerhart, 142–43
      Tate assistance in Berlin, 148–54
      zoo visits, 148, 150, 155n10
   on Leipzig book burnings, 46–47
   life after Gerhart's election, 22–23
   on life in Dessau/Anhalt, 19, 34n6
   on life in Dessau without Gerhart, 48
   Otto Marx, interactions with, 111–13, 127, 131, 135, 137
   on May 1 holiday, 47
   meeting and marrying Gerhart, 18–19
   memoir
      vs. Gerhart's memoir, differences, 9, 10, 32
      importance of, 8
      origin of, 2–3
   mother-in-law (*see* Seger, Hedwig)
   mother's visit, Dessau, 71
   new apartment, Nazi neighbor interactions, 65–66
   new apartment, search for affordable, 62–65
   new apartment, social interactions, 66–67, 78
   Norwegian tour, with Gerhart, 165–69, 189–90
   outlook on Germany, changing, 105
   political engagement, 10–13
   Posses
      care for Renate, 68, 75, 84, 95, 129–30
      Ilse's mother-in-law at, 89–92, 103
      meetings at, 67
   Quisling, encounter with Nazi journalist, 166, 189
   on Reichsbanner and SA tension, 33
   and Reichstag fire, 12, 38–39, 78
   Renate's birth, 24
   resistance, 10–13, 67–70, 78–79, 103–4, 139
   support of Gerhart's escape plan, 74–76, 79
   support of Meinicke, through denazification procedures, 127, 140n10
   and swastika, 23
   view of resistance, 78–79
   visiting brothers in Europe (1974), 225
   visiting Gerhart in Dessau jail, 44–45, 47–48
   visit to Borchardt department store, 68–69, 79
   See also America, life in; exile, France; exile, Switzerland; Heisig, Helmut; London, reunion; Meinicke; Oranienburg concentration camp; Posses; Rosslau concentration camp; Seger, Gerhart
Seger, Johann Friedrich (Gerhart's father), 10, 17
Seger, Renate (Ilse's daughter). *See* America, life in; Brandt, Renate; Seger, Ilse
Sender, Toni
   on Hitler as chancellor, 10, 16n43
   on Nazi speech interrupts, 34
   on Reichstag legislative work, 32–33
   USPD member, 10

Shanghai, German and Austrian Jews
    emigration to, 67, 81n15
Sharp, Ingrid, on post-WW I political
    landscape, 10
Silver, Hillel (Rabbi), 168, 192n8, 203
Social Democrats, German
  and Communists, 137–38
  greeting Ilse at Rosslau arrival, 110
  in Prague exile, 9
Socialist Democrats and Communists,
    division and united front, 137–38
Society for Exile Studies (Gesellschaft für
    Exilforschung), 7
Sozialdemokratische Partei Deutschlands
    (SPD). *See* SPD
Spartacus League, 4
SPD (Social Democratic Party of Germany),
    33, 35n15
  assaults on, 50
  creation and rise, 3–4
  elections (1930), 116
  executive committee in Prague, 95, 104
  Gerhart, member, 1
  Gerhart's book, distribution, 9
  Ilse's connection to, 11–12
  and KPD, division and united front,
    137–38
  leadership escape to Prague, 37, 46
  member betrayal, 142
  member's fears (1933), 77
  Nazi restrictions on, 37
  office ransacking, by SA and SS, 50, 77
  party apparatus establishment, Prague, 37
  underground, supporting Ilse, 8, 12–13, 78,
    104
  union with USPD, 17–18
  Weimar Coalition, formation, 33, 35n15
  in Weimar Republic, 4
  working-class inmates at Oranienburg, 53
SS (Schutzstaffel)
  elections, monitoring of, 37
  military NSDAP branch, 19
  Rosslau concentration camp, control of, 97,
    106n6, 136–37
  and SA, Hitler's private army, 19, 23
  Sachsenhausen camp, opening, 54
  SA members, murder of, 9, 177, 190
  SPD offices, ransacking of, 77
storm troopers (Sturmabteilung). *See* SA
Sturmabteilung (SA). *See* SA
swastika, 23
Switzerland, exile. *See* exile, Switzerland

Tate, Marvis (MP)
  assisting Ilse in Berlin, 148–54
  Hanfstaengl meetings, 145, 148, 154
  Ilse's release and reunion with Gerhart,
    responsible for, 142
  interview, London arrival, 157
  interview in *American Hebrew and Jewish
    Tribune*, 154
Thälmann, Ernst (KPD leader), 6
Third Reich, start of, 46
Three-Arrows anti-Nazi flag, 24, 109, 136,
    140n3
torture sites, 50
trade unions
  abolishment of, 50
  border offices, 104
  Christian labor, 7
  clothing workers, 17
  community centers, conversion to
    concentration camps, 105, 106n6
  Czechoslovakia, support in, 104
  Nazification, 81n12
  ransacking of offices, 77
Three arrows, political symbol,
    140n3
Travel Diary of a German Emigrant (Seger), 3,
    143, 180, 191, 206, 218
Twenty-Five Points, NSDAP platform, 5

Unabhängige Sozialdemokratische Partei
    Deutschlands). *See* USPD
unemployment, Germany 1933, 49
unions. *See* trade unions
united front, 123
United States Holocaust Memorial
    Museum, 50
USPD (Independent Social Democratic
    Party), 4, 10, 14n13, 16n43, 17

Vereinte Front (united front), 123
visits at Lady Astor's house, 142, 145, 159,
    161–62
Völkischer Beobachter (People's Observer), 59,
    77, 81n11, 166
Volksblatt für Anhalt (Gerhart Seger, chief
    editor), 32
von Papen, Franz (chancellor), 6, 7
von Schleicher, Kurt (chancellor, 1932), 7

Wachsmann, Nikolaus
  on arrests and the law, 106n16
  on number of detainees, 80

Weimar Coalition, formation, 33, 35n15
Weimar Constitution, 15n22
　Article 48, invoked by Hindenburg, 5–6, 15n17, 15n19, 36
　vs. US Constitution, 22
Weimar Republic, 32, 33
　end of, 3–5
　Ilse's insights, 10
　overthrow by NSDAP, 5
　weakening of, 6
Wesemann, interactions with Segers, 157–58, 159–61, 189, 192n3, 192n5
Wesemayer. *See* Wesemann
wild camps, 53–54, 80n1, 106n6
Wilhelm II (Kaiser), 3
women
　in concentration camps, 8, 10
　defiance to Hitler, 11
　in German émigré stories, 8
　Ilse's account of, 2, 8, 10, 11
　indoctrination of, 140
　memory and gender, relationship, 9
　resistance to National Socialism, 11
　supporting Ilse, 88, 104
Women in Exile (Society for Exile Studies, working group), 7

MELISSA KRAVETZ is Associate Professor of History and Co-Director of Women, Gender, and Sexuality Studies at Longwood University. She also teaches K–12 educators at the Alexander Lebenstein Teacher Education Institute at the Virginia Holocaust Museum. She is author of *Women Doctors in Weimar and Nazi Germany: Maternalism, Eugenics, and Professional Identity*.

MARK BRANDT is Professor of Chemistry and Biochemistry at the Rose-Hulman Institute of Technology. He is Ilse Seger's grandson.

For Indiana University Press

Lesley Bolton, *Project Manager/Editor*
Allison Chaplin, *Acquisitions Editor*
Anna Garnai, *Editorial Assistant*
Sophia Hebert, *Assistant Acquisitions Editor*
Samantha Heffner, *Marketing and Publicity Manager*
Brenna Hosman, *Production Coordinator*
Katie Huggins, *Production Manager*
Dan Pyle, *Online Publishing Manager*

www.ingramcontent.com/pod-product-compliance
Lightning Source LLC
Chambersburg PA
CBHW030617230426
43661CB00053B/2023